L.F.

GERSHOM SCHOLEM

Modern Critical Views

These and other titles in preparation

Modern Critical Views

GERSHOM SCHOLEM

Edited and with an introduction by
Harold Bloom
Sterling Professor of the Humanities
Yale University

CHELSEA HOUSE PUBLISHERS ◊ 1987
New York ◊ New Haven ◊ Philadelphia

© 1987 by Chelsea House Publishers, a division
of Chelsea House Educational Communications, Inc.,
  95 Madison Avenue, New York, NY 10016
  345 Whitney Avenue, New Haven, CT 06511
  5014 West Chester Pike, Edgemont, PA 19028

Introduction © 1987 by Harold Bloom

Printed and bound in the United States of America

∞ The paper used in this publication meets the minimum
requirements of the American National Standard for Permanence
of Paper for Printed Library Materials, Z39.48–1984.

Library of Congress Cataloging-in-Publication Data
Gershom Scholem.
  (Modern critical views)
  Bibliography: p.
  Includes index.
  1. Scholem, Gershom Gerhard, 1897– .
2. Mysticism—Judaism—Historiography. 3. Cabala—
Historiography. I. Bloom, Harold. II. Series.
BM755.S295G465 1987   296.8'3   86–34319
ISBN 1–55546–274–X (alk. paper)

Contents

Editor's Note

This book gathers together a representative selection of critical essays devoted to the work of Gershom Scholem, the great interpreter of Jewish mysticism and esoteric speculation for our time. The essays are reprinted here in the chronological order of their original publication. I am grateful to Hillary Kelleher for her aid in researching this volume.

My introduction, originally published in 1975, as a review-essay on Scholem's *Kabbalah,* is at once an overview of Kabbalah and an appreciation of Scholem as the Miltonic scholar of Kabbalah. Robert Alter begins the chronological sequence of commentary upon Scholem with two essays, the first of which relates Scholem's interpretation of the false Messiah, Sabbatai Zevi, to a story by S. Y. Agnon and a play by Haim Hazaz. The second sums up Scholem's achievement as the definitive scholar of Jewish mysticism.

David Biale, in the first of his two commentaries reprinted here, works out some of the complex relations in Scholem of counter-theology, language, and historicism. The Christian theologian, W. D. Davies, addresses himself to Scholem's Sabbatian interests, and movingly registers a dialectical attraction-and-repulsion in regard to the antinomian elements in the Sabbatians' apocalyptic yearnings.

In his second contribution, David Biale presents (in German, due to copyright restrictions) the text of Scholem's fascinating "Ten Unhistorical Aphorisms on Kabbalah." Biale's acute commentary and my own paraphrase (in the last essay of this volume) combine to give the gist of Scholem's most surprising legacy to us.

The novelist Cynthia Ozick, herself a fierce polemicist for the normative Jewish tradition, writes a superbly vivid appreciation of Scholem's personal authority. In another appreciation, the scholar Hyam Maccoby, himself an iconoclast, salutes Scholem as having changed absolutely our sense of the religious history of the Jewish people.

Scholem's principal disciple in the study of Kabbalah, Joseph Dan, reconstructs the master's reconstruction of early Kabbalah. Louis Jacobs, himself an eminent scholar of Jewish mysticism, centers upon Scholem's study of Hasidism, with its deep correction of the work of Martin Buber. In an account of Scholem "as Zionist and believer," Rabbi Arthur Hertzberg emphasizes Scholem's refusal to be disillusioned by some of the ideological trends in the later history of institutional Zionism in the state of Israel.

This volume concludes with my own essay on Scholem's ambiguously prophetic stance in regard to an elitist Judaism of the future, which would remove the Platonist elements from both the Kabbalah and from the normative tradition. Though my own view is speculative, it seeks to develop much that is implicit in the burden of Scholem's ongoing prophecy.

Introduction

"Kabbalah" has been, since about the year 1200, the popularly accepted word for Jewish esoteric teachings concerning God and everything God created. The word "Kabbalah" means "tradition," in the particular sense of "reception," and at first referred to the whole of Oral Law. But there existed among the Jews, both in their homeland and in Egypt, during the time of ferment when Christianity began, a considerable body of theosophical and mystical lore. These speculations and beliefs appear to have been influenced by Gnosticism and Neoplatonism, and it seems fair to characterize the history of subsequent Kabbalah as being a struggle between Gnostic and Neoplatonic tendencies, fought out on the quite alien ground of Judaism, which in its central development was to reject both modes of speculation. But Kabbalah went out and away from the main course of Jewish religious thought, and uncannily it has survived both Gnosticism and Neoplatonism, in that Kabbalah today retains a popular and apparently perpetual existence, while Gnosticism and Neoplatonism are the concern of only a few specialists. As I write, the desk in front of me has on it a series of paperback manuals, purchased in drugstores and at newsstands, with titles like *Tree of Life, Kabbalah: An Introduction, Kabbalah Today,* and *Understanding the Kabbalah.* There are no competing titles on Gnosticism today, or on understanding Neoplatonism, and it is important that the continued popularity of Kabbalah be considered in any estimate of the phenomenon of the current survival and even revival of ancient esotericisms.

Popular handbooks of Kabbalah are not always very exact in their learning, and tend to be dangerously eager to mix Kabbalah up with nearly everything else in current religious enthusiasms, from Sufism to Hinduism. But this too by now is a Western tradition, for Christian popularizations of Kabbalah starting with the Renaissance compounded Kabbalah with a variety

1

of non-Jewish notions, ranging from Tarot cards to the Trinity. A singular prestige has attended Kabbalah throughout its history, and such prestige again is worth contemporary consideration. Accompanying this prestige, which is the prestige of supposedly ultimate origins, is an extraordinary eclecticism that contaminated Kabbalah with nearly every major occult or theosophical strain in the Renaissance and later in Enlightened Europe. A reader deeply versed in the interpenetrations of Kabbalah with these strains learns to be very tolerant of every popular version of Kabbalah he encounters. The five I have read recently were all terribly confused and confusing, but all were palpably sincere and even authentically enthusiastic in their obfuscations.

Yet educated readers need not rely upon such manuals. The lifework of Gershom Scholem of the Hebrew University, Jerusalem, was summed up by him, magnificently, in the various articles on Kabbalah in the *Encyclopaedia Judaica,* only a few years ago. These entries, revised by Scholem, are now available in one large volume of nearly five hundred pages, published under the title *Kabbalah.* Most of what follows in this essay is based upon either this book or on Scholem's other major studies of Kabbalah, several of which are easily available in American paperback reprints. Where I will depart from Scholem cannot be on any factual matters in kabbalistic scholarship, but will concern only some suggestions on the continued relevance of Kabbalah for contemporary modes of interpretation, and a few personal speculations on how Kabbalah itself might be interpreted from some contemporary perspectives.

Scholem's massive achievement can be judged as being unique in modern humanistic scholarship, for he has made himself indispensable to all rational students of his subject. Kabbalah is an extraordinary body of rhetoric or figurative language, and indeed is a theory of rhetoric, and Scholem's formidable achievement is as much rhetorical or figurative as it is historical. In this deep sense, Scholem has written a truly kabbalistic account of Kabbalah, and more than any other modern scholar, working on a comparable scale, he has been wholly adequate to his great subject. He has the same relation to the texts he has edited and written commentaries upon that a later poet like John Milton had to the earlier poems he absorbed and, in some ways, transcended. Scholem is a Miltonic figure in modern scholarship, and deserves to be honored as such.

II

Any brief account of Kabbalah has to begin with descriptions of Gnosticism and of Neoplatonism, for these opposed visions are the starting points of the more comprehensive vision of Kabbalah. To most modern sensibilities, Gnosticism has a strong and even dangerous appeal, frequently under other names, but Neoplatonism scarcely moves anyone in our time. William James reacted to the Neoplatonic Absolute or God, the One and the Good, by saying that "the stagnant felicity of the Absolute's own perfection moves me as little as I move it." No one is going to argue with James now, but a thousand years and more of European cultural tradition would not have agreed with him.

Neoplatonism was essentially the philosophy of one man, the Hellenic Egyptian Plotinus (205–70 C.E.), whose seminars in Rome were subsequently written out as the *Enneads* ("sets of nine"). Seeing himself as the continuator of Plato, Plotinus sought vindication for the three mystic and transcendent realities that he called "hypostases": the One or the Good, Intelligence, the Soul. Beneath these hypostases was the world of nature, including human bodies. To bridge the abyss between the unified Good and a universe of division and evil, Plotinus elaborated an extraordinary trope or figure of speech, "emanation." The One's plenitude was so great that its love, light, glory brimmed over, and without the One itself in any way decreasing, its glory descended, first into the realm of Intelligence (the Platonic Ideas or Ideal Forms), next into a region of Soul (including each of our souls), and at last into the body and nature. On this bottom level, evil exists, but only by virtue of its distance from the Good, its division of an ultimate Oneness into so many separate selves, so many objects. The body and nature are not bad, in the vision of Plotinus, but merely have gone too far away from their beloved fatherland. By an intellectual discipline, Plotinus held, we can return to the One even in this life.

Plotinus had a strong dislike for the Gnostics, against whom he wrote an eloquent treatise, calling them "those who say that the Maker of the world and the world are evil." There is no great scholarly book of our time on Neoplatonism (for many of the same reasons that there are no drugstore manuals) but there is a superb work, *The Gnostic Religion*, by Hans Jonas, a worthy complement to Scholem's *Kabbalah*. Jonas usefully compares Gnosticism to nihilism and existentialism, citing many analogues between Valentinus, the greatest of the Gnostic speculators, and the philosopher Heidegger. Gnosticism, according to Jonas, is the extremist version of the syncretic, general religion that dominated the eastern Mediterranean world during the first two Christian centuries. Jonas refers to this general religion of the period as a "dualistic transcendent religion of salvation." "Dualistic" here means that reality is polarized into: God against the creation, spirit against matter, good against evil, soul against the body. "Transcendent" here means that God and salvation are alike transmundane, beyond our world. Gnosticism takes its name from *gnosis,* a Greek word for "knowledge." Though the Church Fathers attacked Gnosticism as a Christian heresy, it appears to have preceded Christianity, both among the Jews and the Hellenes. Gnostic "knowledge" is supposed knowledge "of God," and so is radically different from all other knowledge, for the *gnosis* is the only form that salvation can take, according to its believers. This is therefore not rational knowledge, for it involves God's knowing the Gnostic adept, even as the Gnostic knows Him.

Gnosticism was always anti-Jewish, even when it arose among Jews or Jewish Christians, for its radical dualism of an alien God set against an evil universe is a total contradiction of the central Jewish tradition, in which a transcendent God allows Himself to be known by His people as an immediate presence, when He chooses, and in which His creation is good except as it has been marred or altered by man's disobedience or wickedness. Confronted by the Gnostic vision of a world evilly made by hostile demons, the talmudic rabbis rejected this religion of the alien God with a moral passion surpassing the parallel denunciations made by Plotinus. We can contrast here the most famous formula of Valentinian *gnosis* with an equally famous rabbinic pronouncement of anathema upon such speculations:

> What makes us free is the knowledge who we were, what we have become; where we were, wherein we have been thrown; whereto we speed, wherefrom we are redeemed; what is birth and what rebirth.

> Whosoever speculated on these four things, it were better for him if he had not come into the world—what is above? what is beneath? what was beforetime? and what will be hereafter?

The rabbis believed such speculation to be morally unhealthy, a judgment amply vindicated by the sexual libertinism of many Gnostics. Since Kabbalah, in all of its earlier phases, remained a wholly orthodox Jewish phenomenon, in belief and in moral behavior, it seems a puzzle that Kabbalah had so large a Gnostic content. This puzzle can be clarified by even the briefest account of the origins of the Kabbalah. Kabbalah proper begins in twelfth-century Provence, but Scholem and others have traced its direct descent from the earliest Jewish esotericism, the apocalyptic writings of which the Book of Enoch is the most formidable. This earliest Jewish theosophy and mysticism centered about two biblical texts, the first chapter of the prophet Ezekiel and the first chapter of Genesis. These gave impetus to two modes of visionary speculation, *ma'aseh merkabah* ("the work of the Chariot") and *ma'aseh bereshit* ("the work of creation"). These esoteric meditations were orthodox parallels to Gnostic reveries on the *pleroma,* the unfallen divine realm, and can be considered a kind of rabbinical quasi-Gnosticism, but not yet Kabbalah.

III

Some eight centuries after the Gnostics subsided, a short book, the *Sefer Yetzirah* ("Book of Creation"), became widely circulated among learned Jews. There are at least half-a-dozen English translations of *Sefer Yetzirah* available, and the little book probably will always be popular among esotericists. In itself, it is of no literary or spiritual value, but historically it is the true origin of Kabbalah. The date of its composition is wholly uncertain, but it may go back to the third century. Later kabbalist gossip attributed it to the great Rabbi Akiba, whom the Romans had martyred, which accounts for much of the book's prestige. What matters about *Sefer Yetzirah* is that it introduced, in a very rudimentary form, the central structural notion of Kabbalah, the Sefirot, which in later works became the divine emanations by which all reality is structured. Since the next kabbalistic text of importance, the *Sefer ha-Bahir,* was not written until the thirteenth century, and since that work presents the Sefirot in fuller but not final development, all students of Kabbalah necessarily confront the problematic of a thousand years of oral tradition. All of Jewish medievalism becomes a vast labyrinth in which the distinctive ideas of Kabbalah were invented, revised, and transmitted in an area ranging from Babylonia to Poland. In these vast reaches of space and time, even Scholem becomes baffled, for the very essence of oral tradition is that it should defeat all historical and critical scholarship.

The *Sefer ha-Bahir* (*bahir* means "bright") has been translated into German by Scholem, another service, as this book is incoherent, and its mixture of learned Hebrew and vernacular Aramaic makes it difficult even for specialists. Though fragmentary, the *Bahir* is a book of some real literary value, and truly begins the kabbalistic style of parable and figurative language. Its major figuration is certainly the Sefirot, the attributes of God emanating out from an infinite center to every possible finite circumference. Where the Sefirot, in the *Sefer Yetzirah,* were only the ten primary numbers, a neo-Pythagorean notion, in the *Bahir* they are divine properties and powers, and supernal lights, aiding in the work of creation.

But this was still only a step toward the true emergence of Kabbalah, which took place in thirteenth-century southern France, and then spread across the border to find its home among the Jews of Spain, a process culminating in the masterpiece or Bible of Kabbalah, the *Sefer ha-Zohar*. The Zohar ("splendor") was written by Moses de Leon between 1280 and 1286 in Guadalajara, and with its circulation Kabbalah became a full-scale system of speculation. After seven hundred years the Zohar, with all its faults, remains the only indubitably great book in all of Western esotericism. Most of the Zohar is written in Aramaic, but as an artificial, highly literary language, rather than as a vernacular. There is an adequate five-volume English translation (published by the Soncino Press) still in print, and well worth reading, but it represents only a portion of the Zohar, which is, however, a unique book in that it is impossible to say what a complete version of it would be. The book (if it is a book) varies from manuscript to manuscript, and seems more a collection of books or a small library than what ordinarily we would describe as a self-centered work.

Rather than attempt a description of the Zohar here, I shall pass on immediately to a summary account, largely following Scholem, of the basic concepts and images of Kabbalah, and then return to glance at the Zohar before giving a sketch of the later Kabbalah, which was created after the Jews were exiled from Spain. For the Zohar is the central work of classical Kabbalah, centering on the doctrine of the Sefirot, but Kabbalah from the sixteenth century until today is a second or modern Kabbalah, largely the creation of Isaac Luria of Safed in Palestine (1534–72), and needs a rather different exposition.

Classical Kabbalah begins with a Neoplatonic vision of God. God is the *ein-sof* ("without end"), totally unknowable, and beyond representation, all images of Whom are merely hyperboles. As *ein-sof* has no attributes, His first manifestation is necessarily as *ayin* ("nothing"). Genesis had said that God created the world out of nothing. Kabbalah took this over as a literal statement, but interpreted it revisionistically as meaning just the opposite of what it said. God, being "*ayin*," created the world out of "*ayin*," and thus created the world *out of Himself*. The distinction between cause and effect was subverted by this initial kabbalistic formula, and indeed such rhetorical subversion became a distinctive feature of Kabbalah: "cause" and "effect" are always reversible, for the kabbalists regarded them as linguistic fictions, long before Nietzsche did.

Kabbalah, which thus from the start was revisionary in regard to Genesis (though asserting otherwise), was also revisionary of its pagan source in Neoplatonism. In Plotinus, emanation is a process *out from* God, but in Kabbalah the process must take place *within* God Himself. An even more crucial difference from Neoplatonism is that all kabbalistic theories of emanation are also theories of language. As Scholem says, "the God who manifests Himself is the God who expresses Himself," which means that the Sefirot are primarily *language*, attributes of God that need to be described by the various names of God when He is at work in creation. The Sefirot are complex figurations for God, tropes or turns of language that *substitute* for God. Indeed, one can say that the Sefirot are like poems, in that they are names implying complex commentaries that make them into texts. They are not allegorical personifications, which is what all popular manuals of Kabbalah reduce them to, and though they have extraordinary potency, this is a power of signification rather than what we customarily think of as magic.

Sefirah, the singular form, would seem to suggest the Greek "sphere," but its actual source was the Hebrew *sappir* (for "sapphire"), and so the term referred primarily to God's radiance. Scholem gives a very suggestive list of kabbalistic synonyms for the Sefirot: sayings, names, lights, powers, crowns, qualities, stages, garments, mirrors, shoots, sources, primal days, aspects, inner faces, and limbs of God. At first the kabbalists dared to identify the Sefirot with the actual substance of God, and the Zohar goes so far as to say of God and the Sefirot: "He is They, and They are He," which produces the rather dangerous formula that God and language are one and the same. But other kabbalists warily regarded the Sefirot only as God's tools, vessels that are instruments for Him, or as we might say, language is only God's tool or vessel. Moses Cordovero, the teacher of Luria and the greatest systematizer of Kabbalah, achieved the precarious balance of seeing the Sefirot as being at once somehow both God's vessels and His essence, but the conceptual difficulty remains right down to the present day, and has its exact analogues in certain current debates about the relationship between language and thought.

The Sefirot, then, are ten complex images for God in His process of creation, with an interplay between literal and figurative meaning going on within each Sefirah. There is a fairly fixed and definite and by now common ordering for the Sefirot:

1. *Keter Elyon* or *Keter* (the "supreme crown")
2. *Hokhmah* ("wisdom")
3. *Binah* ("intelligence")
4. *Gedullah* ("greatness") or *Hesed* ("love")
5. *Gevurah* ("power") or *Din* ("judgment" or "rigor")
6. *Tiferet* ("beauty") or *Rahamim* ("mercy")
7. *Nezah* ("victory" or "lasting endurance")
8. *Hod* ("majesty")

9. *Yesod* ("foundation")
10. *Malkhut* ("kingdom")

It is best to consider these allegorical images as carefully as possible, for the interplay of these images in some sense *is* the classical or zoharic Kabbalah, though *not* the later Kabbalah of Luria, out of which finally the Hasidic movement was to emerge. It is not a negative criticism of Scholem to say that the Sefirot have not interested him greatly. Scarcely a dozen pages out of the five hundred in *Kabbalah* are devoted to the details of Sefirot symbolism, just as only ten pages of the four hundred and fifty of Scholem's earlier *Major Trends in Jewish Mysticism* were concerned with expounding the Sefirot. Scholem is impatient with them, and prefers to examine larger mythological and historical aspects of Kabbalah. In contrast, popular expositions of Kabbalah for many centuries down to the drugstore present tend to talk about nothing but the Sefirot. What is their fascination for so many learned minds, as well as for the popular imagination? Contemporary readers encounter the Sefirot in curious places, such as Malcolm Lowry's *Under the Volcano* or Thomas Pynchon's *Gravity's Rainbow,* where these fundamental images of Kabbalah are used to suggest tragic patterns of overdetermination, by which our lives are somehow lived for us in spite of ourselves. Like the Tarot cards and astrology, with which popular tradition has confounded them, the Sefirot fascinate because they suggest an immutable knowledge of a final reality that stands behind our world of appearances. In some sense the Sefirot have become the staple of a popular Platonism or Hegelianism, a kind of magic idealism. Popular kabbalism has understood, somehow, that the Sefirot are neither *things* nor *acts,* but rather are *relational events,* and so are persuasive representations of what ordinary people encounter as the inner reality of their lives.

Keter, the "crown," is the primal will of the Creator, and is scarcely distinguishable from the *ein-sof,* except as being first effect to His first cause. But, though an effect, *keter* is no part of the Creation, which reflects *keter* but cannot absorb it. As it cannot be compared to any other image, it must be called *ayin,* a "nothingness," an object of quest that is also the subject of any search. As a name of God, *keter* is the *ehyeh* of the great declaration of God to Moses in Exodus 3:14; God says, *ehyeh asher ehyeh,* "I Am That I Am," but the kabbalists refused to interpret this as mere "being." To them, *keter* was at once *ehyeh* and *ayin,* being and nothingness, a cause of all causes and no cause at all, beyond action. If Kabbalah can be interpreted, as I think it can, as a theory of influence, then *keter* is the paradoxical idea of influence itself. The irony of all influence, initially, is that the source is emptied out into a state of absence, in order for the receiver to accommodate the influx of apparent being. This may be why we use the word "influence," originally an astral term referring to the occult effect of the stars upon men.

Below *keter* as crown, the Sefirot were generally depicted as a "tree of emanation." This tree grows downward, as any map of influence must. Another frequent depiction of the Sefirot is the "reversed tree," in which the emanations are arranged in the form of a man. In either image, the right-hand side begins with the first attribute proper, *hokhmah*, generally translated as "wisdom," but better understood as something like God's meditation or contemplation of Himself, and frequently called the "father of fathers" or the uncreated Tables of the Law. Freud's imago of the father is a close enough contemporary translation.

The matching imago of the mother, on the left side, is *binah*, usually rendered as "intelligence," but meaning something more like a passive understanding (Kabbalah is nothing if not sexist). *Binah* is sometimes imaged as a mirror (very much in a Gnostic tradition) in which God enjoys contemplating Himself. We can call *keter* the divine self-consciousness, *hokhmah* the active principle of knowing, and *binah* the known, or reflection upon knowledge, or the veil through which God's "wisdom" shines. In another kabbalistic image, certainly derived from Neoplatonism, *binah* as mirror acts as a prism, breaking open divine light into apprehensible colors.

The seven lesser Sefirot are the more immediate attributes of creation, moving out from *binah* in its role of supreme mother. Where the three upper Sefirot together form *arikh anpin* (Aramaic for "long face"), the great or transcendental "face" of God, the seven lower emanations form the "short face" or *ze'eir anpin,* the immanent countenance of God, and sometimes are called the Sefirot of "construction." Unlike the great face, the constructive principles are conceived by analogy, and so are nearly identical with the principles of figurative or poetic language. The first, on the father's or right-hand side, most often called *hesed,* is love in the particular sense of God's covenant-love, *caritas* or "grace" in Christian interpretation. Its matching component on the mother's or left-hand side is most often called *din,* "severity" or "rigorous judgment." God's covenant-love requires a limit or outward boundary, which is provided by *din.* This makes *din* the kabbalistic equivalent of the Orphic and Platonic *ananke* or necessity, the law of the cosmos. Creation, for the Kabbalah, depends upon the perpetual balance and oscillation of *hesed* and *din* as antithetical principles.

It is an unintentional irony of the Sefirot that they increase enormously in human and imaginative interest as they descend closer to our condition. Even the most exalted of kabbalist writers relax and are more inventive when they reach the lower half of the Sefirotic tree. With the sixth Sefirah, *tiferet,* the "mercy" or heart of God, we are in the aesthetic realm of God's "beauty," which for the Kabbalah is all the beauty there is. *Tiferet* is the principle of mediation, reconciling the "above" and the "below" on the tree, and also drawing together the right side and the left side, masculine and feminine. All kabbalistic references to centering are always to *tiferet,* and *tiferet* sometimes stands by itself for the "small face" or God's immanence, and is frequently spoken of as the dwelling-place of the *shekhinah* or "Divine Presence" (of which more later). In kabbalistic dialectic, *tiferet* completes the second triad of *hesed-din-tiferet,* and governs the third triad of *nezah-hod-yesod.*

Nezah or God's "victory" emanates from *hesed,* and represents the power of nature to increase itself, in a kind of apotheosis of male force. *Hod,* the female counterpart emanating from *din,* is a kind of equivalent to "mother nature" in the Western Romantic sense (a kabbalist would have called Wordsworth's or Emerson's Nature by the name of *hod*). *Hod* is "majesty" of the merely natural sort, but for the Kabbalah nothing of course is merely natural. Out of the creative strife of *nezah* and *hod* comes *yesod,* "foundation," which is at once human male sexuality and the ongoing balance of nature.

The tenth and last of the Sefirot is properly the most fascinating, *malkhut* or "kingdom," where "kingdom" refers to God's immanence in nature. From *tiferet, malkhut* inherits the *shekhinah,* and manifests that glory of God in His world. So *malkhut* is called the "descent," meaning the descent of the *shekhinah. Malkhut* is also called the "lower mother" as against the "higher mother" of *binah.* As the closest of the Sefirot to us, *malkhut* sums them up, and makes the world of emanation a pragmatic unity. The kabbalist encounters the Sefirot only through *malkhut,* which makes of kabbalism necessarily a sexual mysticism or erotic theosophy.

IV

In their total structure, the Sefirot are identified with the *merkabah* or "celestial chariot" in which the prophet Ezekiel saw the Divine manifest Himself. This identification led to a series of further symbolic analogies or correspondences—cosmological, philosophical, psychological, indeed every area in which overdetermined meanings could be plotted out. Popular kabbalism concerns itself with these overdeterminations, but they are not the prime spiritual significance of the Sefirot. That significance comes in the interrelationships of the Sefirot, their reflections of one another within themselves.

The great master of these reflections was Moses Cordovero (1522–70), the best example of a systematic thinker ever to appear among kabbalists. But the movement from the Zohar to Cordovero and on to Cordovero's pupil and surpasser, Luria, returns us from doctrine to history, for the later Kabbalah is the product of a second and intensified Exile, following the expulsion of the Jews from Spain in 1492. Perhaps Scholem's greatest achievement as a scholar has been his analysis of Lurianic Kabbalah as a myth of exile. The Sefirot, though they lend themselves to such a myth, are too close to the unfallen worlds fully to accommodate fresh onsets of historical suffering. I touch here upon what I take to be the deepest meaning of Kabbalah, and will digress upon it, before returning to problems of theosophical meaning.

Louis Ginzberg, one of the greatest of modern talmudists, introduced the Palestinian Talmud by remarking that post-biblical Jewish literature was "predominantly interpretative and commentative." This is true even of Kabbalah, which is curious for a body of work professedly mystical and speculative, even indeed mythopoeic. But this emphasis upon *interpretation* is finally what distinguishes Kabbalah from nearly every other variety of mysticism or theosophy, East or West. The kabbalists of medieval Spain, and their Palestinian successors after the expulsion from Spain, confronted a peculiar psychological problem, one that demanded a revisionist solution. How does one accommodate a fresh and vital new religious impulse, in a precarious and even catastrophic time of troubles, when one inherits a religious tradition already so rich and coherent that it allows very little room for fresh revelations or even speculations? The kabbalists were in no position to formulate or even reformulate much of anything in their religion. Given to them already was not only a massive and completed Scripture, but an even more massive and intellectually finished structure of every kind of commentary and interpretation. Their stance in relation to all this tradition became, I think, the classic paradigm upon which Western revisionism in all areas was to model itself ever since, usually in rather indirect emulation. For the kabbalists developed implicitly a psychology of belatedness, and with it an explicit, rhetorical series of techniques for opening Scripture and even received commentary to their own historical sufferings, and to their own, new theosophical insights. Their achievement was not just to restore *gnosis* and mythology to a Judaism which had purged itself of such elements, but more crucially to provide the masses of suffering Jewry with a more immediate and experiential personal faith than the strength of orthodox tradition might have allowed. Hasidism was the ultimate descendant of Kabbalah, and can be regarded as the more positive ultimate achievement of a movement that led, in its darker aspects, to morasses of magic and superstition, and to false messiahs and even apostates.

The Zohar, astonishingly beautiful as it frequently is, is not in itself greatly representative of what became, from the Spanish exile on, the true voice of Kabbalah. Though Cordovero and Luria derived fundamentally from the Zohar, their systems and visions actually have little in common with it. The Zohar is organized as an apparent commentary upon Scripture, just as much of the later Kabbalah is organized as an apparent commentary upon the Zohar, but it is the genius of revisionism to swerve so far from its canonical texts as to make the ancestral voices into even their own opposites. A contemporary reader encountering the Zohar will have trouble finding in it a clear statement about the structure and function of the Sefirot, let alone any of the more complex refinements of Kabbalah. Such a reader will find himself confronted by hundreds of homilies and little stories, many of them haunting in their enigmas, but finally compelling the reader to wish that the Zohar would obey its own injunction about how to interpret Scripture or the Torah:

> As wine in a jar, if it is to keep, so is the Torah, contained within
> its outer garment. Such a garment is made up of many stories,
> but we, we are required to pierce the garment.

To pierce the garment of the Zohar is almost impossible, but in some sense that was the achievement of Cordovero and of Luria.

V

Scholem makes the point that after 1492 and the fresh dispersal of the Jews, the Kabbalah ceased to be esoteric and became "public property." From about 1530 on, Safed in Palestine became the center of the new Kabbalah, and from Safed there emanated out to the Diaspora what became a new popular religion, which captured much of Judaism, and has left an influence (now much diminished) on it ever since. Isaac Luria was much the largest source of this new religion, and will receive more analysis here, as he does in Scholem, but Cordovero was a clearer and more systematic theorist, and some account of his ideas remains the best introduction to the intricacies of the Lurianic Kabbalah.

As early as the 13th century, kabbalists spoke of the Sefirot reflecting themselves within themselves, so that each "contained" all the others. Complex systems of pathways of Sefirot within Sefirot were set up, and meditation upon these pathways became the characteristic kabbalistic exercise, whether in vision, prayer, or intellectual speculation. This theosophical pathbreaking becomes in Cordovero what Ginzberg and other scholars have described accurately as a theory of influence. Cordovero invented a new category, *behinot,* to convey the multiform aspects within each Sefirot, aspects that account for the links between Sefirot. These are the six *behinot* or phases of the ten Sefirot, as differentiated by Cordovero: (1) Concealed before manifestation within the preceding Sefirah; (2) Actual manifestation in the preceding Sefirah; (3) Appearance as Sefirah in its own name; (4) Aspect that gives power to the Sefirah above it, so as to enable that Sefirah to be strong enough to emanate yet further Sefirot; (5) Aspect that gives power to the Sefirah itself to emanate out the other Sefirot still concealed within it; (6) Aspect by which the following Sefirah is in turn emanated out to its own place, after which the cycle of the six *behinot* begins again.

This cycle may seem baffling at first, but is a remarkable theory of influence, as causal yet reversed relationships. To be understood today it needs translation into other terms, and these can be psychoanalytic, rhetorical, or imagistic, for the six *behinot* can be interpreted as psychological mechanisms of defense, rhetorical tropes, or areas of poetic imagery. Whereas the Sefirot, as attributes of God, are manifestly supernatural channels of influence (or, rhetorically speaking, divine poems, each a text in itself), the *behinot* work more like human agencies, whether psychic or linguistic. Scholem indicates that, in Cordovero, the Sefirot "actually become the structural elements of all things," but they do this only by their aspects, or *behinot.* One might indeed call Cordovero the first structuralist, an unacknowledged ancestor of many contemporary French theorists of the "human sciences."

In order to see precisely the great dialectical leap that Isaac Luria took away from his teacher, Cordovero, it is necessary to expound the true, dark heart of Kabbalah: its vision of the problem of evil. Scholem rightly remarks that Jewish philosophy was not very much interested in the problem of evil, and it seems just to observe that talmudic tradition was also too healthy to brood excessively on evil. But Kabbalah departed both from normative Judaism and from Neoplatonism in its obsessive concern with evil. For Neoplatonism, evil has no metaphysical reality, but Gnosticism engaged evil as the reality of this world, which presumably is why Gnosticism now lives, under a variety of disguises, while Neoplatonism is the province of scholars. Probably, this is why the Lurianic Kabbalah came to dominate popular Judaism for many centuries, giving birth first to a series of false messiahs, and finally to the lasting glory of the Baal Shem Tov and his Hasidism.

The book *Bahir* speaks of the Sefirah *gevurah* or *din* as the left hand of God, and so as a permitted evil. Out of this came the kabbalistic doctrine that located evil in what Freud called the superego, or in kabbalistic terms, the separation of *din* from *hesed,* stern judgment from love. The world of *din* brought forth the *sitra ahra* or "the other side," the sinister qualities that came out of a name of God, but then fell away.

The Zohar assigned to the *sitra ahra* ten Sefirot all its own, ten sinister crowns representing the remnants of worlds that God first made and then destroyed. In one of the great poetic images of esoteric tradition, Moses de Leon compared evil to the bark of the tree of the Sefirot, the *kelippah.* The creatures of this bark—Samael and his wife Lilith, or Satan and the chief of witches (of whom more later)—became in the Zohar almost worthy antagonists of God. *Kelippot,* conceived first as bark, became regarded also as husks or shells or broken vessels of evil. But even in the *kelippot,* according to the Zohar, there abides a saving spark of God. This notion, that there are sparks in the *kelippot* that can be redeemed, and redeemed by the acts of men alone and not of God, became the starting-point of Lurianic Kabbalah.

VI

The problem of original genius in every intellectual area, past a certain date (a date upon which no two people can agree), is always located in the apparently opposed principles of continuity and discontinuity. Yet the very word Kabbalah means tradition, and every master of Kabbalah has stressed his own continuity rather than his discontinuity with previous speculators. Luria is extraordinarily original, indeed he may have been the only visionary in the entire history of Kabbalah whose basic ideas were original, since the entire tradition from the *Sefer Yetzirah* through Cordovero is finally only an amalgam, however strangely shaped, of Neoplatonism and Gnosticism. But Luria had the originality of certain great poets—Dante, Milton, Blake— though since the important accounts of his visions are not written by him, but by rival and contrasting disciples, it is difficult to compare Luria's powers of invention with those of other creators.

Before Luria, all of Kabbalah saw creation as a progressive process, moving in one direction always, emanating out from God through the Sefirot to man, a movement in which each stage joined itself closely to the subsequent stage, without enormous leaps or backward recoilings. In Luria, creation is a startlingly regressive process, one in which an abyss can separate any one stage from another, and in which catastrophe is always a central event. Reality for Luria is always a triple rhythm of contraction, breaking apart, and mending, a rhythm continuously present in time even as it first punctuated eternity.

Luria named this triple process: *tzimtzum, shevirat ha-kelim, tikkun* (contraction, the breaking-of-the-vessels, restitution). *Tzimtzum* originally seems to have meant a holding-in-of-the-breath, but Luria transformed the word into an idea of limitation, of God's hiding of Himself, or rather entering into Himself. In this contraction, God clears a space for creation, a not-God. This cleared point the Zohar had called *tehiru,* or fundamental space. Luria saw the *tzimtzum* as God's concentration within Himself of the Sefirah of *din,* rigor, but part of this power of stern judgment remained behind in the cleared *tehiru,* where it mixed together with the remnants of God's self-withdrawn light, called by Luria the *reshimu.* Into the mixture (out of which our world is to be formed), God sends a single letter, the *yod,* the first letter of His great name, YHWH, the Tetragrammaton. This *yod* is the active principle in creation, even as the *reshimu* is the passive principle.

This creation, according to Luria, was of *kelim,* "vessels," of which the culminating vessel was *adam kadmon* or primal man. Two kinds of light had made these vessels, the new or incoming light that had accompanied the *yod* or word of God, and the light left behind in the *tehiru* after the *tzimtzum.* The collision of lights is an enormously complex process, for which this present essay lacks space, but the crucial element in the complexity is that *adam kadmon,* man as he should be, is a kind of perpetual war of light against light. This war emanates out from his head in patterns of *writing,* which become fresh vessels of creation, newly manifested structures of Sefirot. But though the three upper Sefirot held firm, and contained the pugnacious light, the six Sefirot from *hesed* to *yesod* broke apart. This breaking or scattering of the vessels was caused by the force of the light hitting all at once, in what can be interpreted as too strong a force of *writing,* stronger than the "texts" of the lower Sefirot could sustain. Paradoxically, God's name was too strong for His words, and the breaking of the vessels necessarily became a divine act of *substitution,* in which an original pattern yielded to a more chaotic one that nevertheless remained pattern, the guarantee of which was that the vessel of the tenth and last Sefirah, *malkhut* or the female world, broke also, but less sharply than the other vessels.

Though some of the light in the shattered vessels returned immediately to God, much of it fell down with the vessels, so as to form the *kelippot* or evil forces of the universe. But these *kelippot* still have pattern or design, as well as sparks of light imprisoned within them. Luria appears to have believed that all this catastrophe came about because of an original excess of *din,* a plethora of rigor in God Himself, and it is in the Sefirah of *din* that the smashing-apart begins. Scholem theorizes that Luria saw the whole function of creation as being God's catharsis of Himself, a vast sublimation in which His terrible rigor might find some peace. This is not unlike Freud's extraordinary explanation as to why people fall in love, which is to avoid an overfilled inner self. As man must love, in Freud's view, in order to avoid becoming sick, so Luria's God has to create, for His own health. But He could create only by catastrophe, in Luria's judgment, an opinion again very like that of Freud's disciple, Ferenczi, whose book *Thalassa* also ascribes every act of creation to a necessary catastrophe.

Remarkable as these first two stages of Luria's vision are, both *tzimtzum* and *shevirah* are less important in his doctrine than *tikkun*, the saving process of restoration and restitution, for this is the work of the human, taking place through a complex agency called the *partzufim* or "faces," the Lurianic equivalent of Cordovero's *behinot*. Scholem calls the *partzufim* "configurations" or *gestalten*, but like the *behinot* they seem to be at once psychic and linguistic, defense mechanisms and rhetorical tropes. As patterns of images, the *partzufim* organize the shattered world after the vessels have broken apart, and as principles of organization they substitute for or take the place of the Sefirot. *Keter* or the crown is substituted for by the *partzuf* of *arikh anpin*, or God as the "long-faced one," that is to say, the God who is indulgent or forbearing even in fallen history. *Hokhmah* and *binah* are replaced by what Freud called the Imagos, *abba* and *imma*, "father" and "mother," who together create the fourth and most important *partzuf*, called *ze'eir anpin*, the "short-faced" or "impatient" or "unindulgent" God, who stands in judgment upon history. *Ze'eir anpin* substitutes for the six lower Sefirot, from *din* to *yesod*, the six that broke apart most dreadfully. *Ze'eir anpin* thus substitutes also quite directly for the *behinot* of Luria's teacher, Cordovero, and in some sense this *partzuf* can be considered as Luria's revisionist misprision or creative misunderstanding of his direct precursor's most original and important doctrine. Luria's last *partzuf* is called *nukba de-ze'eir*, the female of the impatient God, and substitutes for *malkhut* or the kingdom.

Together, the *partzufim* make up a new and second *adam kadmon*, for the *tikkun* or restoration of creation must be carried out by the religious acts of individual men, of all Jews struggling in the Exile, and indeed of all men and women struggling in the Exile that Luria saw as the universal human existence. The nature of such religious acts of *tikkun* is again too complex to define in a limited space, but essentially these are acts of meditation, acts that lift up and so liberate the fallen sparks of God from their imprisonment in the shards of the *kelippot*. Such acts of meditation are at once psychic and linguistic, but for Luria they are magical too, so that they enter the sphere of practical Kabbalah, a puzzling world that this essay must conclude by entering also.

VII

As a psychology of belatedness, Kabbalah manifests many prefigurations of Freudian doctrine. Yet most of these stem from the psychological notions of Neoplatonism, and are not original with Kabbalah. Thus, the kabbalistic division of the soul into three parts is Neoplatonic, where the lowest soul is the *nefesh* or vital being with which everyone is born. The *ru'ah* or *anima* comes about later through a spiritual awakening, but only with the highest awakening is the true soul born, the *neshamah* or *spiritus*. Lurianic Kabbalah added further souls, so as to achieve a psychic cartography. But a more truly original notion, and one more prophetic of Freud, is the *tzelem,* or divine image in every man, first set forth in the Zohar and then developed by Luria and his disciples. The *tzelem* is a modification of the later Neoplatonic idea of the Astral Body, a kind of quasi-material entity that holds together mind and physical body, and that survives the death of the body proper.

In Lurianic Kabbalah, the Astral Body also serves the function of determining an individual human personality, so that the difference between one of us and another is not necessarily in any part of the soul, but in the enigmatic joining of soul and body, that is, in the relationship between our consciousness and our body. What makes us individual, our *tzelem,* is the way our particular body feels about our psyche, or the way that psyche feels about the body to which it is linked. Scholem says that "without the *tzelem* the soul would burn the body up with its fierce radiance," and one can add conversely that the body's desires would consume the soul without the *tzelem.* It is as though Luria were saying, in our terms, that the body is the unconscious as far as the soul is concerned, or that the soul is the unconscious from the stance of the body.

It was only a step from the idea of the *tzelem* to the Lurianic version of the transmigration of souls, called *gilgul.* Luria seems to have taught that there were families of souls, united by the root of a common spark. Each person can take up in himself the spark of another soul, of one of the dead, provided that he and the dead share the same root. This leads to the larger idea of a kind of eternal recurrence, with the saving difference that *gilgul* can be the final form of *tikkun,* in which the fallen soul can have its flaws repaired. The legend of the *dibbuk* is a negative version of the same idea.

With the idea of *gilgul,* speculative Kabbalah passes into practical Kabbalah, a world of "white" magic, dependent, however, entirely upon the sacredness of a divine language. It is very difficult to distinguish practical Kabbalah from the whole body of Jewish magic and superstition, the vast accumulation of folklore that so long a tradition brings forth. Very late or popular Kabbalah also became mixed with the "occult sciences," particularly astrology and alchemy, but these have little to do with Kabbalah proper.

Two areas of practical Kabbalah seem most authentic: demonology and what was called *gematria,* the explanation of words according to their numerical values, by set rules. Kabbalistic demonology became absorbed by the wilder aspects of Hasidism, and is now familiar to a wide group of contemporary readers through the fiction of Isaac Bashevis Singer. Such demonology ultimately centers upon two figures, Lilith and Samael. One can wonder why Lilith has not become the patroness of some of the more extreme manifestations of the women's liberation movement, as her legendary career shows a strong counter-current of guilt toward women (and fear of them) moving in Kabbalah.

Kabbalah enshrined the *shekhinah* or Divine Presence in the shape of a woman, an image of splendor-in-exile, and the Sefirot are relatively fairly balanced between male and female sides. Yet kabbalistic texts awaken into a peculiar vividness whenever Lilith is invoked. Though she seems to have begun as a Babylonian wind-demoness, she became very thoroughly naturalized in Jewish contexts. A pre-kabbalistic legend held that she was Adam's first wife, and that she abandoned him on the issue of sexual equality, with the immediate cause of separation being that of positions in sexual intercourse, Adam favoring the missionary posture, while she insisted on the ascendancy. In Kabbalah, Lilith dwindled from a heroic self-asserter into a strangler of infants, and into the muse of masturbation, bearing endless imps to those guilty of self-gratification. Kabbalah also married her off to Samael, the principal later Jewish name for Satan as the Angel of Death. The obsessive emphasis upon Lilith's lustfulness throughout kabbalistic literature is an obvious indication of the large element of repression in all those Gnostic fantasies that inhabit the entire history of Kabbalah.

If Lilith is a Gnostic reversal of the *shekhinah,* a demonic parody of the kabbalistic pathos of attempting to exalt aspects of Exile, then it seems fair to say that the techniques of *gematria* were a kind of parody of the sometimes sublime kabbalistic exaltation of language, and of the arts of interpretation. For *gematria* is interpretative freedom gone mad, in which any text can be made to mean anything. But its prevalence was itself a mark of the desperation that underlay much of Kabbalah. To open an ancient text to the experiential sufferings of contemporary men and women was the not ignoble motive of much kabbalism. *Gematria,* with its descents into occult numerologies, is finally best viewed as an index to how tremendous the suffering was, for the pressure of the sorrow came close to destroying one of the greatest interpretative traditions in cultural history.

"Mysticism" is a word I have avoided in this essay, for Kabbalah seems to be more of an interpretative and mythical tradition than a mystical one. There were kabbalistic ecstatics, and subtraditions of meditative intensities, of prayer conducted in an esoteric manner. But Kabbalah differs finally from Christian or Eastern mysticism in being more a mode of intellectual speculation than a way of union with God. Like the Gnostics, the kabbalists sought *knowledge,* but unlike the Gnostics they sought knowledge in the Book. By centering upon the Bible, Kabbalah made of itself, at its best, a critical tradition, though distinguished by more invention than critical traditions generally display. In its degeneracy, Kabbalah has sought vainly for a magical power over nature, but in its glory it sought, and found, a power of the mind over the universe of death.

ROBERT ALTER

Scholem and Sabbatianism

In circles that have remained closely in touch with Jewish history—which, by and large, has meant among readers of Hebrew or Yiddish—the figure of Sabbatai Zevi, the seventeenth-century pseudo-messiah, has in recent times possessed a strange magnetism. It is suggestive that Avraham Mapu (1808–1867), who initiated the Hebrew novel with a book set in the time of Isaiah, soon afterward began work on a novel called *The Visionaries* (of which only a fragment has survived) dealing with the Sabbatians. The subject has been treated by Sholem Asch (in Yiddish), by Israel Zangwill (in English), by Haim Hazaz (in Hebrew), and, of late, most impressively, by Isaac Bashevis Singer, again in Yiddish. In Jewish scholarship, moreover, during the past thirty years, Sabbatianism has become one of the great subjects of research. Most of this activity has been directly influenced by Gershom Scholem, who first announced the program for a general reassessment of Sabbatianism in an essay written in 1937, *Mitzvah ha-Baah ba-'Aveirah* (the untranslatable Hebrew title, which alludes to a Sabbatian reinterpretation of a talmudic concept, might be roughly paraphrased as "The Way of Holy Sinning"); Scholem's two-volume work in Hebrew on Sabbatai Zevi, published in 1957, stands as one of the major achievements of modern Jewish historiography.

The impression one gets from the usual handbooks of Jewish history or from the standard encyclopedias—all of them based on the hostile and misinformed scholarship of the nineteenth century—is that Sabbatianism was

From *After the Tradition: Essays on Modern Jewish Writing.* © 1969 by Robert Alter. Dutton, 1969.

merely a bizarre and transient episode in Jewish history. A deluded Turkish Jew, his brain addled by mystic studies, pronounces the ineffable name of God to an assembled congregation in Smyrna. After he persists in committing this and other forbidden acts, the local rabbis banish him, and eventually he makes his way to Palestine, where he meets up with a very young man called Nathan of Gaza, who, unlike Sabbatai Zevi, has a genius for both theology and propaganda. Nathan manages to convince the older man that he, Sabbatai, is the Messiah, son of David, something he seems inclined to have believed at times anyway, and the two begin to look fervently for the imminent unfolding of the redemption, perhaps in the next year, 1666. Sabbatai returns to Smyrna to announce his mission while Nathan, his "prophet," busies himself sending out emissaries to the far reaches of the diaspora, bearing the good tidings. Almost everywhere, masses of Jews respond to the call of redemption. Sabbatai Zevi proceeds to Constantinople, where his followers expect him to take the crown from the head of the sultan. Instead, he is imprisoned for inciting insurrection; after being detained in what proves to be grand state in the fortress at Gallipoli—the divinely appointed bastion, his followers believe, from which he will soon emerge for the last great battle with the forces of evil—he is summoned to judgment and offered the choice between death by slow torture and conversion to Islam; unhesitatingly, he assumes the fez.

Sabbatai Zevi's apostasy strikes Jews everywhere with the profoundest consternation and despair; in its aftermath, only small sectarian groups of the "faithful" cling to the belief in his messiahship, explaining that he has entered into the realm of defilement in order to redeem or conquer evil at its very source. Some of the faithful imitate their master by themselves converting; others engage in orgiastic rites in order to emulate the audacious plunge of the redeemer into the sphere of impurity. A century later, when the social, political, and intellectual horizons of the Jewish people begin to enlarge significantly with the advent of the Enlightenment and the French Revolution, Sabbatianism seems like a bad dream, a last sickly residue of what were still the Jewish middle ages.

In contrast to this general image of Sabbatianism, which owes much to the rationalistic bias of nineteenth-century Jewish historiography, Scholem has tried to understand the subject sympathetically, as a manifestation of religious consciousness, not merely of psychopathology. Above all else, he has sought to demonstrate that Sabbatianism, far from being a strange passing episode, is in effect the beginning of modern Jewish history. He is able to establish through a careful and exhaustive examination of contemporary documents that the proportions of Sabbatianism, both in the lifetime of

Sabbatai Zevi and afterward, were far greater than the official "Jewish" versions of the events have led us to believe. During those hectic months of messianic jubilation before the apostasy, opposition to Sabbatai Zevi in all but a few places was negligible or simply did not exist. Revered rabbis, adepts of the Law, pillars of the various communities, believed without question in Sabbatai's messiahship; the minority who had doubts kept prudently silent for the most part in the face of the fervid enthusiasm of the Jewish populace. Until the apostasy, then, there was no Sabbatian "sect"; one must rather say that Sabbatai Zevi, with only minor exceptions, was the acclaimed Messiah of the Jewish people, from Yemen to Galicia, from Tunis to Amsterdam. Scholem also shows that very considerable numbers of Jews still adhered to the belief in Sabbatai, and the imminent redemption he would bring, for nearly a century after his death. The most essential point, however, of Scholem's revisionist history is that for a brief moment almost the whole Jewish people was convinced it was living in the presence of the dawning redemption—the *atḥalta d'geulah*—and that many would never again be able to accept their unredeemed, restricted lives as ghetto Jews in the same unquestioning way. A passage in which Scholem discusses the new relation to rabbinic law into which the Sabbatian experience thrust Jews touches on a crux of his argument and also reveals a chief source for his own fascination with the whole Sabbatian phenomenon:

> The believers were able to develop a new criterion with which to measure ghetto reality. This ghetto Judaism had been and was still upheld by the "infidels" who denied the Redeemer's mission, men who possessed the mere body of the Torah and not its innerness. It would not be long before some of the believers would come, whether in extreme or moderate forms, to a criticism of rabbinic Judaism. And that criticism, it must be emphasized, would be from within, not primarily dependent upon the influence of external causes and historical circumstances, like the criticism evoked in the period of the French Revolution and in the age of struggle for political rights for the Jews. . . . And if the traditional forms no longer fit the paradoxical values upon which the movement stood, they would have to seek new and other expressions for their utopian Jewish consciousness. For their consciousness was Jewish and remained Jewish; even at moments of open conflict with the ruling powers of the traditional Jewish society, the believers did not seek to deny their historical Jewish identity from the start.

The general effect of Scholem's pioneering research into Sabbatianism is to turn inside out many of our preconceptions of what is Jewish and what is not. If we think of Jews as tough-minded rationalists, wryly ironic realists, Scholem shows us a whole people emotionally caught up in the most fantastic faith, men and women alike wildly dancing, rolling on the ground, foaming at the mouth, uttering prophecies. If we think of Jews as people living within tightly drawn lines of legal restriction and self-imposed restraint, Scholem shows us Jews casting off all bonds, entering, so they thought, into a new world of unlimited freedom where, according to the Sabbatian maxim, "the abrogation of the Torah is its true fulfillment." If we think of Judaism as a broad antithesis to Christianity in some of its most essential assumptions, Scholem shows us Jews insisting on the primacy of faith over works, Jews coming to believe in a trinitarian God of which the Son, or Messiah, is part, Jews arguing—with the traditional method and idiom of rabbinic discourse as well as of the Kabbalah—that the Messiah has taken upon himself seeming disgrace and outward defeat in order to redeem a sinful world. If our stereotype of the premodern Jew tends to be a puritanical figure, stern, pale, enveloped in somber cloth, following a faith in which the dominant symbols and institutional arrangements are masculine, Scholem discovers for us a Messiah who awakens the hearts of Jews to the possibilities of serving God through the pleasures of the body, who sings this poignantly sensual Spanish song to the *Shekhina* at the holy ark, Torah in hand:

> When I went up to the mountaintop
> When I came down to the river's edge
> I met Meliselda
> Who is the Emperor's daughter
> Coming up from the bath
> From the bath where she had washed.
> Her face flashed like a sword
> Her brows were like the bow
> Her lips were like corals
> And her flesh whiter than milk.

This is not to suggest that Scholem, the disciplined scholar and patient reasoner, so clearly an "Apollonian" figure, is preaching through his scholarship the adaptation of a "Dionysian" form of Jewish life. But what he construes to be the vitality manifested in Sabbatianism is what especially draws him to it, and it is this which he himself emphasizes in the preface to his *Shabbtai Tzvi*: "The degree of vitality in these phenomena surprises us no less than the degree of daring in them, and the eyes of recent generations

have learned to see the spark of Jewish life and the constructive longings
even in phenomena which Jewish tradition fought against with all its soul."
Now, vitality is a concept which, when it is not completely self-evident,
becomes oddly elusive, and I must say that I find this to be the case with
Scholem. One man's vitality is another man's sickness, as opposing interpretations of Sabbatianism vividly illustrate. Scholem seems to connect vitality almost axiomatically with antinomianism, though it could easily be
argued that antinomianism in general, especially as it moves toward the
unbridled excesses to which its inner logic drives it, is rather an expression
of cultural, moral, and psychological disintegration, sharing with vitality only
the superficial similarity of violent motion. More plausibly, Scholem appears
to associate vitality with the return to the full life of the senses that is at
least implicit in the urgent messianic expectations of the Sabbatian movement. If the early talmudic masters had taught their disciples to imagine this
world as an "anteroom" to the "main hall" of a true world elsewhere, the
Sabbatians thought they were seeing the anteroom transformed before their
eyes into the inner hall of the palace, and so there is, paradoxically, a powerful
impulse toward realizing the fullness of life here and now in the very movement so intoxicated with the heady mysteries of the divine Beyond. Finally,
Sabbatianism is an expression of national vitality for Scholem because it
begins to look like a movement of autoemancipation miscarried only because
the age in which it occurred made its political implementation unfeasible:
Sabbatai Zevi, the manic-depressive kabbalist, is no Theodor Herzl, but it is
undeniable that at his call thousands upon thousands of Jews in all parts of
the diaspora actually began to pack up their possessions and prepared to
march after him to Zion.

   "Vitality" has been a great will-o'-the-wisp of Hebrew literature at least
since the time of Berditchevsky, Schneur, Tchernichovsky—the first generation of Hebrew writers to be influenced by Nietzsche—and I think that it is
against this background that Scholem's emphasis on the vitality of Sabbatianism has to be seen. The Sabbatian movement plays much the same role
in Scholem's imaginative vision—and he is a historian who clearly possesses
such a vision—as the cults of Baal, Astarte, and Tammuz play in the poetry
of Tchernichovsky and the latter-day Canaanites after him. Both the pagan
gods and the more recent messianic movement embody possibilities of a
dramatic "transvaluation of values" for the Jewish people, and Scholem in
fact uses the Hebrew equivalent of that Nietzschean formula, *shinui 'arak-
him,* more than once in describing the Sabbatian program. The Canaanite
gods, however, are a convenient literary fiction, a cultural alternative borrowed from the outside that at best merely impinged once upon ancient

Israel. Scholem's model of vitality, on the other hand, is the product of a process immanent in Jewish historical experience. The Sabbatians see themselves as the legitimate heirs of the Jewish past; even as they set about radically transforming the practices and values of Jewish tradition, "their consciousness was Jewish and remained Jewish." Scholem argues, moreover, that there is some causal connection between them and the nineteenth-century modernizing movements that sought to change the basic conditions of Jewish existence.

Scholem's encompassing interpretation of Sabbatianism is so subtly developed that it is hard to know how much of it is really cogent, how much merely seductive. The subject, at any rate, has a seductive allure for him, and I think his relationship to it is finally Faustian, as Faust in Part Two of Goethe's poem plunges into the depths of the past to capture a beauty and power that will always elude him. This, if I read him right, is what S. Y. Agnon is suggesting about enterprises like Scholem's in his remarkable tale, *Edo and Enam*. According to literary gossip in Jerusalem, Dr. Ginath, the enigmatic discoverer of unknown ancient cultures in the story, is in fact an oblique allusion to Agnon's old friend, Gershom Scholem. (The character's name might be a clue: there is a medieval kabbalistic work entitled *Ginath Egoz*, which, like all other kabbalistic works has been discussed in print by Scholem. The word refers to the "garden" of mystic contemplation.) Twice in the story, a character wonders, jokingly, whether Dr. Ginath might not be sitting in his room writing a third part to Faust. Ginath's key to the mysteries of the primal past is, in a strangely denatured way, erotic: in the somnambulistic Gemulah he holds the Helen of a civilization older than Troy whom he will never really possess, as Faust never really possesses Helen. There is something both poignant and ghoulish in her love for him, his use of her; and the intrinsic logic of their relationship brings them to mutual destruction. If, at the end of the tale, Ginath leaves after him the luminous life and beauty of the past he has captured in his work for every man to "make use of its light," that final phrase echoes another a few pages earlier about the ambiguous light of the moon, magically linked to the doomed Gemulah, of which the narrator must warn: "Happy is the man who can make use of its light and come to no harm."

Agnon, in his symbolic treatment of the characteristically modern quest for sources of renewal in the past, is concerned with the ultimate spiritual dangers of such pursuits, but Scholem's own scholarly enterprise also has more immediate implications, and as a useful gloss upon them I would like to offer another imaginative work in Hebrew, Haim Hazaz' play, *In the End of Days*. The Hazaz play, written in 1950, is in no way a direct comment

on Scholem, but it provides an instructive parallel, making explicit the ideological message of Sabbatianism that seems to be implicit for Scholem. The
action is set in a German town during the time of Sabbatai Zevi's ascendancy.
Yuzpa, the fiery messianist who is eventually excommunicated for his rebellion against the traditional order, can be taken, with little qualification, as
Hazaz' spokesman in the play, and the doctrine he preaches is the annihi-
lation of the Exile, which for him means a tearing apart of the institutional
bonds that held life in the diaspora together: "The strength of the Exile is
in Torah, commandments, and the fear of heaven. . . . Torah has been absorbed by Exile, has become synonymous with it." It begins to be clear why
Sabbatian antinomianism should be associated with vitality, for all the heavy
restrictions, sodden with the weight of Exile, must be cast off in order to
enter the new world of freedom and life: "We will bury ourselves, a burial
of the dead, in license, in promiscuity and raw instinct, in order to arise
from the void and chaos of this world like the sleepers of the dust who are
destined to be resurrected, pure and clean and seven times more alive."

Hazaz, let me emphasize, is not really interested in moral anarchy but
rather uses such anarchy as a dramatic symbol for what he conceives as the
desperate need to smash the Exile, to extirpate all bonds and allegiances with
the world of Exile. The main referent of messianism in his play is not individual and anarchic but collective and political. When Yuzpa interprets Sabbatianism as a call for Jews to seize the reins of their own destiny, we hear
in his words a distinctly Zionist modernization of the seventeenth-century
movement; Scholem, as a meticulous scholar, is careful to represent his subject in its own premodern religious terms, but he often leads us to infer the
same analogy with the modern secular movement of redemption that is forced
upon us by Hazaz' protagonist: "Heaven is in our hands . . . understand
that, my friend, understand that. The Redemption depends on us; more than
on God Almighty and more than on the Son of David, it depends on us.
Not the Messiah alone, but us as well, the whole people of Israel and every
single Jew! Great is the Redemption we possess, for we ourselves have conceived it. . . . We decreed and He—must carry it out."

Although I do not think that Scholem's superb scholarship can justly
be called tendentious, there is surely some connection between his ideological
commitment to secular Zionism and his professional commitment to the
study of Sabbatianism. If we are generally accustomed to place the rise of
Zionism in the context of nineteenth-century European nationalism, Scholem's reassessment of Sabbatianism emphasizes a powerful desire for immediate national redemption working through the entire people, an
exhaustion of patience with life in exile, which are not dependent upon

external influences or the imitation of European models. Scholem finally sees Sabbatianism as a preparation of the ground for modern Jewish nationalism, and he even tries to establish a lineal descent—somewhat sketchily, it must be said—from known Sabbatian families to the first Jewish proponents of Enlightenment, who in turn prepared the way for the beginnings of Zionism. Scholem has been vehemently attacked on this point by Baruch Kurzweil, the Israeli literary and cultural critic, who claims that it represents a spurious attempt to legitimize secular Zionism in Jewish terms, to set it up as the logical and authentic product of a process working within Jewish history before its exposure to the great innovating forces of the modern world. Kurzweil vigorously denies any causal connection between Sabbatianism and the Hebrew Enlightenment, though he bases his argument less on historical documentation than on common sense—perhaps a dangerous criterion in history—and on his deep personal conviction that Sabbatianism is a pathological "borderline phenomenon" from which little can be learned about Judaism in its strength or about the Jewish people as a whole.

I cannot pretend to the competence needed to resolve the complex question of Sabbatianism's role in the concatenation of modern Jewish history, but it does not seem to me that the proof of historical causation is indispensable to Scholem's implicit argument for the contemporary relevance of his subject. The ultimate importance of Sabbatianism for our age, even in Scholem's case, is as a paradigm and not as an ancestor. In a period when many conscious Jews are trying to sort out the confusions of their own Jewish identity by a renewed confrontation with the variety of the Jewish past, the Sabbatians embody possibilities of Jewish existence, lived in the fullness of "utopian Jewish consciousness," which are—despite Kurzweil—imaginatively stirring, in any case challenging, and in certain obvious ways deeply disturbing as well. We adopt figures from the past as our contemporaries out of our own needs, regardless of the lines of historical connection with them, and Sabbatai Zevi, the grandly and pathetically deluded Messiah, reaching out for a lustrous world of redemption over the precarious brink of an abyss of anarchy, is, for better or for worse, a distinct contemporary.

ROBERT ALTER

The Achievement of Gershom Scholem

The cabalist from whom the creature took
Its inspiration called the weird thing Golem—
But all these matters are discussed by Scholem
In a most learned passage in his book.
                              —J. L. BORGES, "The Golem"

I would believe only in a God who could dance.
                              —NIETZSCHE, *Thus Spake Zarathustra*

"The desire to destroy," wrote Bakunin, "is also a creative desire," and he managed to inflame—indeed, his ideas still inflame—tens of thousands of minds through his incandescent vision of "the whole of Europe, with St. Petersburg, Paris, and London, transformed into an enormous rubbish-heap." A century before Bakunin, precisely the same ecstatic lust for destruction joined with the same messianic fervor had flared up in the teachings of an obscure Polish Jew named Jacob Frank, though Frank's initial field of reference was theological, not political: "Wherever Adam trod a city was built, but wherever I set foot all will be destroyed, for I came into this world only to destroy and to annihilate. But what I build, will last forever." Bakunin's impact, of course, has been, quite literally, terrific: the Russian anarchist's doctrine has haunted the modern literary imagination and has provided political fanaticism an unfailing source, down to the Bomber Left of our own days, for the dream of redemption through a purifying rite of cataclysmic destruction. Frank, on the other hand, is not likely to have come

From *Commentary* 55, no. 4 (April 1973). © 1973 by the American Jewish Committee.

to the attention of anyone but a serious student of Jewish history, yet this self-chosen messiah of an antinomian sect, both in his psychology and his program of action, offers us, no less than Bakunin, a disturbingly instructive instance of the paradoxes of modernity. Both show us modern man, deformed by his personal and cultural past, in the awful desperation and contradictions of his effort to smash the old molds at whatever cost and create a shining new order.

The juxtaposition of Bakunin and Frank may suggest something of the peculiarity of Gershom Scholem's enterprise as a historian. His work on Jewish mysticism, messianism, and sectarianism, spanning now half a century, constitutes, I should think, one of the major achievements of the historical imagination in our time. I would contend that it is of vital interest not only to anyone concerned with the history of religion but to anyone struggling to understand the underlying problematics of the modern predicament. Yet all along Scholem has been laboring in a forgotten vineyard choked with thorns, a field whose very existence was scarcely recognized before he began his researches in Germany after World War I. The figures he has illuminated—Frank, Sabbatai Zevi, Eleazar of Worms, Abraham Abulafia, Moses de Leon, Isaac Luria—are names virtually unknown outside the orbit of Hebrew culture, and many of the myriad texts he has edited, analyzed, used to reconstruct a vanished past, had been buried in oblivion even within that orbit. Yet Scholem has never exhibited the slightest trace of nervousness about "parochialism" in his chosen specialization. On the contrary, his books and articles are informed by a serene confidence that these are eminently worthy objects of study for anyone curious about man and his culture, and in fact one can think of few more impressive demonstrations that human experience has been more various and devious, more intriguingly complex, than our stubborn stereotypes of it.

Gershom Scholem was born in Berlin in 1897, the son of an assimilated bourgeois Jewish family. In his adolescence he became a convinced Zionist, began learning Hebrew, and for this egregious failure in his duties as a patriotic German was peremptorily banished from his father's house. He studied mathematics and physics, then Semitic philology, in Berlin, Jena, and Berne, completing a doctorate at the University of Munich in 1922. A year later he emigrated to Palestine, and from the founding of the Hebrew University of Jerusalem in 1925 until his retirement in 1965 he lectured there on Jewish mysticism, creating a new department as he had virtually created a new field of study, over the years making a deep impact on generations of Israeli students while his reputation among historians of religion steadily grew through his publications in German and English and his frequent visits to American and European institutions of higher learning.

It is symptomatic of the neglect Jewish mysticism had suffered that the first two decades of Scholem's career had to be devoted chiefly to the editing and explication of the basic mystical texts and to compiling bibliographies for the field. His first substantial work of synthesis and historical overview is *Major Trends in Jewish Mysticism* (1941), initially published in English (from a German manuscript version) and based on a series of lectures given in New York in 1938. This "first work," however, is the mature fruit of twenty years of scholarship—an introductory survey that is, in fact, the definitive book on the subject, and gives every prospect of remaining so. Scholem's subsequent books have, then, necessarily been explorations in depth of subjects already covered in single packed chapters in *Major Trends*. In 1948 he published in Hebrew *Reshit Ha-Kabbalah* ("The Origins of the Kabbalah," not available in English), a study of the mystical movement in Provence and Spain in the twelfth and thirteenth centuries that led to the creation of the *Zohar*. In 1957, again in Hebrew, he published his major two-volume biography of the seventeenth-century pseudo-messiah of Smyrna, Sabbatai Zevi, with extensive consideration of the mass movement inspired by Sabbatai and of Sabbatianism's larger historical reverberations. American readers will soon have an opportunity to examine this work, the most sustained example of Scholem's formidable thoroughness as a historian, with the forthcoming publication in English of *Sabbatai Ṣevi: The Mystical Messiah*. Both *Major Trends* and *Sabbatai Ṣevi* have become landmarks of modern Jewish scholarship, the one a comprehensive summary and synthesis, the other, at the opposite pole, a study in detail of a particular crucial phenomenon. *On the Kabbalah and Its Symbolism* (German original, 1960; English, 1965) offers a general description of the phenomenology of Jewish mysticism, explaining the psychological and institutional categories with which it works, the dynamics and tensions peculiar to it as well as those shared with other mystical systems. In 1960 there also appeared his technical study, *Jewish Gnosticism, Merkabah Mysticism, and Talmudic Tradition*. Finally, *The Messianic Idea in Judaism* (1971) is a generous selection of Scholem's major papers, chiefly from the late fifties and the sixties, again exploring the phenomenology of Jewish mysticism and of Jewish messianism, with particular attention given to Hasidism, to Sabbatianism and its exotic heirs, and to the problematics of tradition in all these currents of Jewish experience.

What, briefly, are the nature and scope of the mystical heritage that Scholem's pioneering work has brought to light? The nine chapters of *Major*

Trends firmly delineate the field. I shall return later to Scholem's general definition of mysticism, but for the moment let me suggest that the common tendency of Kabbalism as he sees it is to work feverishly—and unwittingly—against the grain of classical Judaism while adhering passionately to the classical Jewish system of belief. That is, Judaism, as an institutionalized religion, establishes an abyss between man and God, while Jewish mysticism devises strategies for spanning the chasm; classical Judaism is anti-mytho-logical, Kabbalistic theology "attempts to construct and to describe a world in which something of the mythical has again come to life, in terms of thoughts [those of Jewish tradition] which exclude the mythical element"; conversely, the biblical faith conceives of revelation as the direct utterance of a personal God, while Kabbalism is heavily influenced by gnostic concep-tions of an impersonal divine reality of which God the Creator who addresses man is merely an intermediary manifestation. Many of these tendencies are common to other mysticisms, but the Kabbalists put a very special stress on the eschatological impulse implicit in much mystical thought, and they are distinctive in their central notion of language as a profound reflection of ultimate spiritual reality, in their concomitant devotion to exegesis as a mys-tical activity, in their extravagant claims for the authority of the very tradition they radically reshape, and in the special status of their teaching among mystical legacies as "a masculine doctrine, made for men and by men."

The historical phenomenon of Jewish mysticism as Scholem traces it in *Major Trends* stretches from esoteric doctrine taught in Pharisaic circles in the days of the Second Temple down to the Hasidic movement that flourished in Eastern Europe during the later eighteenth and nineteenth centuries. The earliest recoverable phase is Merkabah (Divine Chariot or Throne) mysticism, a gnostic tradition rooted in Hellenistic thought. Its literary remains, scat-tered over most of the first millennium C.E., are peculiarly not speculative but descriptive—of the glittering reality imaged in the Divine Throne or the Divine Palaces (*Hekhalot*). Accordingly, the Merkabah mystics are perva-sively conscious of God's otherness, even in mystical ecstasy; their vision fixed on the radiance of the Godhead, they exhibit little interest in man or in the moral dimension of spiritual life. The next major mystical movement, the Hasidism of twelfth- and thirteenth-century Germany, in some ways moves to the opposite pole, being less concerned with the mysteries of the Godhead than with man's acts, and assuming a deeply pietistic, penitential, ascetic, and often thaumaturgic character.

The most brilliant development of Jewish mysticism comes with the emergence of the Kabbalah proper in southern France and in Spain around the year 1200. Scholem distinguishes two strands of Kabbalah, ecstatic and theosophical. The former, dominated by the figure of Abraham Abulafia (b. 1240), involves an elaborate system of meditation (especially on the letters of the Hebrew alphabet) and even breathing exercises which are reminiscent of yoga and which may ultimately derive from the same Indian source as yoga. It was the theosophical strand, however, which was to be the more influential, receiving its supreme expression in the *Zohar,* or Book of Splendor, composed, as Scholem has conclusively demonstrated, by a Spanish Jew named Moses de Leon toward the end of the thirteenth century. The intricacies of its doctrine of the Godhead defy brief summary, but the haunting imaginative power of Moses de Leon's literary mélange—"a mixture of theosophic theology, mythical cosmogony, and mystical psychology and anthropology"—proved to be of vital historical importance. Through this remarkable power, the book quickly attained immense popularity, indeed, became the only text after the Talmud to achieve the rough Jewish equivalent of canonical status. It was the basis for the last major theoretical development of Jewish mysticism, the Lurianic Kabbalah that arose in Safed in the early sixteenth century. Isaac Luria and his disciples placed a new central emphasis on cosmogony, conceived creation as a breaking of divine vessels, an emanation of divine light, sparks of divine essence entrammeled in husks of evil from which they must be redeemed. In short, the Lurianic doctrine elevated Exile to a powerfully dramatic principle of cosmic process; it represented a boldly original mystical theology that was also ideally suited to the propaganda of mass movements of spiritual revival. Like the *Zohar* itself, Lurianic teaching was taken up enthusiastically by most segments of the Jewish people, all over the Diaspora. Finally, Lurianism provided the ideological apparatus for two successive movements which shook the structure of traditional Jewish society—the mystical heresy of Sabbatianism that enveloped most of the Jewish world around the year 1666, and Hasidism, the popular mystical movement stirred by charismatic leaders that sprang up in Podolia and Volhynia nearly a century later and profoundly affected East European Jewry at the dawn of the modern period.

Now, Scholem's work is clearly of far more than antiquarian interest, but it is important first to recognize his enormous value as a sheer archaeologist of culture, digging tirelessly through vast moldering mounds of literary remains neglected for the most part by others. He has, ultimately, a definite interpretative view and a clear commitment to certain values, but his work cannot be faulted for tendentiousness because it is based on such painstaking research, always intent on determining the precise and particular facts no matter how much they may upset anyone's established views, including his own. His biography of Sabbatai Zevi is surely a model for the patient reconstruction of a life and a movement (three centuries distant) from all the available sources, and at the same time an instance of revisionist historiography at its most acute. Scholem has rare gifts for synthesis and generalization, as several of his more recent essays on Jewish messianism and tradition demonstrate, but his mind is equally remarkable for the way it adheres to the smallest particles of particular historical experience.

One sees this faculty operating on a small scale with dazzling effect in the essay on the history of the Star of David as a symbol, included in *The Messianic Idea in Judaism*. Scholem discards a series of old chestnuts, follows the forerunners and occasional occurrences of the device through some twenty-five-hundred years of iconography, necromancy, and occult symbolism, distinguishing its shifting and overlapping uses until its final adoption in nineteenth-century Germany as a "Jewish" symbol that could be for German citizens of the Mosaic persuasion completely analogous to the cross for Christians. The sifting of texts and facts concludes with a wryly pointed observation: "Just at the time of its greatest dissemination in the nineteenth century the Shield of David served as the empty symbol of a Judaism which itself was more and more falling into meaninglessness." This sort of essay, one assumes, is a relatively easy spin-off project for a scholar like Scholem, but precisely because it seems so unlike labored scholarship I find the experience of reading it a little dizzying, for the mind that has made it is able to contain in lucid simultaneity such a welter of disparate, far-flung fragments of the lived past. Islamic amulets and Christian manuals of sorcery, alchemical handbooks from the early Middle Ages to the late Renaissance, Kabbalistic tracts from everywhere; the politics, ritual practices, art, and folkways of Christians and Jews in thirteenth-century Anagni, fifteenth-century Prague, sixteenth-century Budapest, seventeenth-century Vienna—all these give the impression of having been not merely surveyed but somehow securely *possessed* in all their concrete particularity. Reading such a historical essay, one is forced to revise one's limited notions of what knowledge can be.

To contain so many materials is a capacity of mind; to possess them is a quality of imagination, and it is this that makes a serious technical scholar like Scholem also a writer of compelling general interest. He writes always with respect for the integrity of his subjects, even those that previously have been considered marginal or "pathological," and so he can enter into them empathetically at the same time as he views them analytically in historical context. One vivid case in point is his commentary on the hymns of the *Hekhalot* mystics in *Major Trends in Jewish Mysticism:* "The immense solemnity of their style, the bombast of their magnificent phrases, reflect the fundamental paradox of these hymns: the climax of sublimity and solemnity to which the mystic can attain in his attempt to express the magnificence of his vision is also the *ne plus ultra* of vacuousness." One might note that "paradox" is one of Scholem's favorite words, and few scholars have had such a deep understanding of how sickness and health, destruction and creation, nonsense and profundity, have intermingled in the same spiritual phenomena. "Vacuousness," in context, is not so damning as it may sound here since it has a precise theosophic referent and hence a definite psychological function. In any case, Jews familiar from the liturgy with repetitious acrostic hymns like *Ha-Aderet v'Ha-Emunah* will be startled to learn that these poems were composed to serve a hallucinogenic function for their original users in the early centuries of the Christian era. Scholem makes this clear without resorting to clinical vocabulary, illuminating the experience he describes as if from within while analyzing it from without:

> Almost all the hymns from the *Hekhalot* tracts . . . reveal a mechanism comparable to the motion of an enormous fly-wheel. In cyclical rhythm the hymns succeed each other, and within them the adjurations of God follow in a crescendo of glittering and majestic attributes, each stressing and reinforcing the sonorous power of the word. The monotony of their rhythm—almost all consist of verses of four words—and the progressively sonorous incantations induce in those who are praying a state of mind bordering on ecstasy.

Scholem's endowments as a historian can hardly be in question, but that is not to say that he has not had his detractors in the world of Jewish scholarship, who have generally acknowledged his gifts while arguing that he has used them for dubious, if not nefarious, ends. It is the general orientation of his enterprise that has laid him open to attack, and that needs some setting in perspective. Modern academic historiography was invented as a serious discipline in early nineteenth-century Germany, and modern Jewish historical scholarship developed very soon thereafter in the same cultural sphere, using the same intellectual tools. There was, however, an important ideological disparity between the two scholarly movements, as Scholem pointed out in a 1959 lecture at the Leo Baeck Institute on the *Wissenschaft des Judentums,* or Science of Judaism. The early generations of German historians, inspired by the ideals of German Romanticism, were nationalists, and what they sought was an "active comprehension of the organism of their own history in the sense of a positive, nationally oriented perspective and future." The proponents of the *Wissenschaft des Judentums,* on the other hand, were at bottom cosmopolitan in outlook, perhaps, indeed, the most dogged heirs of the already fading cosmopolitan vision of the Enlightenment. Though their subject was the national experience of one people, their standpoint was as men of a larger European culture in which an experience so fiercely particular, so redolent of other times and places, could only be an anachronism; and so they often tended to study Judaism as the dead remains of a completed past, not as a living body pregnant with the future. Gerson D. Cohen has recently proposed that Scholem be viewed as a neo-Romantic historian, and in fact the brief notation I have quoted on the Romantic quest for an organism of national history and a perspective on a national future could well be taken as the thumbnail program of Scholem's own enterprise. If, however, that enterprise can in one aspect be described as Romantic, it is a hard-headed, shrewdly skeptical Romanticism, and a Romanticism, as we shall see, steeped in the bitter juices of modern experience, impelled by the concerns of a characteristically modern imagination.

The founders of Jewish historical scholarship, I would add, were motivated not only by the ideology of an intellectual movement but at least as much by the vulnerable sensibility of a new social class. Only a generation or two beyond the ghetto, in an era when assimilation was a beckoning horizon, they sought to confirm in their study of Judaism the values of propriety, prudence, practical reasonableness, and rational faith on which their newly acquired German *Bürgerlichkeit* rested. When Scholem observes that "their bias represents a form of censorship of the Jewish past," thinking chiefly of a post-Enlightenment ideological bias, one could also note that this bias is equally composed of a bourgeois recoil from all that might offend a sense of decency in "good" society. Thus, the *Wissenschaft* scholars developed a peculiar notion of what came to be known as normative Judaism. What was central to Jewish experience tended to be thought of as legalistic, rationalist, prudential, this-worldly, and fundamentally conservative; spiritual phenomena sharply diverging from this general norm had to be viewed as suspect aberrations. In this manner, Jewish mysticism, Jewish enthusiastic and antinomian movements, the profound involvement of Jews through the ages in magic and the occult, all were studied grudgingly as manifestations of the sickly medieval spirit that temporarily beclouded the clarity of Jewish devotion to eternal verities and rational ideals.

Scholem's work, then, might helpfully be viewed as a sustained act of social rebellion, somewhat like the rebellion of the Nietzschean movement of early twentieth-century Hebrew poets and writers to which it is closely allied. One might almost say that he has uncovered for moderns the heritage of a historical Jewish counter-culture, except for the fact that, as his investigations have proven, it was very often the dominant culture. In any case, he has managed to rescue from the murk of the past a rich body of vitally Jewish experience that challenges many of the comfortable values of German middle-class respectability in which the Science of Judaism developed and in which he himself grew up. His writing, in other words, has been not only a decisive revocation of that censorship of the Jewish past which he mentions but also a deftly wielded weapon, for all its heavy apparatus of scholarly footnotes, used to *épater les bourgeois*.

Although Scholem's influence in the world of Jewish scholarship has been enormous, the inertia of established views he has had to overcome has also been considerable. The fact that he is not merely fencing with nineteenth-century ghosts in his historical revisionism was recently made strikingly clear in a review-essay of *The Messianic Idea* by Jacob Agus in *Judaism* (Summer 1972). Agus is a man of serious Jewish knowledge, a prolific writer on theological matters, and, preeminently, a figure of the American rabbinical establishment—which, as it turns out, is in some matters not so unlike the old German-Jewish bourgeois establishment as one would like to think. Agus has, to be sure, the highest praise for the scope and intelligence of Scholem's undertaking, but the ease with which in the very act of praise he closes his mind to the major conclusions of Scholem's researches is quite breathtaking. Thus, Scholem's studies of Sabbatai Zevi, both in the two-volume biography and in a series of scholarly articles, early and late, have forcefully demonstrated that, contrary to nineteenth-century views, the Sabbatian messianic movement of the 1660s had immense reverberations, at its peak enveloping most of the Jewish people in all the far reaches of the Diaspora, and continuing as a highly ramified and active underground for nearly a century and a half. Scholem in effect sets Sabbatianism at the beginning of modern Jewish history, as the first concretely realized historical moment when the whole Jewish people experienced its own incipient emergence from the ghetto world into a radically transformed existence. A world thrown so violently askew would for many never resume its old balance. Though the exact role of Sabbatianism as a causal factor in the various movements that followed it is still open to debate, Scholem has unearthed a current of Sabbatianism (there were good reasons why the participants themselves should have kept it hidden) running through the rabbinical leadership for a century after the death of the apostate messiah, feeding into Hasidism, the Hebrew Enlightenment, the Reform movement, even the French Revolution.

With all this, Agus, after reading, we can assume, Scholem's thousand pages of carefully documented argument, can still blandly assert—revealingly, in a "word of caution" to the reader unversed in Jewish sources—that "one must see the Sabbatian eruption in perspective, as a marginal aberration." It is true, he concedes, that the movement briefly swept the whole people and that the energies of its aftermath were not quickly spent, "But the intellectual leaders of the people, in spite of their anguished situation, quickly regained their equilibrium." No evidence at all is offered for this flat assertion. Apparently, it is sufficient simply to see things "in perspective," and a rabbi's commitment to reasonable faith is taken to be a self-validating measure of what really happened in Jewish history.

As a historian, Scholem is a modernist in much the same sense that Conrad, Kafka, Mann, and Faulkner are modernists. Like these imaginative writers, his insights are often deeply troubling, and it is the business of an establishment figure like Agus to blunt or deflect such an argument wherever it is most probing. But it may be helpful to consider in detail how Scholem is a modernist both in his choice of subject and in the qualities of imagination he brings to bear on it. What, to begin with, is the peculiar appeal of mysticism to a writer whose work begins in the very peak years of European literary modernism, whose mature life has witnessed two world wars, the Holocaust, and the bloody rebirth after two millennia of a Jewish commonwealth? Mysticism, Scholem states at the outset of *Major Trends in Jewish Mysticism,* approvingly quoting Rufus Jones, "is religion in its most acute, intense, and living stage." Clearly, acuteness, intensity, and vitality have been among the great desiderata of the modern spirit in its quest for personal authenticity against what has often seemed the dead and empty formalism of the cultural heritage. The specific meaning of these three qualities as they are associated with mysticism is worth pursuing. I think that implicit in all of Scholem's work is an assumption that mysticism is, finally, the most authentic variety of religious experience because it is the most daring, aspiring to a naked directness of confrontation with divinity, seeking to break through the intervening barriers of institutionalization and received tradition.

Along with the definition of Rufus Jones, Scholem cites Aquinas's characterization of mysticism as *cognitio dei experimentalis,* the experiential knowledge of God. Elsewhere, in his masterful essay on revelation and tradition, he emphasizes the mediated nature for rabbinic Judaism of every experience after the initial revelation. As a result, exegesis becomes the characteristically Jewish means to knowledge and perhaps even the characteristically Jewish mode of religious experience. What the Kabbalists, with their letter-and-word mysticism, sought to get back through exegesis to a species of revelation, to work or contemplate their way through the mediating words of the sacred text to the unmediated Word out of whose infinite declensions and permutations all language and all being come into existence. The Kabbalah is fundamentally a linguistic mysticism, at least in method, and this is surely part of its fascination for Scholem, who shares with his friend Walter Benjamin an abiding interest in the paradoxical ways language, as civilization's endlessly refined and conventionalized instrument, can put man in touch with the potent wellsprings of ultimacy that underlie and antedate all civilization.

Scholem is, of course, equally concerned with how mysticism fits into, or obtrudes from, particular historical contexts, and in this regard his generalization on the relation between mysticism and history in *On the Kabbalah and Its Symbolism* throws a good deal of light on his interest in the subject as a modern: "Mysticism as a historical phenomenon is a product of crises." His inquiries have shown how Jewish mysticism responded to the most terrible historical traumas with apocalyptic systems that renewed the hope of redemption and sustained the life of tradition. To cite the major instance of recent centuries: the Kabbalah, crystallized in late thirteenth-century Spain, provided the vocabulary of spiritual explanation for the banishment of 1492, was then articulated as a general doctrine of cosmic redemption by the Lurianic school in sixteenth-century Palestine, and in its subsequent dissemination decisively shaped minds and offered the ideological tools for the great messianic upheaval of the seventeenth century. It will be apparent even from this hasty sketch that Scholem conceives mysticism not only as the product of historical crisis but as an active force generating further crisis. The Lurianic doctrine of cosmic exile, developed among the refugees from Spain in the decades after the expulsion, did not encourage the exiles to accommodate themselves to their harsh circumstances. On the contrary, "The emotions aroused by these sufferings were not soothed and tranquilized, but stimulated and whipped up."

Though he is not merely a historian of ideas, Scholem writes with a profound respect for the autonomy of the spiritual realm in historical experience, and though he exercises a fine awareness of contexts, he emphatically rejects the "modern naiveté" of sociological or psychological determinism, with its roots in the simplistic positivism of nineteenth-century science. Thus, the actual social composition of the Sabbatian movement makes it quite impossible to reduce it to a rebellion of disadvantaged classes; the movement's special appeal to the most prosperous and legally liberated centers of seventeenth-century Jewry preclude explaining it simply as a response to the persecutions of the period; and even Sabbatai Zevi's manic-depressive psychosis, discussed at great length, does not diminish the power and complexity of the theology built around his personality. "If there was one general factor underlying the patent unity of the Sabbatian movement everywhere, then this factor was essentially religious and as such obeyed its own autonomous laws."

What is it about mysticism that makes it the most appropriate religious response to historical crisis? To begin with, as Scholem points out in a variety of ways, there is a constant tension in mysticism, precisely because it is a *cognitio dei experimentalis,* between imperative personal experience and the religion of fixed norms outside the experiencing self. When a historical crisis occurs, the contradictions within the body of tradition are made manifest, and the new discoveries of a daring self avid for intensities come into the foreground of theological explanation, helping to reconcile the promises of tradition with the sharp disappointments of history. Mysticism, to invoke another of Scholem's favorite words, is by its very nature dialectical, continuously mediating between the absoluteness of the self and the inviolability of tradition, and as such it is ideally suited to coping with a historical reality that vacillates between opposite poles, violently overturning preconceptions and expectations. The Sabbatians after the apostasy of their messiah constitute an extreme case in which "all reality became dialectically unreal and contradictory," but such radical confusions have in one way or another challenged most mystical movements, just as again and again they seem to have engulfed historical experience in our own century.

The fitting response to this kind of traumatic and contradictory historical reality was a religion of extremes, and here again Scholem's explorations of Jewish mysticism jibe with a deep-seated conviction of modernism, that the truth is to be sought in extremes, the historical Judaism revealed in his work being distinctly a Judaism for the readers of Dostoyevski, Kafka, and Rimbaud. Looking back over Scholem's *oeuvre,* one sees a crowd of sharp visual images that forever unsettle one's complacent assumptions about what Jews may have done or been: the early Hasidic ascetics of thirteenth-century Germany, plunging themselves into snow and ice, exposing their bodies in summer to ants and bees; the Jewish women and children of Safed, Aleppo, Smyrna, writhing in prophetic paroxysms, reciting verses in automatic speech, flung to the ground in a self-induced hypnotic trance at the advent of Sabbatai Zevi; the bizarre psychosexuality of Sabbatai himself, who devised weirdly erotic rites, such as a marriage ceremony between himself and the Torah, while his first two flesh-and-blood marriages were unconsummated and the third was to a woman whose promiscuity was notorious in the Jewish world from Amsterdam to Cairo; the orgiastic cult of the Frankists in Poland, or of their Turkish counterpart, the crypto-Jewish Dönmeh sect, which celebrated a spring festival of ritual fornication unwittingly drawing on the old worship of the Magna Mater indigenous to Asia Minor.

Scholem treats all this with the utmost seriousness, fitting it into a large imaginative perspective of interpretation. Here, there is a third key term, in addition to "paradox" and "dialectic," which he invokes again and again. If the two already mentioned terms describe both historical process and the nature of deity, the third term, "abyss," does that and more, representing in an image a kind of ultimate principle of ontology in Scholem's vision of the world. Thus, Jewish mysticism in general attempts "to make visible that abyss in which the symbolic nature of all that exists reveals itself." Sabbatianism and its sundry offshoots are repeatedly described as opening an abyss at the very heart of Judaism. The implicit logic of messianism itself, once it becomes a real operative force in history, is to thrust toward a hitherto sealed abyss of chaotic possibilities: "Every acute and radical messianism that is taken seriously tears open an abyss in which by inner necessity antinomian tendencies and libertine moral conceptions gain strength." Franz Rosenzweig, as the most probing of modern Jewish theologians, is said to have "ripped open the abyss in which the substance of Judaism lies hidden." (True knowledge for Scholem often turns out to be forbidden knowledge.) The apocalyptic element in Rosenzweig's thought "provided a recognition of the catastrophic potential of all historical order in an unredeemed world." Even the legend of the Thirty-Six Hidden Just Men is characterized, perhaps a bit gratuitously, as being sustained by a "somewhat anarchic morality" because it confronts us with the idea that "we can never fathom" the nature of our neighbors. The mystic, Scholem tells us at the beginning of *On the Kabbalah and Its Symbolism,* wants to encounter "Life" (the quotation marks are his); but this primordial Life, ceaselessly engendering and annihilating form, "is the anarchic promiscuity of all living things. Into this bubbling cauldron, this continuum of destruction, the mystic plunges."

Scholem generally avoids psychoanalytic vocabulary—because, I think, it might seem clinically reductive in its application to phenomena that above all need rescuing from the contempt of the learned—but it is hard to escape the parallel between his notion of an abyss upon which the lid of civilization sits precariously and Freud's view of culture in *Civilization and Its Discontents.* In any case, the abyss for Scholem seems to be not just the function of pent-up psychological forces but also the substantive nature of reality outside the human psyche, and here a more apposite source for his vision could well be the Nietzsche of *The Birth of Tragedy.* Nietzsche's notion of a Dionysian truth in excess, of contradiction at the heart of nature; his guiding concept of a dangerous dialectical tension between the Apollonian love of form and order and the Dionysian impulse to orgiastic release, to fusion with the inhuman chaotic potency that underlies existing things—all these have their parallels in Scholem. Even Nietzsche's contempt for the self-deceiving optimism of Socratic culture (essentially, nineteenth-century German academic culture) with its anti-mystical bias has its analogue in Scholem's rebellion, less visionary, more grounded in an exacting intellectual discipline than Nietzsche's, against the bias and tacit censorship of the *Wissenschaft des Judentums*. Finally, that abyss of formlessness from which culture arises implies the necessity of myth for Nietzsche: only through myth can man remain in touch with the realm of the irrational that is the matrix of reality and also give it an imaged order, a sequence of dramatic actions, which can be grasped by a finite human consciousness. "Without myth," Nietzsche asserts, "every culture loses the healthy natural power of its creativity: only a horizon defined by myths completes and unifies a whole cultural movement."

Now, myth has always been a problematic phenomenon for Judaism. One might well say, as the late Yehezkel Kaufmann repeatedly argued, that the whole tendency of biblical monotheism was to conduct a systematic purge of myth, leaving only a few vestigial literary allusions whose original meanings were no longer even understood. The need for myth, however, might be driven underground but could not be entirely extinguished. Scholem quite candidly describes the Kabbalah in the opening chapter of *Major Trends* as a "revival of myth" from the innermost recesses of historical Judaism, and it is clear that he shares the modern fascination with myth that begins signally in *The Birth of Tragedy* and flowers in some of the major imaginative works of the earlier twentieth century. His exemplary exposition of the theosophic doctrine of the *Zohar* excites the imagination as it does largely because he perceives so surely the resurgence of old mythological images in the new mystical lore, male and female gods coupling in cosmic exultation, confirming the unity of the world and the eternal meaning of transient human life through the power of their divine sexuality.

Scholem, let me stress, is a student of mysticism, not a mystagogue, and he has none of that peculiar nostalgia for primal mud that has characterized many latter-day myth-mongers. He lucidly recognizes that the Celestial Bridegroom and the Celestial Bride of the *Zohar* are only a step and a half away from the pagan excesses of the Dönmeh sect adoring a mother goddess in orgies. For all his interest in antinomian extremes, Scholem is committed to civilized restraints and to the values and ordered achievements that can be realized within those restraints. Nevertheless, his entire study of Jewish mysticism implicitly argues that a spiritual tradition entirely cut off from myth is cut off from living connection with ultimate reality and so doomed to wither.

I hope the foregoing will suggest something of the range of implication in the qualities of acuteness and intensity that Scholem associates with mysticism. The third of Rufus Jones's intertwined categories, vitality ("religion in its most . . . living stage"), calls for further commentary because it bears a rather special relationship to Scholem's Zionist commitment. He is perfectly open about the nature of that commitment in the brief Foreword to *The Messianic Idea*. The essays are addressed, he tells us, not to dilettantes but to people with a passionate interest in Judaism and its past; moreover, "This book is written by a man who believes Judaism to be a living phenomenon which . . . has not yet exhausted its possibilities" and whose future forms one cannot presume to predict.

Scholem's primary period of research is precisely the era of Jewish history considered in many older views to be a period of decadence after the peak achievements of the Bible, the Talmud, the Spanish philosophers and poets. In this era, running from the later Middle Ages to the threshold of modernity, he discovers a mysticism richly developing until it becomes the dominant force in the Jewish people, manifesting great spiritual boldness, intellectual subtlety, and an unflagging sense of national vigor in the most dire historical circumstances. At the core of the Kabbalah, especially as it received its definitive formulation in the school of Isaac Luria, "lay a great image of rebirth," and what is especially remarkable about this image of rebirth is that it remained strongly particularist in its Jewishness while at the same time achieving an embracing universalism of outlook, erecting a splendid cosmogony out of the historical experience of the Jews. "Kabbalistic myth had 'meaning,' because it sprang from a fully conscious relation to a reality which, experienced symbolically even in its horror, was able to project mighty symbols of Jewish life as an extreme case of human life pure and simple."

This understanding of the Kabbalah offers a new perspective on the rise of modern Jewish nationalism. Zionism may be seen not as an act of historical desperation, the implicit admission of what Georges Friedmann has called "the end of the Jewish people," but, on the contrary, the last of the great visions of rebirth that began driving the Jews toward new horizons some six centuries before Herzl, a movement not only stimulated from without but animated from within by a deep source of national vitality. (It might be noted that the organic conception of national history mentioned by Scholem in connection with the German Romantics is in fact his own implicit view of Jewish history.) In the model of the Lurianic Kabbalah, moreover, one glimpses the possibility that the reborn Jewish state may somehow amplify its nationalism with the universalist vision of Jewish tradition and not subside into being a Bulgaria of the Middle East. These historical precedents

of national renascence are all the more convincing because they are not
presented tendentiously: Scholem is careful not to interpret the messianic or
mystical movements as "proto-Zionist" in any simplistic sense; he in fact
argues at length that Hasidism through its stress on the goal of ecstatic
communion (d'vekut) aimed at a "neutralization" of messianism after the
great Sabbatian outburst; and in his studies of the antinomian movements
he is sharply conscious of the fact that the other face of the coin of redemption is destruction.

The dialectical play, however, between redemption and destruction is
intimately associated with the vitality Scholem attributes to the Kabbalah.
Seeing in the regnant rabbinic tradition during this period an acquiescence
in the passivity and abjectness of Exile, an increasingly arid—perhaps one
might say, bourgeois—religion estranged from the sources of living religious
experience, he writes out of the ultimate conviction that rebellion was a
historical necessity, though he knows that the aftermath of any rebellion may
be chaos. This is one reason why he is so deeply fascinated by the Sabbatian
movement, for the Sabbatians destroyed the world of rabbinic Judaism from
within while remaining thoroughly Jewish in their consciousness. They were,
as Scholem puts it in his classic essay, "Redemption through Sin," "revolu-
tionaries who regarded themselves as loyal Jews while at the same time completely overturning the traditional religious categories of Judaism." There is
surely a good deal of enthusiastic empathy with the Sabbatian rebellion in
Scholem's studies of it—one is struck, for example, by his vivid description
of a contemporary portrait of Jacob Sasportas, the arch-opponent of the
Sabbatians, showing "the face of a Jewish Grand Inquisitor," dour, stern,
harsh, irascible, arrogant. One should add, however, that this imaginative
identification with the rebels does not dim Scholem's perception of the pathological elements among them, the reign of terror (the phrase is his) they
imposed during the months of their total ascendancy, and the ultimate futility
of their rebellion.

In any case, what emerges from the multifarious mystical matters discussed by Scholem is a powerful sense of the protean nature of Jewish experience. Where we might have been inclined to view the various modern
ideologies of Jewish survival as a splintering of classical Jewish unity, a fateful
breaking away from the grand continuity of the Jewish past, Scholem shows
us a historical Judaism itself fissured with sharp divisions and marked by
the most extreme variety. Halfway through the first volume of Sabbatai Ṣevi,
he makes explicit this large implication of his work: "There is no way of
telling a priori what beliefs are possible or impossible within the framework
of Judaism. . . . The 'Jewishness' in the religiosity of any particular period is

not measured by dogmatic criteria that are unrelated to actual historical circumstances, but solely by what sincere Jews do, in fact, believe, or—at least—consider to be legitimate possibilities." This will obviously not sit well with contemporary Jewish dogmatists, spokesmen for the various rabbinical, communal, and Zionist establishments or for ideologized notions of the Jew as enlightened internationalist, but the mass of historical evidence Scholem marshals to support his assertion is formidable. His stress on the vital Jewish consciousness of the pseudo-messianic movements has been attacked as a spurious partisan attempt to validate secular Zionism in terms of Jewish history, but the real point about Scholem's work is that it is post-ideological. Though he is personally committed to the Zionist renascence, what his researches actually do is to open the doors of the mind to a genuine Jewish pluralism, grounded in the spectacular plurality of Jewish historical experience.

Scholem has the kind of ironic intelligence that delights in contradictions, that can hold the multiple attributes of the subjects it scrutinizes in clear simultaneous view, and that is even capable on occasion of a certain teasing archness, for all its scholarly gravity. (The whimsical tone of Borges's poetic allusion to Scholem is not really inappropriate.) As a result, his account of the Jewish past can accommodate the full power of its most seemingly alien manifestations while seeing in overview the distinct limitations of their historical field of operation. Similarly, he can affirm the revolutionary significance in Jewish history of the Zionist fulfillment with an acute awareness of its looming ambiguities. This rare amplitude of perception is beautifully evidenced in the lead essay of *The Messianic Idea in Judaism*. I would like to conclude by quoting an extended passage from this essay because it illustrates so finely Scholem's incisive critical perspective on the very past whose pulsating life stirs his imagination, and shows how his involvement in the past is intellectually linked with a deep concern for the complexities of history unfolding in the present. Celebrations of the noble impulse of Jewish messianism past and present are the great cliché of modern Jewish intellectuals, no matter how distant they may be from any connection with historical Judaism. Scholem, who knows the messianic phenomenon and has appreciated its distinctive power from the most intimate familiarity with all its manifestations, is able to penetrate beyond the banalities of the apologists to the profound historical contradictions at the root of the messianic idea.

> The magnitude of the messianic idea corresponds to the endless powerlessness in Jewish history during all the centuries of exile, when it was unprepared to come forward onto the plane of world

history. There's something preliminary, something provisional about Jewish history, hence its inability to give of itself entirely. For the messianic idea is not only consolation and hope. Every attempt to realize it tears open the abysses [again, the key phrase] which lead each of its manifestations *ad absurdum*. There is something grand about living in hope, but at the same time there is something profoundly unreal about it. . . . Thus in Judaism the messianic idea has compelled a *life lived in deferment,* in which nothing can be done definitively, nothing can be irrevocably accomplished. One may say, perhaps, the messianic idea is the real anti-existentialist idea. Precisely understood, there is nothing concrete which can be accomplished by the unredeemed. . . . The blazing landscape of redemption (as if it were a point of focus) has concentrated in itself the historical outlook of Judaism. Little wonder that overtones of messianism have accompanied the modern Jewish readiness for irrevocable action in the concrete realm, when it set out on the utopian return to Zion. It is a readiness which no longer allows itself to be fed on hopes. Born out of the horror and destruction that was Jewish history in our generation, it is bound to history itself and not to meta-history; it has not given itself up totally to messianism. Whether or not Jewish history will be able to endure this entry into the concrete realm without perishing in the crisis of the messianic claim which has virtually been conjured up—that is the question which out of his great and dangerous past the Jew of this age poses to his present and to his future.

DAVID BIALE

Theology, Language, and History

Scholem's philosophy of Jewish history argues against the dogmatic rationalism of the nineteenth century that Jewish history consists of a productive conjunction of opposites: myth and rationalism, restorative and apocalyptic messianism. The Jewish tradition is governed by the unceasing dynamic conflict between these opposing forces. Behind Scholem's careful studies of Kabbalistic texts lies this fundamentally dialectical view of the development of history. I contend that Scholem's dialectical philosophy of history is rooted in a particular theology which may have something to contribute to the contemporary debate over Jewish theology.

Scholem was, of course, primarily an historian, and a secular one at that. Yet, as the letter to Zalman Schocken suggests, there can be no denying the metaphysical impulse which lurked behind his decision to study the Kabbalah. By piecing together Scholem's theological position, we can discover a fascinating attempt by an historian to wed secular historiography to a religious tradition. In doing so, we shall see why Scholem's importance extends beyond the academic discipline of history to a wider arena of modern Jewish thought. Only by understanding the philosophy that lies behind the historical studies can we begin to appreciate Scholem as a spokesman for modern Judaism as well as an historian of its earlier manifestations.

Scholem's theological reflections must be considered against the backdrop of the crisis of Jewish theology in this century. Partly in response to

From *Gershom Scholem: Kabbalah and Counter History*. © 1979, 1982 by David Biale. Harvard University Press, 1982.

developments in liberal Christian theology, Jewish theologians by the end of
the nineteenth century were attempting to define an "essence of Judaism"
(*Wesen des Judentums*). This movement, perhaps represented best by Leo
Baeck's book of that name, was no more than the culmination of similar
efforts we have already traced in earlier Jewish historiography. Like its Christian counterpart, the "essence of Judaism" was generally defined as rational
or "prophetic" ethics to demonstrate the identity between Judaism and modern culture. But also like its Christian counterpart, rational Jewish theology
quickly encountered a crisis. As theologians came to question modern cultural assumptions, they redefined Judaism as fundamentally *alien* to modern
culture. Buber's argument that Judaism is an oriental religion was part of
this general rejection of occidental culture.

The crisis of Jewish theology is most clearly illustrated in the work of
Hermann Cohen (1842–1918), who articulated in his early writings the most
extreme version of rational religion. Cohen reduced religion to rational ethics
and argued that God is no more than a methodological principle. In his later
writings and particularly in his posthumous *Religion der Vernunft aus den
Quellen des Judentums,* Cohen altered his position. Without abandoning his
abstract methodological God, he argued now that religion cannot be reduced
to universal ethics since religion deals with man as an individual. Man requires something beyond ethics in order to deal with his existential situation.
Cohen's late position became the basis for modern Jewish existentialism as
developed by Franz Rosenzweig and Martin Buber, and, indeed, Buber took
his I and Thou terminology from Cohen himself.

The Jewish existentialists contested the reduction of Judaism to a principle of reason. Buber as a religious anarchist rejected the notion of an
authoritative revelation and historical tradition. Out of hostility toward both
orthodox halakhic Judaism and rational Jewish philosophy, Buber rejected
the burden of tradition and created his counter-history by a subjective,
mythopoeic "act of decision." Scholem also labels himself a religious anarchist, but we shall see that he means something quite different from Buber.
In fact, Scholem's theology must be considered a consistent attack on and
alternative to existentialism. Like Buber, Scholem revolted against the philosophical attempt to define an essence of Judaism and argued that Judaism
actually consists of an anarchistic plurality of sources. However, where Buber's rejection of rationalism led him to ahistorical irrationalism, Scholem's
led to historiography.

Buber and Scholem each offer answers to the crisis of rational Jewish
theology. I believe that the fundamental difference in their responses lies in
their disagreement about the ability of the historical tradition to communi-

cate with the secular Jew. Since the possibility of communication with a religious tradition depends ultimately on one's view of the nature and efficacy of language to transmit divine revelation, my discussion of the theological dimension of the Buber-Scholem controversy will focus to a great extent on language. Though neither Buber nor Scholem ever engaged in technical language philosophy, both developed views on language which were crucial to their theologies. We shall see that Scholem's position is particularly close to that of Walter Benjamin and may well have been derived in part from Benjamin's early metaphysical speculations on language.

The problem of language is particularly acute in the evaluation of mystical experiences, since the mystic must express his experience of the infinite in finite language. Moreover, most mystics feel an extraordinary desire to communicate their experience, even as they acknowledge the impossibility of doing so. How is the historian of religion to evaluate these linguistic expressions? There are two discernible solutions. The first is to argue that language has an inferior status to revelation and is unable to communicate more than a pale shadow of the original experience. In the face of revelation, man is quite literally dumbstruck and only later tries to translate divine silence into inadequate human speech. The essence of the mystical experience is silence; there is no relationship between it and the language used to describe it. This would be Buber's position.

The second position, which both Scholem and Benjamin adopted, argues that language itself is of divine origin and that the experience of revelation is linguistic. Since language is equivocally both divine and human, a basis exists for using language to communicate an experience of the divine. The profound implication of the language question is whether divine revelation must remain a silent, individual experience or whether it can become a public, communicable tradition, for a reliable tradition demands belief in the language in which it is conveyed. . . .

SCHOLEM'S EARLY WRITINGS ON LANGUAGE AND THEOLOGY

In his early attack on Buber's Erlebnismystik, Scholem had sought to affirm the validity of history and tradition for the secular Jew. In order to do so, he adopted a much more positive attitude toward language as the vehicle for transmission of the tradition. Against Buber's "mysticism of silence," Scholem developed a theology in which revelation and tradition were linguistic experiences: he grounded the authenticity of tradition in the efficacy of language. Since Scholem is not a mystic, it would be a grave error to claim without careful consideration that his position resembles the one he attributes to the Kabbalah. However, from a number of articles, both early and late, we can discern that there is a remarkable similarity between his conceptions and the Kabbalah's.

Philosophy of language was one of Scholem's earliest academic interests. As a student of mathematics, he wrote a seminar paper under Bruno Bauch defending mathematical logic as a legitimate approach to language. In 1916 he read Wilhelm von Humboldt's *Sprachphilosophische Schriften* and Fritz Mauthner's *Beiträge zu einer Kritik der Sprache*. After transferring his academic focus from mathematics to the Kabbalah, he initially considered writing a dissertation on the linguistic theory of the Kabbalah, a project he only completed fifty years later. The evidence is compelling that Scholem's intellectual origins cannot be understood without reference to his interest in philosophy of language.

From 1917 to 1923, Scholem undertook many translations from Hebrew to German and from Yiddish to German. His interest in translation and language in general was in part a result of his fervent attachment to Hebrew, which sparked the bitter debate with the Blau-Weiss. In a letter to Scholem in 1917, upon receiving his translation of the Song of Songs into German, Benjamin wrote:

> Your love for the Hebrew language can only express itself in the German as respect before the essence of language and the word . . . In other words, your work remains apologetic because it expresses the love and honor of an object which is not in its own sphere. Now, it is not fundamentally impossible that two languages could go together in one sphere: to the contrary, this constitutes all great translation . . . However, for you, the German language will never be quite as close as the Hebrew and for that reason, you are not the "summoned" translator of the Song of Songs.
>
> (*Briefe*)

This passage is an early reflection of Benjamin's theory of translation, developed later in his "The Task of the Translator," that the translator must consider all languages equally reflective of pure language. While it is possible that Benjamin's criticism of Scholem was accurate when Scholem was young, in later life Scholem came to regard German with virtually the same reverence.

Under the influence of Hölderlin's translation of Pindar, Scholem developed the view, similar to Benjamin's, that translation should not make reading easier for the reader, since the great works of literature and their translations are not written [, as Benjamin says,] "with the reader in mind." In a review of three translations from Yiddish to German by Alexander Eliasberg, Scholem argues that Yiddish is a difficult language to translate because its religious stratum is preserved in Hebrew. Translation of religious terms into German destroys the linguistic levels that make Yiddish a unique synthesis of a number of languages. Under the spell of the "cult of the Ostjuden," Scholem refers to Yiddish as a "warm" language (since it combines Hebrew and German) as opposed to German, which is "cold." Eliasberg responded that Scholem seemed to want not translation but transliteration of the Yiddish text into Latin characters. As Ernst Simon has noted, in his own translations of mystical texts Scholem often preserves certain key terms in the original language of the text to reflect their technical meaning, although they might be equally foreign to the original.

Scholem was also critical of the first samples of the Buber-Rosenzweig Bible translation, which appeared in the 1920s. He set forth his critique in a number of letters to Buber starting in 1926, when Buber sent him the Genesis translation. Buber himself [in *Brief-wechsel*] called Scholem's comments "the most serious I have encountered, actually the only serious critique." Scholem contended that Buber had adopted an elevated style (*Tonhöhe*) or, more precisely, a *niggun* (melody) for the prose passages in Genesis. Buber had imposed the flowery *Jugendstil* he still favored on texts whose original character was much more prosaic. In later years, after his position on language had changed somewhat, Buber toned down the high poetic style of the translations from the 1920s. Scholem praised the final version when it finally appeared in 1961, noting the "distinct urbanity of your new version" as against the "element of fanaticism" in the first.

Buber's problem in the early translations, Scholem implied, was that he considered revelation an ecstatic experience that deserved the poetic language of "pathos." Buber believed that the inability of the mystic to convey his experience forces him to imprecise, poetic expression. Scholem first attacked this idea in 1922 in his critique of Meier Wiener's *Lyrik der Kabbala,* which was inspired by Buber's Erlebnismystik. Scholem rejected Wiener's assertion that "religion is too imprecise (*ungenau*) for [us] to grasp its whole being":

> This is actually a most successful and outstanding formulation
> of a groundless concept of religion which can only be established
> or confirmed by grasping the central fact of religion, revelation,
> as an amorphous, ecstatic experience (*Erlebnis*) which only
> (makes sense), if at all, on the plane of inwardness, while its
> external emanations remain entirely fuzzy. [Revelation should

rather be understood] as an auditory phenomenon, which always
appeared to both the philosophers of religion and theoreticians
of language, as well as to the mystics [including] the Kabbalists,
as exactly definable (*exakt bestimmbar*).

("*Lyrik* der Kabbala?")

Wiener had mistranslated mystical texts because he had assumed that mystics
express their experiences in fuzzy poetic language. Mystical sources often
appear unclear not because the mystic was confused but because the modern
reader cannot decipher the text. For someone who does not know Latin,
even Caesar's *Gallic Wars* might appear to be "mystical."

In his earliest writings on religion, Scholem already began to develop a
different position on the nature of mysticism and revelation. Revelation is
not a silent Erlebnis, but an auditory experience that can be expressed in
language. Translation of Kabbalistic texts is possible because the Kabbalists
themselves considered their language a precise, technical vocabulary and not
arbitrary and emotive poetry. These texts are not well served by poetic translations; they cry out for scientific philology. The very self-conception of the
medieval Kabbalists defines the kind of scholarship required to decipher their
texts. Since the Kabbalists viewed language positively, Scholem believed with
the Wissenschaft des Judentums that the philologian, whose working assumption is the continuity of a linguistic tradition, is the proper interpreter
of Kabbalistic texts.

While in these early reviews (1920–1922) Scholem seems to include all
religions in his argument, he is far more cautious in later formulations to
refer only to Judaism and to distinguish carefully between the Kabbalah and
other mystical traditions. Where Buber and other historians of religion in
the early twentieth century tried to establish the common basis of all religious
experience, Scholem argues [in *Major Trends in Jewish Mysticism*] that, historically, each type of mysticism had its own unique tradition: "Only in our
days has the belief gained ground that there is such a thing as an abstract
mystical religion." Without denying the similarities between mystical traditions, Scholem focuses obstinately on Jewish mysticism as a self-contained
historical tradition.

THE KABBALAH'S LINGUISTIC MYSTICISM

In the introduction to *Major Trends in Jewish Mysticism*, in which he
seeks to establish the unique characteristics of Jewish mysticism, Scholem
focuses on the question of language and, in a footnote, suggests that this
was his major area of disagreement with Buber:

[The mystics] continuously and bitterly complain of the utter in-
adequacy of words to express their true feelings, but, for all that,
they glory in them; they indulge in rhetoric and never weary of
trying to express the inexpressible in words. All writers on mysticism have laid stress on this point. Jewish mysticism is no exception, yet it is distinguished by two unusual characteristics,
which may in some way be interrelated . . . First of all, the striking restraint observed by the Kabbalists in referring to the supreme experience; and secondly, their metaphysically positive
attitude towards language as God's own instrument.

The Kabbalists were less interested in describing their own experiences than
in mystical commentary on earlier texts. The biographical literature, Scholem
claims, is far inferior in Jewish mysticism to the theoretical. Hence, Jewish
mysticism differs from many other traditions in its lack of interest in personal
experience and its emphasis on a tradition of scholarly commentary. Scholem's own studies of the Kabbalah focus on "theoretical" Kabbalah and his
occasional treatment of practical "experiential" Kabbalah, such as the prophetic Kabbalism of Abraham Abulafia, is designed to prove the rule by
reference to the exception.

Scholem believes that the defining characteristic of Jewish mysticism as
commentary on a secret tradition has its origins in a unique and explicitly
positive attitude toward language. Commentary is not only the proper mode
of Jewish mysticism, but is actually required because of the divine origin of
traditional texts. An essential connection exists between commentator and
text [as is pointed out in *Major Trends in Jewish Mysticism*] because of the
divine character of language: "Language in its purest form, that is, Hebrew . . . reflects the fundamental spiritual nature of the world . . . Speech
reaches God because it comes from God . . . All that lives is an expression
of God's language."

In his article on "The Name of God and the Linguistic Theory of the
Kabbalah," Scholem argues that linguistic mysticism developed in two stages.
In the *Sefer Yitzirah*, which he dates to the second or third century, the
twenty-two letters of the Hebrew alphabet and the ten cardinal numbers
were the tools of creation: "the clear opinion of the author is that every
created thing has a linguistic essence which consists in any conceivable combination of these fundamental letters . . . This conception of the essence of
the Creation is closely linked with the linguistic conception of magic." In
the thirteenth century, however, linguistic magic became linguistic mysticism:
the letters and numbers were not tools created by God for magical purposes,

but emanations of God's own essence. God's name was conceived as equivalent to his essence and as the means by which he created the world. Creation was a linguistic process in which God's name became material.

For the thirteenth-century Kabbalists, creation and revelation were identical events: both were linguistic "autorepresentations" of God. The Torah, read mystically, was nothing but a series of esoteric divine names. The hidden structure of the Torah was equivalent to the structure of the world, and the task of the Kabbalist was to decipher the common linguistic essence of creation and revelation: "The Torah, as the Kabbalists conceived it, is consequently not separate from the divine essence, not created in the strict sense of the word; rather, it is something that represents the secret life of God, which the Kabbalistic emanation theory was an attempt to describe."

According to the Kabbalists, the divine language consists solely of divine names and has no grammar. Scholem notes that for the Kabbalists the essential name of God paradoxically "has no 'meaning' in the traditional understanding of the term ... It has no concrete signification." God is not meaningless, but, we might say, "meta-meaningful"; he is the source of all meaning. Words, on the other hand, do have meaning since their purpose is to communicate information. How, then, does the divine language, which has no concrete meaning, become the source of all meaning? Against Buber's "unmediated word of God," Scholem argues that the Kabbalists believed that revelation must be mediated since communication with God can only take place by indirect discourse.

The dialectical translation of the divine revelation into human language is possible because of the equivocity of the divine name. The paradox of a human-divine language is inherent in the Hebrew phrase for the Tetragrammaton, *shem ha-meforash*. Scholem shows how the sixteenth-century Kabbalist Moses Cordovero offered two etymologies for this expression: it could either mean "explicit" (*l'faresh*—to make explicit) or "hidden-separate" (*l'hafrish*—to separate). That the very Hebrew expression for the essential name of God contains these contradictory meanings suggests that language itself, which originates in the name of God, is equivocal. In the process of creation and revelation, God's hidden name becomes an explicit, communicable word. The divine name becomes dialectically the source of all meaning.

Scholem argues that the ability of language to be at once divine and human lies in its capacity to symbolize. He argues that, for the Kabbalists, symbols are the means for describing God indirectly. Unlike allegory, the symbol is not imposed arbitrarily on a mystical event, but has the inherent power to evoke an intuitive understanding:

If allegory can be defined as the representation of an expressible something by another expressible something, the mystical symbol is an expressible representation of something which lies beyond the sphere of expression and communication, something which comes from a sphere whose face is, as it were, turned inward and away from us . . . The symbol "signifies" nothing and communicates nothing, but makes something transparent which is beyond all expression.

(*Major Trends in Jewish Mysticism*)

Symbols, like the divine name, have no concrete signification, but they become dialectically the expression of the inexpressible source of meaning.

For the Kabbalists, symbols are not arbitrary or subjective, but have an essential inner connection with what they symbolize. Symbols are therefore the residue of divine names in human language. The great faith the Kabbalists had in language was a result of their belief in symbols as the bridge between human and divine language. In the modern, technological world in which man's fantasies have been isolated to a private world of subjective symbolism, the disappearance of public symbols has become, according to Scholem, a "great crisis of language." We might add that Buber's linguistic skepticism was a reflection of his own secularism since he could no longer believe in language as capable of symbolizing the ineffable.

THE KABBALAH'S PLURALISTIC CONCEPT OF TRADITION

The Kabbalistic notion of revelation, according to Scholem, is of an auditory experience in which the name of God is translated into human language and thereby becomes comprehensible. The divine name "is not a communication which provides comprehension . . . it becomes a comprehensible communication only when it is mediated." Revelation is therefore a meaningless experience until it is mediated through human language, and this mediation is justified by the divine origin of the language:

Here revelation, which has yet no specific meaning, is that in the word which gives an infinite wealth of meaning. Itself without meaning, it is the very essence of interpretability . . . We now face the problem of tradition as it presented itself to the Kabbalists. If the conception of revelation as absolute and meaning-giving but in itself meaningless is correct, then it must also be true that revelation will come to unfold its infinite meaning . . . only in its

constant relationship to history, the arena in which tradition unfolds.

(The Messianic Idea in Judaism)

Since there is "no immediate, undialectic application of the divine word,"
revelation only acquires concrete meaning in an historical tradition. Revelation is the source of all meaning and, indeed, of all life. In the words of
the sixteenth-century Kabbalist Meier Ibn Gabbai, whom Scholem quotes
extensively, revelation is not a one-time event, but a "fountain [which] is
never interrupted . . . Were it to be interrupted, for even a moment, all creatures would sink back into their non-being." Revelation is continually necessary to sustain the world, but without a tradition of commentary and
interpretation to translate God's word into concrete reality, revelation would
have no relation to the world and the "fountain" would cease.

How did the Kabbalists understand the interpretive tradition created by
revelation? They clearly saw themselves as legitimate interpreters of revelation, even when their interpretations seemed to contradict the literal meaning
of scripture. In fact, the Kabbalists justified the paradoxical character of their
interpretations in theological categories. Ibn Gabbai, for instance, wrote that
the "ever-flowing fountain" generates many "diverse ways of interpretation"
but

> the differences and contradictions do not originate out of different
> realms but out of the one place in which no difference and no
> contradiction is possible. The implicit meaning of this secret is
> that it lets every scholar insist on his own opinion and cite proofs
> for it from the Torah; only in this manner . . . is the unity [of the
> various aspects of the stream of revelation] achieved. Therefore,
> it is incumbent on us to hear the different opinions.
>
> *(The Messianic Idea in Judaism)*

Every interpretation has divine sanction and, indeed, conflict of opinions is
required to "unite the stream." Against a monolithic or dogmatic conception
of Judaism, Ibn Gabbai called for an open marketplace of interpretations.

Scholem believes that the Kabbalistic doctrines of revelation and tradition are the very opposite of those of the nineteenth-century rationalists,
"whose aim was an apologia based on the possible rationality of Judaism in
a context which seemed to admit only unequivocal dogmatic formulations."
For the Kabbalists, since the source of revelation is a name unbound by any

specific meaning, each word in the Torah can be interpreted *equivocally* in an infinite number of ways. The quintessence of revelation, says Scholem,

> is no longer the weight of the statements that attain communi-
> cation in it, but the infinite number of interpretations to which
> it is open. The character of the absolute is recognizable by its
> infinite number of possible interpretations . . . Infinitely many
> lights burn in each word . . . Each word of the Torah has sev-
> enty—according to some, 600,000—faces or facets. Without giv-
> ing up the fundamentalist thesis of the divine character of the
> scriptures, such mystical theses nevertheless achieve an astound-
> ing loosening of the concept of Revelation. Here the authority of
> Revelation also constitutes the basis of the freedom in its appli-
> cation and interpretation . . . Legitimacy was also accorded to
> progressive insight and speculation, which could combine a sub-
> jective element with what was objectively given . . . In principle,
> then, every one of the community of Israel has his own access to
> Revelation, which is open only to him and which he himself must
> discover.
>
>   ("The Meaning of the Torah in Jewish Mysticism")

The right to interpret revelation in an infinite number of potentially contradictory ways comes from revelation itself. Not only was the law revealed at
Sinai, but so was the right, even obligation, to interpret and reinterpret
revelation.

Scholem argues [in "Jewish Theology"] that this potentially anarchistic
theology is moderated and regulated by the concept of tradition. The Kabbalists believed that the tradition is authoritative because it is grounded in
revelation. The infinite meaning of revelation only unfolds gradually in an
historical tradition, which, presumably, is open-ended since there are an
infinite number of possible interpretations. At any given moment in history,
the immediate reality of revelation cannot be recaptured without recourse
to the mediation of tradition. In other words, there is no pure experience of
revelation but only a tradition of interpretations of revelation to which one
can refer. To be sure, revelation guarantees the sanctity of any interpretation,
but only to the one who submits himself to the whole historical tradition of
interpretation. Recognition of the authority of tradition also grants the freedom to reinterpret it in new and radical ways: "That voice which calls forth
incessantly from Sinai is given its human articulation and translation in

Tradition, which passes on the inexhaustible word of Revelation at any time and through every 'scholar' who subjects himself to its continuity."

SCHOLEM'S ANARCHISTIC THEOLOGY

When Scholem speaks of "every scholar," does he also mean himself? In the various articles referred to above on language and theology, Scholem writes in the detached voice of an historian of the Kabbalah, and it is often extremely difficult to discern whether he identifies with the views of his sources. His tantalizing but reticent hints that he himself might hold these positions have driven some of his interpreters to despair. Our examination of his earliest writings suggests certain similarities between his own views on language and theology and those he later ascribed to the Kabbalah. In addition, there exists a little-known article from 1932 where Scholem speaks in his own voice and does not conceal his theology behind the mask of the Kabbalah.

The article is a critique of Hans Joachim Schoeps's book, *Jüdischer Glaube in dieser Zeit*. Schoeps, a well-known historian of religion, is one of the more curious products of the German-Jewish symbiosis. A Prussian monarchist, he believed in the years before the Nazis that German Jews, as opposed to the Ostjuden, could live in harmony with a nationalistic German state. In the early 1930s he was active politically in propagating his right-wing Völkisch ideas. Needless to say, his political views, which were anathema to most German Jews, were enough to guarantee his theological reflections a hostile reception in the Jewish community, but he compounded his difficulties by a radical theological position permeated with Karl Barth's dialectical Protestantism.

With many thoughtful Jews of his generation, Schoeps strongly criticized the liberal rationalist theology of the nineteenth century and searched for a radical religious solution to the problem of secularization. Schoeps rejected the oral law and whole Jewish legal tradition, and wanted to resurrect a biblical theology based on a doctrine of irrational revelation. Man believes in God not because revelation is in harmony with his reason, but precisely the opposite, because the content of revelation is paradoxical. Schoeps borrowed much of his existentialist terminology from Kierkegaard and Barth, but he also found a Jewish source for his ideas in the nineteenth-century iconoclastic theologian Salomon Ludwig Steinheim. In his *Offenbarung nach dem Lehrbegriff der Synagoge* (Revelation According to the Teaching of the Synagogue), Steinheim had argued that the belief in creation out of nothingness is the central dogma of Judaism and runs counter to the teachings of rational philosophy. Against the liberal rationalists of the nineteenth century, Steinheim saw Judaism as a religion of irrational revelation. Like Kierkegaard, with whom Schoeps compares him, Steinheim believed that revelation had no intelligible content and that Jewish tradition was merely conventional and artificial.

Schoeps adopted Steinheim's idea of reconstructing the putative biblical faith in irrational revelation as a solution to the crisis of rational Jewish theology. Like Scholem, Buber, and others, he discovered a counter-tradition in Judaism, running from Judah Ha-Levi to Steinheim, which acclaimed the unique irrational message of Jewish revelation. At the same time, he attacked the Zionists for trying to place Judaism on a secular basis. For Schoeps, Judaism was primarily a religious faith, and in studies of the historical interaction of Jews and Germans, he argued that, from a secular perspective, Jews were part of Germany.

As might be expected, Scholem violently objected to Schoeps's identification of Jewish secular fate with Germany. Although he himself had criticized the "Zionist secularization of Judaism," Scholem considered Jewish fate, both secular and religious, to be unique and distinct from Europe. He particularly criticized Schoeps's emphasis on German Jews, which he believed distorted the unique national character of Jewish history as a product of the totality of world Jewry. Schoeps's counter-history itself was a distortion since it relied on philosophical sources when it could have found a much more fruitful source in the Kabbalah. By constructing his irrationalist critique of nineteenth-century Jewish rationalism on a philosophical counter-tradition, Schoeps fell into the same trap as did the apologists: he construed a dogma of Judaism which excluded the totality of Jewish sources.

Scholem confesses his admiration for Steinheim's irrationalist nonconformism, but he rejects an irrational dogma as vehemently as he does a rational one. By attempting to return to a biblical theology of *creatio ex nihilo,* which Scholem argues is anachronistic for biblical theology in any case, Schoeps had attacked the Jewish concept of tradition. Scholem compares Schoeps's "neutralization of Jewish historical consciousness" to Karaism in the Jewish sphere and Barthian theology in the Protestant. If Schoeps wanted to overcome history with an ahistorical faith, why did he reject only the oral law? Was not biblical revelation equally absurd to a modern man concerned with "the contemporary understanding of existence" (*heutigen Daseinsverständnis*)?

Against Schoeps's abrogation of tradition, Scholem suggests his own theological position in a few sentences that are formulated in terms virtually identical to those he ascribes to the Kabbalah:

> Revelation is, despite its uniqueness, still a *medium*. It is [the] absolute, meaning-bestowing, but itself meaningless that becomes explicable (*das Deutbare*) only through the continuing relation to time, to the Tradition. The word of God in its absolute symbolic fullness would be destructive if it were at the same time meaningful in an unmediated [undialectical] way. Nothing in historical time requires concretization more than the "absolute concreteness" of the word of revelation.
>
> ("Revelation and Tradition")

There is no such thing as an unmediated concrete word of God. God's revelation is abstract and infinite, but because it linguistically "bestows meaning" (*Bedeutung-Gebendes*), it can be concretized by man. The interpretive tradition has its source in revelation, but it is necessary to render revelation comprehensible. Revelation and tradition are an indivisible unity. Schoeps had reduced Judaism to an ahistorical faith because he failed to understand the essential function of tradition and the impossibility of "pure" faith. Without tradition, the "voice" (*Stimme*) of revelation necessarily loses its force:

> The voice which we perceive is the medium in which we live, and where it is not [the medium], it becomes hollow and takes on a ghostly character in which the word of God no longer has [an] effect, but instead circumvents . . . The residue of the voice, as that which in Judaism is the tradition in its creative development, cannot be separated from it [the voice].

Against Schoeps's ahistorical, dogmatic theology of belief, Scholem calls for a return to historical consciousness. Not the suprahistorical Erlebnis of Martin Buber, but concrete historical experience (Erfahrung) must be the basis for revitalized Judaism. Scholem ends his polemic against Schoeps with a phrase from Kant: "I am not orthodox, but it is evident to me that without the restoration of such a 'fruitful *bathos* of experience' (*fruchtbaren Bathos der Erfahrung*), which arises out of the reflection and transformation of human words in the medium of the divine, nothing of your project can be realized." The equivocity of divine-human language creates the historical tradition whose authority must be recognized even by Jews in a secular age.

In his reply to Scholem, [Ja-Nein-und Trotzdem] Schoeps argued that he and Scholem were perhaps representatives of two opposite tendencies in Jewish history, which he syncretistically labeled "critical-protestant" and "ontological-catholic." Could tradition have any meaning without belief in the immediate word of God? Scholem, although he professed belief in God, had only tradition, while he, Schoeps, sought to revitalize tradition by returning to original revelation. Schoeps wrote: "You will not find any answer here through science (*wissenschaftlich*), because to this question [the question of revitalized Judaism] only the answer through existence (*mit der Existenz*) can be convincing." Schoeps thus incisively laid out the fundamental theological dispute between himself and Scholem: faith versus history.

Scholem's "Open Letter" to Schoeps must be read as an antiexistentialist manifesto and, although he specifically attacks Schoeps's dialectical theology, he must have had in mind the other "ahistorical" existential Jewish theologies of that time, notably those of Buber and Rosenzweig. Rosenzweig's view of language as he developed it in his *Star of Redemption* was actually much closer to Scholem's than to Buber's: "The manifestation (*Offenbarwerden*) that we are looking for here must be one that is essential revelation and nothing more. That is to say, however, it should be nothing else than . . . the self-negation of a purely silent essence through an audible word." However, Rosenzweig considered the Jews a people outside history, whereas the essence of Scholem's position is that the Jews are subject to the laws of history. Rosenzweig's opposition to the Zionist attempt to "return the Jews to history," which so enraged Scholem, must be seen as a consequence of his ahistorical view of Judaism. More important, Rosenzweig's "ahistoricity" led him to a different understanding of tradition. The revelation at Sinai, if not literally "law-giving," was at least a "command" (*Gebot*) for Rosenzweig. The command of Sinai created a legal tradition that the secular Jew approaches as a given. One is free to accept or reject parts of the tradition according to one's personal progress on the "path" of the halakhah, but the nature of the tradition is both legal and fixed.

Scholem's understanding of tradition is much broader than Rosenzweig's: "Tradition as a living force produces in its unfolding another problem. What had originally been believed to be consistent, unified and self-enclosed now becomes diversified, multifold and full of contradictions. It is precisely the wealth of contradictions, of differing views, which is encompassed and unqualifiedly affirmed by tradition." Rosenzweig termed Scholem's position "nihilism," but I believe that he misunderstood the difference between nihilism and Scholem's religious anarchism. When Scholem calls himself a religious anarchist, he means that the historical tradition, which is the only source of knowledge we have of revelation, contains no one authoritative voice. All that can be learned from the study of history is the *struggle* for absolute values among conflicting voices of authority.

Scholem is an anarchist because he believes "the binding character of the Revelation for a collective has disappeared. The word of God no longer serves as a source for the definition of possible contents of a religious tradition and thus of a possible theology." Yet we have seen that he affirms belief in God as intrinsically "meaningless" but nevertheless "meaning-bestowing." God stands as the unknowable origin of the tradition and as the guarantor of its legitimacy. But like Maimonides, Scholem does not believe that it is possible to make any meaningful positive statements about Him. Left without direct access to revelation, he still has the literary sources of tradition about which statements can be made because their language is guaranteed by God. Scholem does not abrogate the authority of tradition, as would a secular nihilist, but asserts its pluralistic message.

Against both the Jewish existentialists and their rationalist predecessors, Scholem asserts that commentary and not theology is the correct discipline for understanding Jewish tradition:

> Truth is given once and for all, and it is laid down with precision. Fundamentally, truth merely needs to be transmitted. The originality of the exegete (*Schriftgelehrter*) has two aspects. In his spontaneity, he develops and explains that which was transmitted at Sinai, no matter whether it was always known or whether it was forgotten and had to be rediscovered. The effort of the seeker after truth consists not in having new ideas but rather in subordinating himself to the continuity of the tradition of the divine word and in laying open what he receives from it in the context of his own time. In other words: not system but commentary is the legitimate form through which truth is approached.
>
> ("Revelation and Tradition")

Against the nineteenth-century search for a systematic definition of Judaism, Scholem asserts that the process of commentary is itself the vessel in which the truth of revelation is carried. The commentator is not "original" as a philosopher might be in deductively deriving a definition of Judaism from *a priori* principles. Rather, his originality consists in letting the sources speak through him; the legitimacy of his new interpretation is guaranteed by his subordination to the sources of the tradition.

The "audacious freedom of interpretation" which this theory of tradition suggests derives from Scholem's understanding of the dialectic between the written and oral law in Judaism. Interestingly enough, he quotes as his source none of the numerous Jewish analyses of this relationship, but the Christian Kabbalist, Molitor:

Every written formulation is only an abstracted general picture of a reality which totally lacks all concreteness and individual dimension of real life ... The spoken word, as well as life and practice, must therefore be the constant companions and inter-preters of the written word, which otherwise remains a dead and abstract concept in the mind ... In modern times, where reflec-tion threatens to swallow up all of life, where everything has been reduced to dead, abstract concepts, that old inherent reciprocal relationship between the written and spoken word, between the-ory and practice, has been totally displaced.

(*Philosophie der Geschichte*)

Molitor suggests that the oral law reinvigorates the written by giving it a concrete interpretation: God's revelation can only become concrete through the mediation of revelation. The written word is here a metaphor for reve-lation, while the spoken word suggests the commentary on revelation. The tradition is only called oral metaphorically to suggest its freedom as against the ostensibly fixed and dogmatic character of the written text. Scholem recognizes [in *The Name of God*] that the actual notion of "writing" in Judaism, and particularly in the Kabbalah, is very different from this meta-phorical usage: "For the Kabbalists, linguistic mysticism is at the same time a mysticism of writing. Every act of speaking ... is at once an act of writing and every writing is potential speech."

The notion of an oral tradition, even when actually written down, is Scholem's model for interpretive freedom. The oral tradition gains its efficacy precisely from its detached perspective on revelation: "The Torah is the medium in which knowledge is reflected; it darkens as it brings with it the essence of the tradition, radiating into the pure realm of the 'written,' that is to say, [of] unusable teaching. [The teaching] only becomes usable where it is 'oral,' in other words, where it is transmittable." Because it is expressed in the language of men, the oral tradition can be transmitted, and it is usable because it can be interpreted and commented upon. But because it is already historically removed from revelation, tradition guarantees a certain freedom: it becomes the possession of men who interpret it according to their lights.

The importance Scholem attributes to historical perspective can be seen in his refusal in 1930 to translate Rosenzweig's *Stern der Erlösung* into Hebrew. He found a magical, even demonic connection between the work and the spirit of the German language which made the *Stern* incomprehen-sible. The *Stern* would only become translatable in some future generation "that will no longer feel itself addressed in such an immediate fashion by the themes most pertinent to the present time . . . Only when the enchanting beauty of its language will have worn off . . . shall this testimony to God be able to assert itself in all its undisguised intent." The language of an experience of God requires historical perspective in order to become part of a transmittable and translatable tradition.

The interpreter of tradition, living perhaps centuries after the original revelation, receives revelation through the mediation of tradition, a tradition to which he adds. Interpretation for Scholem is a creative activity that sustains the ever-growing tradition, but only the interpreter who takes upon himself the burden of tradition and does not try to leapfrog directly back to revelation is granted legitimacy.

KABBALIST OR HISTORIAN?

There is a strong suggestion in the preceding argument that Scholem considers the work of the historian to be very similar to that of the Kabbalist. Both are engaged in detached commentary on a tradition. In his rejection of both the rationalist and the existentialist definitions of Judaism, does Scholem adopt the theology of the Kabbalah as a model for his own theological justification of historiography? Does he hold that the secular historian is the modern incarnation of the traditional commentator? Does historiography serve the same function as the oral tradition of the Kabbalah in reinvigorating a decaying written tradition?

The similarity between Scholem's own theological formulations and those he ascribes to the Kabbalah seems too striking to be coincidental. He clearly feels a strong affinity with his sources. The most remarkable evidence of this affinity is the first of his "Zehn Unhistorische Sätze über Kabbala" (Ten Unhistorical Aphorisms about the Kabbalah):

> The philology of a mystical discipline such as the Kabbalah has something ironic about it. It is concerned with a veil of mist (*Nebelschleier*) which, as the history of the mystical tradition, hangs around the body, the space of the matter itself. It is a mist, however, which [the tradition] generates out of itself.
>
> Does there remain for the philologian something visible of the law of the thing itself or does the essential disappear in the projection of the historical? The uncertainty in answering this question belongs to the nature of the philological enterprise itself and thus contains the expectation, from which this work lives, of something ironic which cannot be severed from it. But doesn't

such an element of irony lie already even more in the subject of
this Kabbalah itself and not only in its history?

   The Kabbalist claims that there is a tradition whose truth can
be transmitted. An ironic claim since precisely that truth which
is the issue here is anything but transmittable. It can be known,
but not transmitted and precisely that which is transmittable in
it, it no longer contains. Authentic tradition remains hidden; only
the decayed (*verfallende*) tradition chances upon (*verfällt auf*) a
subject and only in decay does its greatness become visible.

Scholem uses explicitly Kabbalistic language in this extraordinary statement to describe his own enterprise as an historian of the Kabbalah. He is
concerned with an esoteric discipline that can only become the subject of
historiography when it is no longer esoteric, when it has "decayed" into a
public tradition. Hence the historian of the Kabbalah can never be sure if he
is dealing with the thing itself or only with its historical shadow. Similarly,
the Kabbalist claims to transmit the secret essence of revelation; yet the
hidden character of that truth cannot be transmitted. When the Kabbalist
describes the indescribable in human language, he too can never be sure of
the truth of his words. This problematic relationship is reenacted in modern
terms in the tension between Scholem as secular historian and his subject.

   This text also immediately reminds us in style and substance of the letter
to Schocken discussed in the first chapter. Here, too, the source of revelation
is hidden and accessible only by the indirect means of commentary. We are
also reminded of Scholem's reference to Kafka. What Scholem believed that
he found in Kafka now becomes clear: a fictional representation of the theological problem he himself confronted as an historian. Whether or not Kafka
intended works like *The Trial* and *The Castle* primarily as theological allegories, it would seem that Scholem understood them in this light. The paradox that faces the historian is the paradox that faces Kafka's heroes: how
to gain access to the source of revelation, which is intrinsically inaccessible.
For Scholem, the historian's paradox is, in fact, the problem facing every
Jew, whose only approach to revelation lies through the tradition. For the
secular Jew, as for the Kabbalist, revelation remains hidden.

   Still, the very fact of a distance between Scholem and his subject suggests
that he cannot be considered a Kabbalist. The anarchistic theology that underlies his philosophy of history is not identical to the position of the Kabbalah. The Kabbalists were not full-fledged anarchists because they believed
in the authority of normative Jewish law. However, the anarchism that lurked
in potentia in their theology could become explicit in secular historiography,

which is not yoked to this authority. Even if the modern historian believes that there is a God, his assumption is that the only meaningful statements he can make are about the pluralistic historical tradition. Scholem therefore sees the Kabbalists as his precursors and Kabbalistic theology as the precursor to his theological anarchism—but they are not the same. Modern historiography is a new development in the history of commentary in which the Kabbalah was an earlier stage. Unlike Buber, Scholem does not identify fully with his sources, but maintains his historical detachment, a detachment that, however, is characteristic of all commentators, secular or religious. In this way, Scholem is able to claim that secularism, as embodied in the modern historical method, is "part of the dialectic of the development *within* Judaism."

Scholem's transformation of the traditional Jewish notion of commentary into historiography suggests that he views historical science, no matter how "secular" or radical, as the modern form of Judaism. In Scholem we have the fulfillment of the desire of the nineteenth-century Wissenschaft des Judentums to find a secular substitute for religion in historiography. Indeed, in his "Open Letter" to Schoeps, Scholem points out that his own position is much closer to Graetz's historicism than to twentieth-century theology. But as opposed to the Wissenschaft des Judentums, Scholem argues that an anarchistic plurality of interpretations, and not just rationalism, must characterize historical Judaism. It might well be argued that such anarchism of interpretations was already an implicit possibility in nineteenth-century historicism: witness, for instance, Nachman Krochmal's suggestively radical idea that each age has its own legitimate "mode of investigation," a phrase similar to Ranke's claim that "each age is equally close to God." If each period's way of interpreting revelation is legitimate, the historian must treat each with equal favor. Scholem may be seen as the dialectical fulfillment of the original impulse in the Wissenschaft des Judentums, since nineteenth-century Jewish historiography laid the basis for anarchistic historicism but belied its promise by generally succumbing to a rationalist, dogmatic theology. Scholem's anarchism provides Jewish historicism with a theological rationale it did not achieve in the nineteenth century.

BENJAMIN'S INFLUENCE

Scholem's position on language and theology is illuminated by the early writings of Walter Benjamin. Although it is hard to demonstrate the direction of influence in a close friendship, I believe that Benjamin developed his views on language before Scholem, who was five years his junior, and he may be considered one of Scholem's predominant sources. In November 1916, Benjamin promised to send to Scholem his essay "Über Sprache überhaupt und über die Sprache des Menschen," whose linguistic theory bears a remarkable resemblance to that which Scholem ascribes to the Kabbalah. Whether or not Benjamin actually influenced Scholem on these matters, he explicated his point of view much more systematically than Scholem, and Scholem was well aware of Benjamin's formulations.

Scholem regarded Benjamin as primarily a metaphysician of language engaged in "mystical linguistics." He has emphasized this side of Benjamin's work against those who claim the later Benjamin as a genuine Marxist theoretician. In despair over his friend's flirtation with Marxism, Scholem wrote to Benjamin in 1931: "You could be a figure of high importance in the history of critical thought, the legitimate continuer of the most fruitful and genuine traditions of Hamann and Humboldt." Scholem felt that Benjamin's Marxism was only a superficial jargon which hid a much more profound religious sensibility. Like many other Germans in the 1920s, Scholem and Benjamin found certain strains in the Enlightenment and German romanticism which inspired their own thinking. Scholem saw in Benjamin an intellectual heir to the philosophers of language, who, like Humboldt, had tried to discover the "inner spirit" of language common to mankind or, like Hamann, had struggled to define the mystical relationship between human and divine language.

Benjamin's attitude toward language was irreconcilably opposed to Buber's; in fact, the first expression I have found of his position appeared in a letter he wrote to Buber attacking Buber's use of language. Buber had invited Benjamin to contribute to his new journal, *Der Jude*. Like Scholem, Benjamin found repugnant the prowar tone of *Der Jude*, and particularly of Buber's editorial "Die Lösung." In July 1916 he turned down Buber's invitation in a letter whose contents were known to Scholem. Besides protesting that he had not yet developed his Jewish position sufficiently to write an article on a Jewish topic, Benjamin attacked the prowar position of *Der Jude* and particularly the connection between Buber's support for the war and his use of language. Benjamin's first statement on language was, then, a result of his opposition to the war, just as the war prompted Scholem to develop his own position against Buber.

Benjamin accused Buber of writing political propaganda; Buber had put language at the disposal of military action and language had therefore lost its independence. In war propaganda, Benjamin suggested, words have no autonomy of their own but become the obedient servants of action, the "preparation of the motives of action." Buber held that ultimate experiences are ineffable. Benjamin evidently understood Buber to be suggesting that the essence of action is also ineffable: language can, at best, prepare the motivations for action by exciting the emotions, but it has no essential relationship to action itself. Benjamin argued that, in Buber's writing, language had become "impoverished, weak acts."

Benjamin believed that language in itself is a form of powerful action: "I do not believe that the word stands somewhere farther away from the divine (*Göttlichen*) than does 'real' action." He argued against Buber that there is no sphere of experience which is ineffable: the true task of language is "the crystal-clear elimination of the unsayable (*Unsagbare*) in language. Only where this sphere of the wordless in its ineffable pure power is opened up, can the magic sparks spring between word and . . . act . . . Only the intensive directing of the words into the kernel of the innermost silence will achieve true action." Against Buber's mystical depreciation of language, Benjamin proposed a magical theory in which language itself becomes an action: to speak is to make.

Benjamin's new theory of language must also be understood as a pacifist critique of Buber's wartime Erlebnismystik. Satirically employing one of Buber's favorite mystical expressions, the "realization of the correct Absolute" (*Verwirklichung des richtigen Absoluten*), Benjamin implied that the glorification of action above words in prowar propaganda was the consequence of Erlebnismystik. For Benjamin, if language had been conceived as a form of legitimate action, it would have been turned against the war; in his Marxist period in the 1930s, he would see language as one of the only remaining weapons against fascism.

Benjamin's critique of Buber's philosophy of language was part of his general rejection of Lebensphilosophie. As Ernst Cassirer has noted, the "philosophers of life" held that life "seems to be given only in its pure immediacy . . . The original content of life cannot be apprehended in any form of representation, but only in pure intuition." For Benjamin, it was precisely through language that the essence of life could be grasped. Benjamin also argued forcefully against the nominalist theory of language as "an arbitrary game." As he wrote to Hugo von Hofmannsthal in a polemic against the language theory of the positivistic sciences, which could as well have been directed against Buber:

> The conviction which guides me in my literary attempts . . . [is] that each truth has its home, its ancestral palace in language, that this palace was built with the oldest *logoi* and that to a truth thus founded, the insights of the sciences will remain inferior for as long as they make do here and there in the area of language like

nomads . . . in the conviction of the sign character of language which produces the irresponsible arbitrariness of their terminology.

For Benjamin, language is the "essence of the world" and those who consider it an arbitrary collection of signs are "spiritually dumb."

Against the sign theory of language, Benjamin developed a "Kabbalistic" conception of language as symbolic, which explains his affinity with the symbolic poets of the late nineteenth century such as Mallarmé. Words have both communicative and symbolic functions. On the level of communication between people, words are impregnated with conventional meanings, but they can also symbolize an ineffable essence: "Language is in every case not only the communication of the communicable, but equally the symbol of the incommunicable." Following an old distinction that he took from Goethe and that Scholem adopted, Benjamin understood symbols as the opposite of allegories. Allegorization starts with a general concept and then searches for a specific but arbitrary physical representation of the general idea. The allegory therefore corresponds to the arbitrary sign of the sciences. The connection between the allegory and the concept allegorized is never immediately apparent and requires explication. Symbols, on the other hand, "establish a connection which is sensually perceived in its immediacy and requires no interpretation." Since the belief in symbols had waned in the modern world, the task of philosophy, which Benjamin opposed to science, is to "re-establish the symbolic character of the word, in which the idea comes to self-understanding in its primacy." Language is one of the primary cognitive tools with which man gives intelligible form to chaotic sense perceptions. Benjamin saw language as a creative instrument with which the noumenal world could be recaptured from behind the curtain of phenomenal perceptions and conventional meanings.

Benjamin added a theological dimension to his idealistic philosophy of language. In his early essay, "Über Sprache überhaupt und über die Sprache des Menschen," he deals with the question of how divine language can become human. God's word is equivalent to existence, but God could not have created the world by calling it directly into existence with concrete words, since God's language, by definition, is undifferentiated and infinite. Divine language seems incommensurable with human language, and therefore an immediate linguistic relationship between God and the world, Buber's "unmediated word of God," is impossible. Creation and, in fact, all interaction between God and the world must be mediated by man. God is the "source" of language, but it is man who names objects and thereby "brings the world before God." By the process of naming, man concretizes divine language and makes it human. When man names, he repeats the primordial act of Adam and reestablishes the "magic spark" between language and objects which Benjamin referred to first in his letter to Buber. The magic spark is lost when language becomes a merely conventional instrument for human communication, but in every generation man has the capacity to recover the Edenic creativity in language.

The notion of a divine language of names which underlies conventional language is very close to the Kabbalah's theory as interpreted by Scholem of the divine name as meaningless but meaning-bestowing. For Benjamin, words are encumbered with conventional meanings, but names are "the analogue to the knowledge of the object in the object itself . . . The name is superessential; it signifies the relation of the object to its essence." Benjamin distinguished between a "pure language" consisting only of names and language burdened with conventional meanings, but he argued that no particular language can be pure since each language is bound up with its own conventions. Only the totality of all languages constitutes pure language. Translation is therefore one of the best means to liberate men from the conventions of their own particular language: "The task of the translator is to release in his own language that pure language which is under the spell of another, to liberate the language imprisoned in a work in his re-creation of that work."

Translation not only recaptures pure language, but also enriches the vocabulary of a particular language by drawing on the metaphors of another. Like Humboldt, Benjamin believed that language is not a given but an "activity" in which man is constantly creating new forms: language is always growing. Benjamin's divine *Ursprache,* or primordial pure language, could never be fully recovered since language never stands still. The mythical Adam named objects and created language *ex nihilo,* but we inherit our language from the past. As we try to recover the pure language beneath the layers of conventional accretions, we also add to the language by creating new words and reinterpreting old ones. The philosophical job of interpreting language in order to purify it is actually creative since it adds new layers to the pure language. The concept of an Ursprache was therefore only an abstract hypothesis for Benjamin since it could never be isolated without transforming it. Once man concretizes divine language, he irreversibly alters the unmediated relation between God and the world by mediating between them. Although all authentic translation and literary criticism try to recapture the magic spark between word and object which characterizes divine language, this goal remains a utopian absolute that can be approached but never reached.

For Benjamin, divine language, represented by biblical revelation, was a guarantee that ordinary human language is not merely conventional and that it has its source in the noumenal world. The whole phenomenal world is like an esoteric text that demands interpretation. Our effort to understand the essence of this world is guaranteed by the hypothesis of a divine language of names which is equivalent to the "thing-in-itself." Without this theological belief in God as the source of language and in language as the mediating tool between the mind and essential reality, the work of interpretation is meaningless.

I have suggested that Benjamin saw interpretation, of which translation is a special case, as a creative process. The totality of all interpretations constitutes the ever-growing linguistic tradition. Like Scholem, Benjamin was deeply concerned with the category of tradition and with the possibility of recovering tradition in a secular world. In a letter to Scholem in 1917, he criticized Scholem's essay on Blau-Weiss education in which Scholem had argued for education by example. Benjamin urged him to consider tradition as the true basis for pedagogy. Teaching by example renders the student passive and makes the student dependent on the teacher. When student and teacher are both engaged in appropriation of the tradition by creative interpretation, a community of learning is created:

> I am convinced that tradition is the medium in which the student is continually transformed into the teacher . . . Whoever has not learned cannot educate . . . Education (*Unterricht*) is the only point of free unification between the older with the younger generation, like waves which throw their foam into one another. Every error in education ultimately goes back to [the idea] that those who come after us are dependent upon us. They are only dependent on us insofar as they are dependent on God and on language in which we ourselves must submerge our will in some communality (*Gemeinsamkeit*) with our children.

A tradition rooted in language, which itself originates in God's language, is the common source for all generations. This tradition, like the world as a whole, does not lie beyond a passive observer to whom it is given through either education or sense perception. Rather, the tradition is appropriated by the student as he interprets it, and education consists of a community of interpreters from different generations.

In Scholem's own views on education, expressed many years later in a discussion with Israeli educators, there is an echo of Benjamin's concept of an open dialogue with tradition. Education, Scholem insists, should not re-

flect one dogmatic viewpoint but should expose the student to the whole
contradictory wealth of the tradition:

> If I were called upon to teach, I would try to show that Jewish
> history has been a struggle over great ideas and the question is
> to what extent we should be influenced by the degree of success
> achieved in that struggle by values which were formulated and
> defined in the tradition . . . At the same time, I would consider
> with my pupils the failures in history, matters having to do with
> violence, cruelty and hypocrisy.

In his pedagogy, as in his historiography and theology, Scholem believes that,
unless we regard the tradition as a pluralistic constellation of forces to which
each generation contributes, Judaism will lose its vitality.

Benjamin and Scholem agree that the ability of language to symbolize
the ineffable guarantees tradition as the medium which connects man to the
divine source of creation and revelation. For both, tradition consists of creative commentary in an effort to reestablish the essential connection between
man and the source of language. Their metaphysical affirmation of language
and historical tradition departs radically from Buber's ahistorical mysticism
and, I believe, constitutes an important response to the crisis of Jewish theology in the twentieth century.

SCHOLEM AND THE CRISIS OF JEWISH THEOLOGY

Gershon Weiler, in an article on "The Theology of Gershom Scholem,"
argues that Scholem does not define what he means when he says that he
believes in God. In order to make meaningful statements of belief about God,
Scholem should have addressed himself to the Maimonidean problem of the
attributes of God, which he seemingly evades. Weiler claims that Scholem
has fallen into the same logical difficulty as "the modern Protestant theologians, the existentialists and even Buber . . . They all speak as if there is some
hidden [essence] which is revealed in experience alone but they continue to
use the name 'God.'" Weiler posits only two theological alternatives: either
the logically meaningless "experiential" theology of Buber or Maimonidean
rationalism.

I believe that Scholem, along with Walter Benjamin, has charted a third
theological course. He does not accept Buber's conception of revelation as
experience. On the other hand, although he accepts Maimonides' reluctance
to assign any positive attributes to God, he is not interested in rational
theology. With Benjamin, he sees God as the origin and guarantor of the

process of interpretation he calls tradition. The tradition on which he, as a modern historian, comments is itself testimony to the original impetus of divine revelation; yet it does not permit any meaningful statements about revelation itself or its divine source. The only meaningful statements one can make are about the tradition, the province of the historian and commentator rather than of the theologian. Scholem's theology is therefore an antitheological argument for historiography, but historiography conceived as one more interpretive contribution to the ever-growing tradition.

Does Scholem deserve a place in the history of Jewish theology in the twentieth century? I suggested [elsewhere] . . . that the crisis of Jewish theology, embodied in the thought of Hermann Cohen, represented a watershed in theological speculations. The failure of rational theology is normally considered to have led to the existentialism of Rosenzweig and Buber. Scholem's explicit rejection of these two thinkers suggests that his own position may constitute an alternative response to the crisis of theology.

Cohen was the explicit starting point for Buber and Rosenzweig. In the last chapter we saw that the young Scholem was also well aware of Cohen and, although he criticized his contemporaries for not appreciating the Marburg philosopher, Cohen represented for him the dogmatic attempt to purge myth and pantheism from Jewish history. Scholem began his career in conscious opposition to Cohen's rationalism. But it is significant that just as Cohen's late thought pointed toward existentialism, it also hinted at the opposing direction that Scholem himself would pursue in his rejection of the existentialists: historical study of Judaism. Although it would be erroneous to claim that Scholem "borrowed" any of his ideas from Cohen, his position may be judged in retrospect as, dialectically, both a continuation and a refutation of Cohen's rational theology.

In his *Religion der Vernunft*, Cohen suggests two concepts of God. One is a personal God with whom the suffering individual can enter into dialogue, and the other is a restatement of his older concept of God as an abstract methodological principle. Although the new concept was to become a fruitful source for Buber and Rosenzweig, it is striking how closely the methodological God-concept resembles Scholem's theological position. In his chapters on "God's Uniqueness," "Creation," and "Revelation," Cohen argues that God's uniqueness is the exact opposite of the pluralistic world; yet it is not the negation of the world. Instead, God is conceived as an "originative principle" (*Ursprungsprinzip*), meaning a principle that is the origin of other dialectically opposing principles. Revelation is a similar process where "the eternal, which is removed from all sense experience, therefore from all historical experience, is the foundation and the warrant of the very spirit of national history." God is the origin and guarantor of the permanence of the world and of the historical tradition. We immediately recognize that, despite the difference in terminology, Cohen's dialectical concept of God is very similar to Scholem's idea that God is meaningless but meaning-bestowing.

Like Scholem, Cohen considers the tradition a body of exegetical interpretations for which the model is the oral law: "The oral law is spontaneous, as the 'fruit of the lips,' whereas the written tradition is stamped on brazen tablets. [The oral law is also] not an immediately finished product, but an open one, one that always continues to be produced." The tradition contains a variety of principles and interpretations, which Cohen readily admits often appear to contradict one another. This notion of a pluralistic, open-ended tradition looks very much like Scholem's concept of tradition.

There is also a striking resemblance between Scholem and Cohen on the issue of the relationship of the modern interpreter to the tradition. In a rather compressed and enigmatic section of the introduction to the *Religion der Vernunft,* Cohen argues that the exegetical method of the traditional oral law is not "formal logical deduction." In other words, the biblical exegete does not merely deduce his interpretation from the biblical text. Instead, he discovers his own thought in the text by a process of interaction between himself as a thinker and his source (*Quelle*):

> First, thought is thought, whether it occurs in the Haggadah as a moral thought in the imaginative style of poetry, or in the Halachah as a law for which, as for all other thoughts, one will subsequently find the sanction in the Bible . . . Otherwise, it would be almost inconceivable that the memory of the talmudic scholar could find in the great treasure of biblical words and its sentence structure the analogy exactly appropriate to the case at hand . . . Logic confers seriousness upon the imagination, because the imagination is sustained and supported by the stern objectivity of the problem.
>
> (*Religion der Vernunft*)

This exegetical philosophy, in which interpretive originality and the objective message of the text are harmonized, is not only the method of the Jewish tradition—it is Cohen's own method. He too argues that the nature of Judaism can only be determined by a dynamic interaction between the modern philosopher and the historical sources. In other words, for Cohen, the modern interpreter of tradition operates with the same logic and principles of interpretation as can be found in the tradition itself. The philosopher of history therefore continues the work of interpretation and becomes part of tradition. In a similar way, Scholem argues that the secular historical method is already anticipated by the tradition itself. He "discovers" a possible precursor of his own theology in the sources he studies. Since his exegetical philosophy is not alien to the tradition, he, as a modern historian, continues the work of commentary.

Despite these remarkable similarities, there is a fundamental difference between Scholem and Cohen. Cohen claims that the apparent contradictions between interpretations within the tradition are an illusion. All these interpretations are actually united by the concept of reason, and it is the task of the philosopher of Judaism to discover this unifying reason in the sources. Scholem rejects the idea that a philosophical concept can impose unity on an intrinsically pluralistic tradition. The contradictions within the tradition are not an illusion, but an essential consequence of the unfolding of the infinite meanings of revelation. The only possible definition of Judaism is the totality of the contradictory principles that make up Jewish history. Since there is no *a priori* philosophical essence of Judaism, but only a plurality of historical sources, historiography and not philosophy is the proper discipline for the modern Jew. Where Cohen found his precursors in the philosophical tradition, Scholem finds his in the pluralistic commentaries of the Kabbalah.

Although Cohen defined Judaism as solely a religion of reason, his claim that the tradition is pluralistic prepared the ground for the subversion of his own rationalism. By developing the notion of a pluralistic tradition to its logical conclusion, Scholem has overturned Cohen's philosophical rationalism and addressed the crisis of Jewish theology in an original way. Judaism can only be understood on the basis of the totality of Jewish sources, a totality that can be grasped only by historical study of these sources themselves.

It must be emphasized that Scholem has never systematized the theological suggestions discussed in this chapter. The very fact that we have been forced to ask where he speaks in his own voice and where he speaks as an historian of the Kabbalah precludes our calling him a "theologian." Moreover, the ideas outlined here, perhaps because they have not been systematically developed, are surely open to criticism. In a secular world, a struggle goes on to define the meaning of Judaism. While a pluralistic or anarchistic theology may have attractions for those unable or unwilling to accept an orthodox and dogmatic "essence" of Judaism, it fails to answer significant questions. An anarchistic philosophy of Judaism seems to preclude any normative element by definition: it leads, in Scholem's case, to a study of history rather than a prescription for how a Jew should live. While this may have been a personal solution for Scholem as an historian, in what sense can it be generalized and applied to others? Have Scholem's historical studies of neglected and suppressed movements in the Jewish past given us a key to understanding what legitimately belongs to the Jewish dialectic today, or have they added to the difficulty of the task?

Whether Scholem's theological reflections, such as those found between the lines of his historical work, will provide a coherent impetus to modern Jewish thought depends less on Scholem than it does on those centrally concerned with such questions. Perhaps one should not expect more from an historian who is faithful to his sources than to provide fruitful hints rather than a systematic philosophy. Yet, in suggesting the possible nexus between mysticism and modernity, Scholem has opened our perspectives both on our past and on our present.

W. D. DAVIES

From Schweitzer to Scholem:
Reflections on Sabbatai Svi

The place of Albert Schweitzer in the history of the interpretation of the New Testament is secure. Although the predominance of the History of Religions School often led to the neglect of his work, especially in Germany, ultimately it could not be ignored; and that for one reason. Along with Johannes Weiss, Schweitzer established once and for all the eschatological dimensions of the New Testament. Necessary modifications of his work, compelled by C. H. Dodd and others, have not shaken the rightness of his main emphasis. The continuing insistence on eschatology by Schweitzer's fellow Alsacian, Oscar Cullmann, in many influential studies, the recent reiteration of apocalyptic as the matrix of Christian theology by E. Käsemann, U. Wilckens, and others, the emerging concentration on the examination of the apocrypha and pseudepigrapha, especially in this country, and the call by Klaus Koch to rediscover apocalyptic—all implicitly reinforce the significance of Schweitzer's contribution.

"Context determines content." This rediscovery of the significance of apocalyptic for the theological understanding of the New Testament has been stimulated by the temper of our disjointed times, and by certain important discoveries. The Qumran documents (providing first-hand sources especially for the examination of a sect living in the tension of an eschatological situation), and the documents of Nag Hammadi have made possible a deeper understanding of apocalyptic and gnostic attitudes. Here I want to point to

From *The Journal of Biblical Literature 95*, no. 4 (December 1976). © 1976 by the Society of Biblical Literature.

still another sphere (not strictly a source) where we can find illumination for the understanding of the apocalyptic world within which the writers of the New Testament moved. The invitation to prepare this lecture [The Albert Schweitzer Memorial Lecture at the meeting of the Society of Biblical Literature and the American Academy of Religion, 1 November 1975, The Palmer House, Chicago, Illinois,] arrived when I was re-reading Gershom G. Scholem's great work *Sabbatai Svi: The Mystic Messiah, 1626–1676*. Its relevance for the study of the New Testament struck me with renewed force, and I dared offer as a title, "From Schweitzer to Scholem." This theme turned out to be too broad, and I can only deal with the prolegomena to it. I shall offer reflections on the value of Scholem's study for what could lead to a reassessment of Schweitzer's work. These reflections, which have turned out to be more interrogatory than affirmative, are based mainly on *Sabbatai Svi,* but also on Scholem's other profound contributions to the study of messianism and mysticism. I emphasize that it is impossible to do justice to their vast riches and deep penetration here. I rely entirely upon Scholem's interpretation of the sources for Sabbatianism (a fact which he would be the first to admit is not without its dangers) and shall consider the purpose of this lecture fulfilled if only it helps to integrate Scholem's insight into the nature of Judaism more closely into the study of Christian origins.

Sabbatai Svi was born in Smyrna in 1626. In 1648 he proclaimed himself to be the Messiah, but was met with scorn. Three years later the Jewish community outlawed him. But in 1665 Nathan of Gaza, a young rabbi trained in the talmudic schools in Jerusalem, became convinced, through a vision, that Sabbatai Svi was the Messiah. He persuaded a reluctant Sabbatai of his messianic destiny and proceeded to disseminate the astounding news of his identity throughout the diaspora. The movement spread to Jewish communities in Yemen and Persia in the East and to those in the West as far as England, Holland, Russia, and Poland. It was stirred by massive repentance, expressed in fasts and mortifications, and by extraordinary enthusiasm, visions, and miracles. The date of the end of all things was fixed for 1666 but was conveniently moved when necessary. The antinomian acts of Sabbatai Svi failed to dampen the enthusiasm of the believers, who through him were experiencing the emotional reality of redemption. Neither the astounding apostasy of Sabbatai Svi to Islam and his attempts to persuade believers to apostatize, nor even his death destroyed the movement. There still exist a few believers in Sabbatai Svi.

Scholem has traced the history of this Messiah and his movement. Can a seventeenth century messianic movement illumine Early Christianity? The dangers of parallelomania (especially when movements long separated in time are compared) are familiar, particularly since Samuel Sandmel's noted address on this theme. But this being recognized, I welcome one salutary outcome of Protestant-Roman Catholic interchange in our time. Protestants have tended to think that movements are best understood in the light of their origins; Catholics, in terms of their developments. We now see more clearly that both origins and developments help to reveal the essence of movements. We can learn much about the nature of apocalyptic in the first century from the ways in which it expressed itself in the seventeenth. Scholem is right to draw attention to phenomena in early Christianity which seem to be illumined by counterparts in Sabbatianism. Was Sabbatianism directly influenced by Christianity? Scholem faced this question. Sabbatai himself had a real interest in those who claimed to be messiahs before him, especially in Jesus. Some Gentile Christian chiliasts were well informed about Sabbatianism and perhaps were indirectly influential in shaping it. But direct Christian influences cannot be proved, and Scholem prefers to regard Sabbatianism as an independent, indigenous phenomenon within Judaism. In Sabbatianism, we can examine in depth a major Jewish messianic movement, other than Christianity.

One point is of special note. If an early Christian Aramaic literature was ever written, it has not survived. The documents produced by early Christianity are few and are written in Greek. There is a sparse leanness about them. They demand infinite labor to give them flesh and blood, color and substance. The New Testament is a distillation. On the contrary, in Sabbatianism, thanks to the immeasurable labors of Scholem, the documentation is rich. Through it one can feel and know the historical actuality of the movement more directly than is the case with early Christianity. We shall attempt to show what Scholem's work offers the student of the New Testament under three headings: first, the new light it sheds on the nature of Judaism; second, on messianism; and third on early Christianity.

NEW LIGHT ON THE NATURE OF JUDAISM

To begin with, the Judaism which one encounters in Sabbatianism does not conform to the picture of it handed on to us even by Jewish scholars. Long ago, Scholem had emphasized two hitherto ignored facets of Judaism: the deep penetration of it by mystical currents, and the domestication of apocalyptic within Pharisaism. The picture of a predominantly halakic Judaism, largely untouched by mystic experiences and apocalyptic visions, has

had to be abandoned. Scholem has now further unearthed and examined a
world of mystical secrets, symbols, images, enthusiasms, and esoterica which
rabbinic leaders and scholars had considered unworthy of serious attention
and treated with contempt. In doing so, he has further discredited the concept of a normative pharisaic Judaism. He has made such a concept unten-
able, not only by insisting on the two broad aspects hitherto denied to
Judaism referred to, but also in a more detailed way. To illustrate, let us
consider one phenomenon in Sabbatianism which has customarily been taken
to be utterly non-Jewish.

Judaism has usually been described as insisting on the qualitative difference between God and man. The notion of the divinity of a human being
was regarded as one of the marks of Hellenistic religion which sharply differentiated it from the Jewish. The doctrine of the incarnation has always
been regarded as the Rubicon between Christianity and Judaism. But the
case of Sabbatai Svi is instructive. Divided and uncertain of himself as he
was, at certain points he claimed to be divine and he did not offer explanations for his claim. The evidence for all this is ambiguous, but it is not to
be ignored. He was regularly called by the term "Our Lord." It can be
objected that Sabbatai's mind was diseased and that it is illegitimate to
deduce anything about Judaism from his case. Scholem has shown that he
was a pathological figure, suffering from a manic-depressive condition. But
this makes it all the more striking that his followers, including rabbis despite
the criticisms of some rabbinic leaders, do not seem to have objected to his
claim to divinity nor found it, in itself, impossible. Moreover, the role ascribed to Sabbatai Svi by Nathan of Gaza was such as to demand that he
possess divine power because, through his activity and the faith in himself
which he engendered among his followers, the whole cosmos was to be
redeemed, to achieve restoration. In previous studies, Scholem had indicated
that in the Merkabah mysticism of an earlier period in Jewish history the
unbridgeable gulf between man and God remained. But in Sabbatianism this
gulf seems to have been crossed. Within a messianic context a new dimension
of union between God and man had opened.

But before Sabbatai Svi appeared, Judaism had known the long development of a mysticism in the medieval period in which the relationship
between man and God had been constantly pondered under other than simply
scriptural influences. This long development makes any direct comparison
with Judaism in the period before the appearance of Jesus very precarious.
But we can at least say this. Schweitzer drew a sharp distinction between
the mysticism of Paul, that of being "in Christ," and the mysticism of the
Fourth Gospel, that of being "in God." The former he considered Jewish

and messianic, the latter Hellenistic. In the light of the history of Sabbatai Svi, such a distinction need not point outside Judaism. Sabbatai Svi's claims to divinity did not signify or imply any departure from it, nor involve the emergence of a new religion. Given belief in the advent of the Messiah, the possibility for transcending the customary categories of Judaism as they had traditionally been understood, was immensely enhanced.

NEW LIGHT ON MESSIANISM

The reference to the Messiah brings us to the second sphere where Scholem's work is illuminating, our understanding of messianism. In a remarkable way Sabbatianism shows that messianic movements are always likely to have presented certain constants. The same characteristics recur in such movements, although separated widely in space and time. Certain phenomena re-emerge in Sabbatianism which had characterized early Christianity. They are so many that it is tempting to find in Sabbatianism simply a late, distorted replica of Christianity (a temptation that, as we saw, Scholem has taught us to resist). It is impossible to enumerate completely the phenomena to which we refer. We shall divide them into two groups: first, what we shall call, without prejudice, secondary characteristics; and secondly, primary or essential phenomena. The former are very many; the latter can be reduced to two.

As for the secondary phenomena, they may be divided as follows. First, certain strictly religious emphases are common: for example, repentance, prayer, fasting, enthusiasm. Although Paul (in this, he was very unlike Nathan of Gaza) apparently never emphasized repentance directly, early Christianity was preceded by or accompanied by a movement of repentance which Jesus himself joined. The same phenomenon in an even more marked form emerged at the birth of Sabbatianism. Sabbatai Svi himself, but in particular his prophet, Nathan of Gaza, inaugurated a vast movement of repentance and mortification of the flesh, a mortification which Paul at times might have exemplified (1 Cor. 9:27). The sources for Sabbatianism reveal the extremes to which such pre-messianic repentance was liable: some followers of Sabbatai Svi died from fasting. Doubtless, had we more sources, early Christianity would reveal the same. Similarly in the strictly religious dimension, the habits of prayer of Sabbatai Svi recall the immediacy of the prayer of the Jesus of the Synoptics. The religious intensity of Sabbatai Svi, his experience of mystical absorption and ecstasy, and the almost bizarre unrealism of some of the Sabbatian believers recall the kind of enthusiasm which one detects both in and behind the Synoptics. Käsemann's brilliant detection of an early

Christian enthusiasm has probably simply raised the lid of a cauldron. The enthusiasm, for example, which led to the so-called communism of Acts finds its parallel at the advent of Sabbatai Svi in the sale of their property by countless rich Jews in many quarters.

Secondly, the miraculous is as marked in Sabbatianism as in early Christianity. For example, the manner of the birth of Sabbatai Svi was dwelt upon in a way reminiscent of the birth narratives in Matthew and Luke; and Sabbatai Svi urged a cult of his mother, comparable with later Christian Mariolatry. There was a tradition that between 1648 and 1650 Sabbatai Svi was miraculously saved from drowning: "He rose from the sea and was saved," as was Jesus when he walked on the sea. Magical elements which have been discovered in the Synoptic tradition have their parallels, in a very enhanced form, in Sabbatianism. Sabbatai Svi seems at times to have inaugurated a magical enterprise. There were attempts to force the end by what has been called a "practical Qabbala," which amounted to magic. That Jesus' work could be and has been regarded in a similar magical fashion the studies of A. Schweitzer himself show; in the end the Jesus of Schweitzer is an apocalyptical magician who seeks to "force" the end.

Thirdly, the nature and activity of Sabbatai Svi and Jesus as messiahs are often similar: for example, that the Messiah could be in the world unknown reappears in Sabbatianism; and also he is parallel with Moses and Adam; his coming inaugurates or is accompanied by the "birth pangs of the Messiah." Like Jesus, Sabbatai Svi chose twelve to represent the Twelve Tribes of Israel. Like Jesus also, Sabbatai Svi was a messiah without armies. In a strange way, but with a great difference in the nature of their pains, both Jesus and Sabbatai were suffering messiahs.

Fourthly, among these secondary phenomena, if such a term be permitted in this connection, both Sabbatai Svi and Jesus were conceived to have overcome death, the former by occultation and the latter by resurrection. And both were expected to return again to earth to complete their work.

Fifthly, we note the striking phenomenon that the roles of John the Baptist and Paul in early Christianity and that of Nathan of Gaza in Sabbatianism are parallel. *Mutatis mutandis,* Nathan of Gaza in himself was to Sabbatai Svi what both John the Baptist and Paul were to Jesus. Until Nathan convinced him, Sabbatai Svi was uncertain of his messianic identity. Though more directly so (the Synoptic and Johannine materials are here so varied), Nathan was a witness to Sabbatai in a way parallel with that of John the Baptist to Jesus. But it was Nathan also who later provided the theological structure for the interpretation of Sabbatai Svi and in this played the role of Paul to Jesus. Like Paul, Nathan refused to be impressed by or to demand

"signs" that the Messiah had come. But this single parallel of Nathan with
the Baptist and Paul must not be pressed. It is altogether natural that the
founder of any movement should have significant interpreters.

Finally, much as many scholars urge that there was little interest in the
life of Jesus even on the part of Paul, Sabbatianism flourished apparently
without much active interest among the masses of believers in the history
and character of Sabbatai. What mattered was *that* the Messiah had appeared, not *who* had appeared as Messiah. The strange behavior of Sabbatai
Svi, a manic-depressive, caused consternation among the rabbis, and others,
who believed in him, as among those who did not. He changed the calendar,
ignored the food laws, pronounced the ineffable Name, and was sexually
irregular. His conduct was often, to use Scholem's vivid phrase, "an Exodus
from the Law." The justification of Sabbatai's behavior, his attitude to and
disobedience of the Law, culminating in his monstrous apostasy to Islam,
posed a problem for his followers, comparable with that facing early Christians by the free attitude of Jesus to the Law and by his suffering and death.
The theology of both movements began with an initial disappointment which
had to be explained. Both turned to the same exegetical methods to do so,
and both concentrated on the Suffering Servant of Isaiah 53 for illumination.
Both developed a doctrine of the parousia; both demanded faith, unattested
by works or signs. Perhaps, in early Christianity a new element had entered
Judaism, that is, faith in a pure or neat form, not necessarily associated with
good works, became the mark of redemption, and that a faith in a paradoxical messiah. Such a faith re-emerged in Sabbatianism. Both movements
produced a doctrine of Incarnation. In both a deeply felt faith, an immediate
experience of being in a new eon, a "realized eschatology" of incalculable
emotional intensity, enthusiasm and exultation led to a radical criticism of
Jewish tradition, a new standard of measurement being applied to it. The
experience of the freedom of the children of God led to antinomian tendencies, especially and unrestrainedly in Sabbatianism, but also in early Christianity, which at times broke out into license.

Taken together, the phenomena to which we have pointed—and many
more such could be noted—are extremely valuable. To read the history of
Sabbatai is to encounter the emotional intensity of a messianic movement at
first hand, a temper or an atmosphere strikingly like the very enthusiastic,
ecstatic world of feeling which was the "new creation" of early Christianity.
This is not all. The history of Sabbatai suggests that a messianic movement
of any depth is most likely, almost inevitably, to call forth certain phenomena—ecstasy, mortifications, visions, miracles, enthusiasms and certain inescapable parallel responses. The reason for this is simple. The messianic

tradition had developed into a popular tradition, so that the advent of a messiah at any time stirred up among the masses certain age-long, stereotyped expectations. Discouraged as they might be to do so even by the messiah himself, the believing masses found "signs" everywhere. Moved by the age-old concepts and symbols of messianism rooted in the Scriptures and enlarged upon in tradition, they were eager to clothe their messiah, in every age, with the kind of characteristics they thought proper to him.

Probably in every messianic movement, certainly in Sabbatianism and early Christianity, a distinction should be clearly recognized between the understanding of it among the masses and among the more sophisticated leaders. Attempts to explain Sabbatianism and early Christianity in predominantly political or economic or sociological terms have generally failed to convince. Believers in Sabbatai Svi were drawn from the rich and the poor, the underprivileged and the established, from the ignorant 'am hā'āreṣ and the rabbinic authorities. Similarly, early Christianity was probably indifferent to barriers of wealth, class, and learning, although the evidence is not as clear as in Sabbatianism. Nevertheless there were real differences of comprehension among the believers in both movements. Nathan of Gaza and Paul of Tarsus understood the respective messiahs in whom they believed in a far more theologically informed manner than most of their fellow-believers. One is tempted to find here a suggestive datum for the interpretation of the symbols of apocalyptic in both movements. Recently we have been urged to distinguish between "steno symbols" and "tensive symbols." This distinction should probably be related to differences between the masses and the more subtle believers in early Christianity as in Sabbatianism. Because in both movements most believers belonged to the masses, they both tended to take on, especially incipiently, the marks of the popular understanding of the messianic age to which we have drawn attention. But it would be very unwise to find the essence of any messianic movement in the kind of phenomena which such an understanding magnified. Bizarre miracles, the froth of enthusiasm and ecstasy must not be given equal weight with, or (perhaps better) must not be understood apart from the underlying formative factors in a messianic movement, to which we now turn.

More important than the secondary phenomena, then, are certain fundamental similarities, accompanied by equally fundamental differences, between early Christianity and Sabbatianism. These we have called primary phenomena. They may be introduced under two rubrics.

First, in both movements there was a radical confrontation with the established order, focused on the ultimate authority within Judaism, the Torah. In both, social, political, and religious loyalties and oppressions were challenged, so that there emerged an inevitable concentration on the person of the messiah in whose name the challenge was issued. In both, faith in the messiah became the primary mark of the believer.

Secondly, both movements within a very short period spread extensively. Sabbatianism and early Christianity are in one thing peculiar. Most of the many messianic movements in Judaism have been short-lived and concentrated in specific localities. But Sabbatianism and Christianity are alike in having had an ecumenical appeal. Within two years, Sabbatianism spread throughout Europe and the Near East. Confined almost exclusively to Jews, it affected almost the whole of Jewry. Within a slightly longer period, Christianity spread from Palestine to Rome in the West and eastwards as well, to some extent among Jews but also, and particularly, among Gentiles. This means that both Sabbatianism and Christianity were understood to satisfy the spiritual needs of Jews and especially, in the case of the latter, of Gentiles. Movements do not spread without reason: emotionally at the least both early Christianity and Sabbatianism conveyed the living experience of redemption.

At first sight, these two rubrics seem to justify Scholem's claim that messianism is essentially constituted by two fundamental elements. First, there is the emergence of a messianic figure. He serves as a catalyst, negatively, for radical criticism of the existing order; positively, of dreams at long last come true, of barriers long-standing being broken down, of a new creation—all this accompanied by an impulse to propagate the good news. And then, secondly, this messianic figure must meet a widespread need and be understood to satisfy that need in terms of an interpretative ideological structure of magnitude and depth. Infinitely complex as are all historical movements, Scholem claims that significant messianic movements are usually born of a coincidence—that of the interpretation of this person within a large conceptual framework which can illumine his significance for that need. To put the matter concretely, a significant messianic movement demands the coincidence of a Jesus and a Paul or of a Sabbatai Svi and a Nathan of Gaza. The catalyst of a messianic movement is a messianic figure, but its spread and significance are necessarily determined by the scope and profundity of the conceptual framework or myth within which such a figure can be or is interpreted.

This dual aspect of messianic movements is especially clear in Sabbatianism. Owing to the absence of contemporary sources of sufficient richness, it is not so immediately clear in early Christianity. Does Scholem's analysis help in the clarification of early Christian history?

Scholem points out that among Jews in the seventeenth century, when Sabbatianism arose, there was one single, dominant theology, Lurianic Qabbala, which constituted a rich, comprehensive myth. It varied in its forms but was profoundly united in essentials and was almost universally accepted by Jews. It was the universal dominance of a single theology or myth that enabled Sabbatai Svi, through Nathan of Gaza, to initiate such a widespread messianic movement. The reason for the hold of Lurianic Qabbala on Jews everywhere was that it provided a key to the mystery of their suffering at the hands of the Gentile world and made that suffering tolerable. In medieval Europe, the one inescapable fact about Jews was that they were in exile, at the mercy of the whims of their Gentile rulers. In 1492 they had been expelled cruelly from Spain; in 1648–49 there were horrendous massacres in Poland. How could Jews continue to bear the burden of their exile? Lurianic Qabbala provided the answer in subtle, mystical terms which satisfied. At first the doctrine, absorbed in strictly theological concerns, had not been particularly concerned with the question of exile as such. But it had developed in such a way as to provide a sustaining explanation for the terrible experiences of Jews in exile: it spoke directly to their needs. It did so by setting their exile in a cosmic, divine perspective: it connected the historical exile of Jews with a supramundane exile of man from God, and indeed, with a rupture in the very being of God himself. By enduring their exile, while remaining loyal to the disciplined, austere, ascetic tradition of the Torah, and the knowledge of it supplied by the Qabbala of Luria, suffering, exiled Jews were assured that they were making possible a cosmic reintegration and with this the restoration of man to God and a reconciliation within God himself. The technical term for this process of restoration was *tiqqûn*. Lurianic Qabbala was not simply a mystical and intellectual structure of vast complexity and insight; it became the strength and stay of a despairing people, crushed in the ghetto. In their insignificance, it gave to Jews cosmic significance. It enabled them to believe not only that even *this* world, in which they knew exile, *could* be saved or undergo *tiqqûn,* but that through their obedience to the Torah it was they who were to be its saviors. When that obedience would have reached its fulfillment, the Messiah would appear. It was not the Messiah who would make the restoration possible; rather he would be a sign that it was near. He would usher in the end, made possible by the Jews' own obedience.

Within this context the impact of Sabbatai becomes understandable: without it, his name would probably by now be forgotten like that of many another messiah in Jewish history. As we already noted, his claim to be the Messiah was at first ridiculed. But when a recognized prophet interpreted that claim in the light of the all-pervasive Lurianic Qabbalistic expectations, a new movement was born: the interpretation was as crucial as the claimant, the myth as the fact. Jews became convinced that the ultimate *tiqqûn* or restoration had now begun. The end was at hand; deliverance was at the door. The results of this conviction were staggering. The one decisive factor was *that* the Messiah had appeared. Who he was, or what he was like, was for many unimportant. Interest in the personal character and conduct of Sabbatai was at best secondary and probably, among the majority of believers, nonexistent. What made him significant was his role as the Messiah, proclaimed and authenticated by Nathan. In the Lurianic world, among Jewish hearts made sick by hope deferred, the magic word, Messiah, was enough to set the world on fire. That among certain at least of the Sabbatians the neglect of a radical assessment of the character of Sabbatai Svi was to bring its terrible nemesis will become clear as we turn now to our main concern: the light that Sabbatianism throws on early Christianity.

EARLY CHRISTIANITY AND SABBATIANISM

Before we deal with the most significant questions that Scholem's works have provoked, it is desirable first to recognize their contribution to our understanding of the apocalyptic terminology of the New Testament. I am acutely conscious of my incompetence in dealing with this. I am versed neither in linguistic analysis nor in literary criticism as it is currently practised. I can simply point to certain facts. Sabbatianism used the terminology of apocalyptic as symbolic of a supernatural, unseen reality; this it did as heir to the Qabbala. But equally certainly it took that terminology quite literally. For example, when Sabbatai's messiahship was accepted at Smyrna, he proceeded forthwith geographically to carve up the world, which he was soon to rule. He ascribed to several of his followers different parts of the world as their dominions. Some of his wealthy followers sold their possessions convinced that the end of the old order was literally at hand. The Turkish authorities took very seriously the political implications of Sabbatai's activity. On his side, he behaved like a monarch. Much modern discussion of the meaning of apocalyptic language which overmuch spiritualizes it must be regarded as misguided. For example, to understand the term "kingdom of God," as used in early Christianity, as non-political and non-terrestrial is unjustifiable, if it be taken to have been so used universally. Whatever their limitations, in their tenacious insistence on a literal understanding of the messianic prophecies chiliastic movements are doubtless true to much in Sabbatianism and in early Christianity. There was a literal dimension to apocalyptic language which must not be evaded, and it had a catastrophic political and social relevance. In particular, the political and sociological implications of early Christianity and their actual impact would be more adequately recognized if this literalism were taken more seriously. This would help us to comprehend that all messianism has a revolutionary, subversive potential. This is not to underrate the symbolism of apocalyptic. A literary critic might do justice to our point by claiming that apocalyptic terminology is both conceptual and symbolic.

This applies especially to the understanding of early Christianity among the masses, which embraced apocalyptic literally and uncritically. To bear this in mind is to see both Jesus and Paul as corrective of a popular messianic political revolutionary enthusiasm and, therefore, despite the new wine which they dispensed, as, in a certain sense, conservative. In this light they both emerge as reductionists of a fecund apocalyptic enthusiasm that sometimes led to political theatrics and discovered in the new creation a legitimation of license.

But even more important are the two factors, the coincidence of which, according to Scholem's analysis, is necessary for the emergence of a significant messianic movement. Do they apply to early Christianity? First, can we point with equal clarity, as we did in the case of Sabbatianism in the seventeenth century, to a dominant ideological or theological framework in the first-century Judaism into which Jesus of Nazareth was fitted as Messiah to give birth to early Christianity? Or, to put it in another way, does first-century Judaism present an ideological counterpart, equivalent in depth and extent, to the Lurianic Qabbala in seventeenth-century Judaism which made Sabbatianism possible?

The answers given to this question will be familiar. As representative, we refer to those of E. R. Goodenough and W. Bousset. Goodenough was concerned to explain how a Palestinian movement so quickly penetrated and prevailed over the Greco-Roman world. His answer was that by the first century certain Jews in the Hellenistic world had opened their minds to pagan notions and made them "at home" in Judaism. When Hellenistic Jews became Christians, they carried over these notions into their understanding of their new faith. This rapidly enabled the gospel to penetrate the Hellenistic-Roman world. But did such a Hellenistic Judaism as Goodenough describes exist universally among first-century Jews as did Lurianic Qabbala among those of the seventeenth, and was it as theologically dominant and accepted? Goodenough's position has not won the assent of those best qualified to assess Judaism. His treatment of the extent and potency of rabbinic influence as over against the almost autonomous Hellenized Judaism which he delineates remains questionable.

Bousset, whose work *Kyrios Christos* often seems to anticipate much in Goodenough, nevertheless points to another alternative. For him nascent

Christianity employed ideas anticipated in the apocalyptic tradition in Judaism. For example, a christology of pre-existence lay hidden in the idea of the Son of Man of Jewish apocalyptic. In the first century an apocalyptic structure was ready into which Jesus, as Messiah, could be fitted, as Sabbatai Svi was fitted into Lurianic Qabbala in the seventeenth. Faith in Jesus had merely to clothe itself with apocalyptic. How others have followed Bousset in this view we need not trace. But here again the difference between the role of apocalyptic in the first-century Judaism and Lurianic Qabbala in that of the seventeenth is unmistakable. The relative importance of apocalyptic in the complex of first-century Judaism is much disputed. The older view that apocalyptic was as peripheral in first-century Judaism as, let us say, the chiliastic sects in modern Christianity is no longer tenable. Apocalyptic belonged to the main streams of Judaism; but that Judaism was extremely variegated and certainly not dominated by a single apocalyptic ideology. In isolation, apocalyptic, although it has taken up Alexander the Great's notion of world empire, cannot provide a universal, dominant theological parallel to the Lurianic Qabbala of the seventeenth century.

The two clear answers, then, to the question whether there was a dominant theological counterpart to Lurianic Qabbala in first-century Judaism do not satisfy. Does a combination of them do so? This might be suggested by the very nature of Lurianic Qabbala itself. In it two things were fused: an eschatological ideology derived from Jewish apocalyptic, modified and reinterpreted in terms of the notion of the *tiqqûn*, and a form of gnosticism tracing its lineage apparently back to the early Christian centuries. This fusion enabled Lurianic Qabbala to connect the terrestrial messianic hopes with an inward and supernal order and constituted its extraordinary dynamism. Scholem's work prompts the question whether in the first century too—in an inchoate form at least—a comparable fusion of a modified apocalyptic and proto-gnosticism had occurred to provide the framework for interpreting Jesus. P. D. Hanson has recently insisted on the prophetic connections of the origins of apocalyptic. But by the first century, what Hellenistic and other influences, including possibly pre- or proto-gnostic ones, had penetrated it? Unfortunately the New Testament is so laconic that it allows no certainty as to any one dominant framework, apart from the Scriptures, into which Jesus was fitted. Moreover, whereas Sabbatai Svi had one outstanding, almost unique interpreter in Nathan of Gaza, Jesus had various interpreters at least as different as Matthew, Mark, John, and Paul. And again sources outside the New Testament are either insufficiently examined or too confusing to allow for certainty. There are increasing, although disputed, indications of the fusion or interaction of apocalyptic with pre- and

proto-gnosticism, if not gnosticism, in the first century and that before
70 C.E. But even allowing for such a fusion before that date, can we claim
that it provided a dominant theological outlook for first-century Judaism as
did Lurianic Qabbala for that of the seventeenth? He would be a bold man
who would claim this. If a unified ideology was the mark of seventeenth-
century Judaism, we have long been taught that diversity was that of the
first. But is this the whole truth? In reaction to G. F. Moore, have we over-
emphasized that diversity and overlooked a possible overarching unity provided by a rich fusion of Law, apocalyptic, and pre- or proto-gnosticism?
This question is made more and more pressing by Scholem's understanding
of messianism.

Perhaps the problem as to what theological framework most governed
early Christianity can best be approached obliquely. The social and political
structures favoring the spread of Christianity are clear—a ubiquitous synagogue, made accessible by Roman imperial roads and favored by Roman
policy, provided a ready-made platform for Christian missionaries. We may
ask what particular need had arisen among Jews in the first century. Sabbatianism met the needs of Jews in exile. Was there a dominant need that
first-century Judaism had to face? *The* crucial question which it confronted
was that posed by the Gentile world. In the first century, Jews, although
occasionally living apart as in Alexandria, were not in a ghetto. They were
free to respond to the fascination of Gentile life. This constitutes a crucial
difference between the larger context of Sabbatianism and early Christianity.
At the time of Sabbatianism, Judaism was turned in upon itself, cabined,
cribbed, and confined. Sabbatianism arose within a suffering ghetto to meet
its peculiar needs. By no means was the Gentile question central to it. By the
seventeenth century that question had been closed; Gentiles had rejected
Jews. Jews in turn had largely rejected Gentiles and had become introverted;
the references to Gentiles in a thousand pages of Scholem's work are few.

It was otherwise in the first century. Then the question of how to relate
to the Gentile world pressed ubiquitously upon Jews. There was a vast missionary movement to the Gentile world. Before 70 C.E. there were elements
in apocalyptic which directly occupied themselves with the fate of Gentiles
and that with hope for them. The relation of such elements to any pre- or
proto-gnosticism we cannot pursue. But these elements did speak with particular force to the need of first-century Jews to come to terms with Gentiles.
That they were a marked aspect of first-century Judaism before 70 C.E., after
which date apocalyptic became more discredited, seems clear. Based on the
Scriptures of Judaism, they were also the outcome of three centuries of the
exposure of Jews to Hellenism—an exposure that time and again created a

crisis: the crisis constituted by the insidious attraction of Gentile life. It could be resolved either by greater and greater intensity to achieve a total obedience as at Qumran, or by reinterpretation and adaptation as in Pharisaism, or by a blind hatred as among Zealots; or, on the other extreme, by acceptance and assimilation and interpenetration. Whatever the solution adopted, first-century Judaism faced at boiling point the fascinating impact of Hellenism. Within that context apocalyptic, in those elements of it to which we refer, provided a hope for the final redemption of Gentiles. Was it apocalyptic, characterized by this universalist hope, that provided the framework for presenting Jesus as the "Savior of the World"? And, although it reflected a challenge produced by the attraction of the outside world, while Lurianic Qabbala was the product of an internal crisis produced by the rejection of Jews by the outside world, can we regard this apocalyptic, modified by Hellenistic influences, as a first-century counterpart to Lurianic Qabbala in the seventeenth?

There are two difficulties. First, there is that already mentioned with reference to Bousset's position. How significant in first-century Judaism was the kind of apocalyptic to which we refer, among other matters, concerned with the Gentiles and possibly infiltrated by a pre- or proto-gnosticism? How pervasive was the hope for the Gentiles within it? That the hope existed is clear, but was it widespread, not to say dominant? The answer is not easy. The wide infiltration of apocalyptic ideology into the Greco-Roman world would seem to be likely. It began, according to M. Hengel, before the third century B.C. J. Daniélou insisted that up to the Council of Nicea the substructure of Christian theology remained Semitic and largely apocalyptic in its terminology. The bog of terminological inexactitude must be avoided, but if gnostic thought was from the beginning related to apocalyptic, it is significant that R. M. Wilson writes of "something of an atmosphere in which the people of the early Christian centuries lived and moved." The work of such scholars gives us pause. They justify the question which Scholem's work compels us to ask. Behind the variety of first-century Judaism did there perhaps exist a single, widely-diffused and popular eschatological frame of reference in both Palestinian and Hellenistic Judaism (to use a distinction now largely obsolete)? Sweeping generalizations are out of place. In the present state of our knowledge it is as difficult to give an affirmative answer as a negative one. For example, R. M. Grant, who once urged that gnosticism was born of the collapse of apocalyptic, now denies this outright. Daniélou's evidence is more abundant than convincing. Unless or until new texts from Nag Hammadi, Qumran and elsewhere enlighten us further, we must tentatively assert that the role of apocalyptic, however modified and reinterpreted under Hellenistic influences, cannot have been so important in the spread of Christianity as was Lurianic Qabbala in that of Sabbatianism. Such apocalyptic did not dominate the whole of Judaism—which was not in the first century a ghetto but spanned several cultures. We conclude that one element in the twofold coincidence to which Scholem points as necessary to significant messianism is not clear in early Christianity. Whereas in Sabbatianism there was a decisive conceptual framework or myth in the dominant Lurianic Qabbala, to judge from the sources we now have, the conceptual background in early Christianity appears to have been far more complex and varied.

We referred to the need of Jews to come to terms with Gentile life. The opposite must not be underestimated: the need that Gentiles often felt to embrace Judaism. The multiplicity of God-fearers, and proselytes, which, according to some, largely accounts for the magnitude of the diaspora, indicates that the primordial and nuclear certainty of Jewish monotheism and the sustaining discipline of life under the yoke of the Torah exercised a deep attraction for Gentiles. Any simple conceptual framework which should—on Scholem's terms—dominantly sustain the interpretation of Jesus would have to embrace the Jewish and the Gentile worlds. Where is it to be found?

This brings us to the second apparent difficulty in finding a dominant apocalyptic, oriented towards the Gentiles, one of the two decisive factors in the spread of Christianity. It springs to the eye. To judge from the gospels, the Gentile question, although recognized, was not central to Jesus of Nazareth. This disturbing fact leads to the question, What role did the person of Jesus of Nazareth play in early Christianity? Was it as decisive as that of Sabbatai Svi in Sabbatianism? Despite the comparative infrequency of Jesus' engagement with Gentiles, we suggest that the answer to this question is in the affirmative, because Jesus had his Paul and others to interpret him, as Sabbatai Svi had Nathan. Where was the heart of the matter for Paul? He found the significance of the emergence of Jesus as the Messiah particularly in the grace that he had shown to the 'am hā'āreṣ, and then, why not to Gentiles? The Gentile mission was for Paul implicit in the ministry of Jesus. His call was to the Gentiles. This is a fundamental datum. There was little if any ground for a concern for Gentiles in the life of Sabbatai Svi. It is this ultimately that explains why Christianity became more than a Jewish but also a Gentile movement, whereas Sabbatianism remained Jewish.

We enter here disputed ground. There probably existed in both Sabbatianism and early Christianity many believers for whom the personalities of Sabbatai Svi and Jesus, respectively, were a matter of indifference and even unknown. But this must not mislead us. Ultimately, it was the personality of each messiah that gave to the movements they inaugurated their peculiarity. One ventures to urge that, in the end, what moved Sabbatianism was *that* the Messiah had appeared, incidentally as Sabbatai Svi; whereas what astounded early Christians was that it was Jesus of Nazareth who had come as the Messiah. The difference between Sabbatai Svi and Jesus, draped as they both came to be in the traditional messianic mantles, is ultimately a difference, quite simply, of what we might call "character." Rabbinic leaders were so embarrassed by Sabbatai Svi's conduct that they sought to destroy the evidence for it. In Sabbatai Svi, despite his appeal to the masses, there seems to be no real concern for them such as breaks through the Jesus of the gospels. There is an insensitivity to the ostentatious and bizarre which is unthinkable in Jesus and, unless (paradoxically) antinomianism be an expression of such, an absence of sensitive moral concern. Sabbatai Svi was not a teacher of morality. The difference between the two messiahs comes to clearest expression in the apostasy of Sabbatai Svi, and the death of Jesus on the cross. Scholem calls the apostasy the most execrable act possible in the Jewish mind.

Two ways were open to Sabbatians after Sabbatai Svi's apostasy, either to follow his actions, to imitate him, or to see in his fate a call to ever greater rigor in obedience to the Law. Sabbatianism developed along both ways. Some believers followed the latter course and showed a zeal in piety and morality which outshone that of other Jews and, indeed, became a mark of their heretical faith. Such Sabbatians recognized that while Sabbatai lived on the brink of the new eon, they themselves did not and could not follow his freedom from the Law. Their attitude could be compared with that of early Jewish-Christians who retained their zeal for the Torah, even though believing in Jesus as the Messiah. In the course of time these nomistic Sabbatians declined and reverted to the main stream of Judaism; historically they were not significant. Other Sabbatians took the former of the two possible courses noted. They took Sabbatai Svi as a paradigm and an example to be imitated. To do so, they had to call evil good. They had to justify apostasy itself as messianic and redemptive. To do so in the end was to destroy all values dear to Judaism. It implied an ultimate cynicism and nihilism, born doubtless of a profound despair, in which the demand of God was mocked. It is no accident that the most distinctive doctrine of Sabbatianism came to be that of redemption through sin. The infinitely complex and even pathological reasons for the conduct of Sabbatai Svi excite our pity. In the radical Sabbatian wing, its theological and practical consequences were disastrous. Despite the indifference of the masses of Sabbatians to the character of their messiah, his passive surrender to the power of impurity and iniquity, even as he persisted in his messianic mission, stamped itself upon his radical followers. In loyalty to their apostatized redeemer, they too were led to strange acts. Like the Messiah himself, they too had to descend into impurity; for them too good had to become evil. The very weakness of Sabbatai Svi they took for strength. And it was the radical Sabbatians who persisted; it was they who became historically significant. As time went on, the figure of Sabbatai Svi, within Sabbatianism itself, became vague almost to the point of anonymity. Perversely, his lack of integrity alone remained significant, and that diabolically.

Scholem has referred to the gulf that separates the character of Sabbatai from that of Jesus of Nazareth. As we indicated, the interest of much of primitive Christianity in the history and personality of Jesus has been denied. But while we recognize the force of the arguments of those who hold this view and the support it receives to a degree from developments in Sabbatianism, it is wiser to urge that, as the very emergence of the gospels indicates, the character of Jesus at least, if not the inner recesses of his personality and the minute biographical details of his life, in various degrees and dimensions, remained central for early Christianity. That *he* was the messiah was significant for early Christianity, in a way that Sabbatai Svi as a person was not for Sabbatianism. We consider it legitimate to speak of the personality of Jesus or his character and do not find the suggestion, recently made by Dean S. W. Sykes of Cambridge, that the heart (I reject the word essence, as did R. W. Funk) of Christianity lies in the character of Jesus, easily dismissible. But because so many find difficulty in speaking of or in picturing the personality of Jesus, we shall seek to pinpoint the essential difference between Sabbatai Svi and Jesus, not in terms of their characters, but in terms of another dimension, the Law.

Judaism lived by a moment, that of revelation, and by a dimension, that of tradition, the latter being the explanation and application of the former. The meaning of the revelation at Sinai was variously interpreted. As the Temple Scroll at Qumran has illustrated with astonishing force, the extent to which the Law itself was examined and even questioned in first-century Judaism was far greater than we had often assumed. Currents emerged in Judaism in which in the messianic age even a new *tôrâ* was anticipated. Whether these currents were as early as the emergence of Christianity is questioned; certainly they existed in the Judaism that Sabbatai Svi knew. Messianic freedom, as Sabbatai understood it, allowed him to live beyond the Law. His position led to antinomian nihilism. If allowed to develop unchecked, the freedom of early Christianity could have had the same result. But whereas in Sabbatianism the messianic founder (who was, we repeat, not a teacher) could supply no check to antinomianism but only a stimulus, in early Christianity there could be found such a check in the ministry, character, and teaching of Jesus. The attitudes of Jesus and Paul to the Law cannot be discussed at the tail end of a long lecture. Perhaps the Fourth Gospel best sums up that attitude when it speaks of the new commandment of the gospel as constituted by *agapē*. The concentration on *agapē* as the quintessence of the Law is not a negative dismissal of the tradition of Judaism, but its radical reduction to one dominating dimension. The life of Jesus of Nazareth, as understood by his followers, was consonant with this dimension, an expression of *agapē*. It could, therefore, always provide a corrective to any antinomian messianic license that might emerge. This did not prevent antinomianism from emerging in early Christianity. Over against the concentration on the Law in Jewish-Christianity stood the amorality and immorality of gnostics and other Christians. The situation in both early Christianity and Sabbatianism was highly dialectical and complex. But at the root of the Christian tradition was a founder, whose impact could provide a salutary control in a way that Sabbatai could not. The Lord with whom the Christian tradition was sometimes virtually identified was such that he could be a constant corrective, even though misinterpreted in both nomistic and antinomian terms. As we have expressed it elsewhere, Jesus became the Torah of Christians. Here lies the heart of the matter, not in the apocalyptic imagery and fantasies with which he, like Sabbatai Svi, came to be clothed.

We have sought to apply Scholem's categories to early Christianity. With regard to one of the two essential dimensions which he finds behind significant messianic movements, caution is necessary. It is easier to isolate Lurianic Qabbala as the one Sabbatian framework than to point to such a single conceptual framework, apart from the Scriptures, governing early Christianity. As for the role of the messianic figures, Jesus and Sabbatai, they were both significant in their respective movements not only as catalysts or initiators but as formative factors. The constructive constraint of Christ's ministry in early Christianity stands markedly over against the negative, distorting, and ultimately nihilistic influence of Sabbatai in Sabbatianism.

One final word. Lurianic Qabbala was far too complex and comprehensive a phenomenon to be simply labelled as apocalyptic. But it had absorbed apocalyptic elements. So ingrained in our minds is the halakic conception of Judaism, especially after 70 C.E., that it requires an effort to grasp that apocalyptic, messianic expectations which had emerged before the common era persisted in strength throughout the medieval period and down to the seventeenth century so that Sabbatai Svi could easily draw upon their dramatic dynamism. Jewish engagement with apocalyptic did not cease with the fall of Jerusalem in 70 C.E., and so one cannot read the history of Sabbatai

Svi, at least with Albert Schweitzer in mind, without being compelled to reflect upon the significance of apocalyptic. One might gather from Schweitzer that it is a dead end; from others that it is a kind of collective megalomania. But using the term in a broad sense at this point, apocalyptic presents both positive and negative aspects. To assess these would require a knowledge of the meaning of symbols which is beyond my competence. An examination of the nature of the symbolism of apocalyptic, such as has been begun by Amos Wilder and others, is a crying need. On the positive side, apocalyptic, emerging and re-emerging again and again in times of extreme suffering and despair, is the expression, in the light of the divine purpose, of a legitimate critical response to the iniquities, corruptions, and distortions of this world, to which, alas, most of us are at least half-blind. It is the element of divine discontent, of the desire for something afar, of the aim which exceeds our grasp. Without this discontent, the dead hand of custom, stagnation, and insensitivity throttles life, and even ancient good becomes uncouth. From this point of view, apocalyptic is the leaven of history. Its societal and cosmic imagery, symbols and hopes, which turn human longings to vivid expectations, are always necessary as a spur to sensitivity and a corrective against a false, irresponsible, individualistic piety. Even more, these expectations themselves—unrealistic as they often are—have a creative impact and, against themselves, modify societies even when those same societies reject them. Such hopes open up new possibilities, new pathways to Utopia, even if they never arrive there. A literature produced when man is at the end of his tether has its own stark, unblinded, and penetrating insight, even though its actual practical counsels, born of despair, are often dubious. The plea of K. Koch for the rediscovery of "apocalyptic" is understandable.

But, on the negative side, it needs careful control. A good stimulant, does it constitute a good diet? The ivied walls of the academy in which we dwell at ease make the appreciation of apocalyptic difficult for most of us. But this being admitted, again to use the term in an undifferentiated sense, apocalyptic has an ugly face. To read Scholem's work is to stand amazed, overwhelmed, and—it is to be stated—alienated by the bizarre, unhealthy, and unsavory possibilities of apocalyptic, messianic, political, and other indulgence. Despite its suffering and courage, its moral and intellectual striving and daring, the practical consequences of what we normally refer to, without differentiation, as apocalyptic are no less baffling and even terrifying than its often lurid imagery. The rabbinic reaction to such apocalyptic as a pernicious menace is understandable. In Sabbatianism, an unrestrained utopian apocalyptic-mysticism worked itself out in antinomianism. Early Christianity knew the same temptation, but in its main developments, though not in all its expressions, it was often spared from the more undesirable tendencies by the constraint of its founding figure. Early Christianity was apocalyptic, but it was such under the constraint of the *agapē* (to risk distortion through brevity) of Christ. The sum of the matter is this: if we are to continue to describe early Christianity as apocalyptic, it seems to me that we can only do so by carefully differentiating what we mean. P. D. Hanson has led the way by drawing a distinction between prophetic eschatology and apocalyptic eschatology, a distinction which is not without parallel with that drawn by Scholem for a later period between restorative and utopian messianism. . . .

In this centennial lecture I have referred only very sparingly to the great Albert Schweitzer. But I have tried to recall you to the haunting question which he bequeathed to us. How are we to preserve visionary intensity without an illusory fanaticism? It is because it offers a sobering warning against any uncritical concentration on and endorsement of an undifferentiated apocalyptic that I have reflected with you on Scholem's great work.

DAVID BIALE

Gershom Scholem's Ten Unhistorical Aphorisms on Kabbalah: Text and Commentary

In 1958, Gershom Scholem published [in *Geist und Werk: Festschrift zum 75. Geburtstag von Dr. Daniel Brody*] a series of ten aphoristic statements entitled "Zehn unhistorische Sätze über Kabbala." Although later republished in the third volume of his collected German essays, *Judaica*, these aphorisms have received little or no attention in the English-reading world, despite their considerable interest both for Scholem's own thought and as philosophical reflections on some fundamental issues in the Kabbalah. The word "unhistorical" in the title immediately suggests Scholem's intention to take off the hat of historian and philologian which he wore in most of his writings and to look at his material from a different perspective. Since Scholem's primary achievements lay in the history and philology of the Kabbalah, his more philosophical and theological reflections have often been treated as occasional pieces, peripheral to his main contribution. I have argued elsewhere that an understanding of Scholem as an historian requires an examination of these writings and attention to his place in modern Jewish thought. From the beginning of his career, when he planned to write a dissertation on the Kabbalah's philosophy of language, he was attracted to the Kabbalistic treatment of philosophical and theological issues which have contemporary resonance. While it would be a mistake to assert that he imposed these modern categories on his historical studies, they did influence the themes which he chose to address and in many instances dictated the language in which he cast his writing.

From *Modern Judaism* 5, no. 1 (February 1985). © 1985 by the Johns Hopkins University Press.

One of the main characteristics of these aphorisms is just such an interplay between historical theses and modern philosophical language. Scholem boldly suggests parallels between modern schools of thought and the Kabbalah: dialectical materialism and the Lurianic Kabbalah, phenomenology and Moses Cordovero, Franz Kafka and the eighteenth-century Frankist, Jonas Wehle. At the end of aphorism 4, he notes: "the conception of the Kabbalists as mystical materialists with a dialectical tendency would certainly be thoroughly unhistorical, yet anything but meaningless." At first blush, to impose modern categories on an historical subject would certainly seem unhistorical. Yet, Scholem assumes that the philosophical issues treated by both the Kabbalah and modern philosophy are universal, even as they are addressed historically in different terms by different movements. The seemingly "unhistorical" procedure of these aphorisms is therefore philosophically meaningful: modern philosophy and the Kabbalah illuminate and explicate the same problems and can therefore shed light on each other. But it is also historically meaningful because it allows the modern sensibility to grasp a system of thought that appears initially alien and remote.

This telescoping of historical ideas by viewing them through modern prisms is not, however, a subject only for "unhistorical" aphorisms. It lies at the heart of one of the classic problems of all historical work: what changes do ideas necessarily undergo as they are refracted through the eyes of an historian whose categories of thought are historically different? The very ability of the historian to reconstruct the past lies in his finding a common ground or common language between himself and his sources: if the past is utterly alien, it cannot be reconstructed. Hence, the historian must engage in a delicate balancing act between past and present, maintaining the bridge between them without collapsing one into the other. The fact that Scholem gives explicit consideration to this issue in these aphorisms does not mean that he ignored it in his historical work. On the contrary, one can find repeated instances where he consciously used modern categories to illuminate and explicate problems in the Kabbalah. Indeed, one of the keys to Scholem's success as an historian of the Kabbalah was in turning an ostensibly alien system of ideas into one with a contemporary resonance and urgency. Yet, unlike Martin Buber, who also found striking parallels between modern thought and the Kabbalah, Scholem was largely able to maintain the distinction between them.

That Scholem chose to express these ideas in the form of aphorisms and in language which is much more opaque than his normal German style deserves some comment. The tradition of aphoristic writing in German goes back to Lichtenberg in the eighteenth century and Feuerbach in the nineteenth. But it was Nietzsche who exploited the aphoristic form as a vehicle for his attack on systematic philosophy. What better way to destroy the idea of systems than by writing in a deliberately fragmentary and elusive style which hid as much as it revealed? The aphoristic style was particularly effective in conveying paradoxes, which also suited Nietzsche's anti-rationalist intent.

Nietzsche's influence can be detected in a variety of German writers in the twentieth century, and particularly starting in the 1920s. Theodor Adorno, Ernst Bloch and Walter Benjamin, among others, all composed some of their best writing in aphorisms. Scholem was close to all of these German Jewish thinkers, although, as is well known, was not at all sympathetic to their neo-Marxism. Yet, it is quite likely that his own attempt at aphoristic writing may have owed much to their influence. In particular, Walter Benjamin's "Ten Theses on the Philosophy of History," written in 1940, must have evoked in Scholem the desire to set down some of his ideas in the same style as that adopted by his martyred friend. Although the aphorisms presented below lack the literary flair of Benjamin's theses, it seems to me that Scholem was attempting to imitate Benjamin's late work.

An additional influence which Scholem suggests in the tenth *Satz* is that of Franz Kafka. Scholem saw in Kafka's writings, and particularly in his parables, a modern form of Kabbalah. Like Nietzsche's aphorisms, Kafka's parables are characterized by ironic twists and reversals. The expulsion from Paradise turns out to have been "a stroke of luck, for had we not been expelled, Paradise would have had to be destroyed." By making daring use of counter-factual conditionals, Kafka explored alternative interpretations of biblical and other classical stories, a procedure that might well be termed "midrashic." It was this ability to explode the conventional reading of well-known texts and reveal their secrets that must have reminded Scholem of the Kabbalah and made him see in Kafka a kind of neo-Kabbalist.

For Scholem's own purposes, the aphoristic style clearly held particular attraction. Although these aphorisms are "on" or "about" (*über*) Kabbalah, they are, in their own way, Kabbalistic in both style and content. In order to convey the parallels between the intellectual problems of the modern historian and those of the Kabbalists, Scholem adopts Kabbalistic formulations which he, of course, avoided in his more historical essays. The aphorism conveys a sense of mystery and impenetrability: opaqueness is almost part of its definition. The sense of secrets hidden behind the explicit text in an aphorism is thus reminiscent of the Kabbalah for which truth is by nature secret (*sod*). Aphorisms mirror the Kabbalistic concept of esoteric truths. That which is hidden cannot be expressed without altering its meaning and, therefore, the aphorism, which suggests more than it expresses, is a better vehicle for these reflections than direct exposition. Hence, Scholem's choice of aphorisms is itself proof of the relationship between the historian of the Kabbalah and his subject matter.

Indeed, the very number of aphorisms—ten—hints at a Kabbalistic "subtext," for that is the number of *sefirot* (divine emanations). And just like the *sefirot* themselves, these aphorisms are at once discrete and seemingly unlinked to one another, yet, at the same time, unified by a common theme which is treated in each from a different angle. That theme, to which we have already alluded, is the fundamental tension or even paradox of communicating a truth which is by definition secret or hidden. What is the definition of a "secret" (*Geheimnis*)? On the one hand, it may be something which is known but deliberately hidden, or, it may be that which is essentially inaccessible (hidden by nature rather than by design). It is this latter sense of a secret which Scholem has in mind here. Kabbalistic truth is inaccessible because God is transcendent. Historical truth is inaccessible because the past cannot be known in the same way we know the perceptual world. Both Kabbalist and historian face the same problem of how to convey a truth which is hidden.

The subtle influence of the Kabbalah on Scholem as an historian becomes particularly apparent in deciphering the language of the aphorisms. Scholem writes in German but often thinks in the technical language of the Kabbalah (either Hebrew or Zoharic Aramaic). Thus, a correct understanding of the text requires sensitivity to the Kabbalistic language lurking behind it. For instance, in discussing the epistemology of the Kabbalah, he uses the term *Erkenntnis* ("knowledge"). Yet, it becomes clear in the context that he has in mind the Kabbalah's understanding of knowledge in the form of the *sefirah* (divine emanation) called *hokhmah* ("wisdom"). One is thus faced with the problem of grasping both the philosophical vocabulary and its Kabbalistic background in reading the text. The function of the commentary to each aphorism will be in part to point out the Kabbalistic dimension which is concealed behind the text.

SATZ 1

Die Philologie einer mystischen Disziplin wie der Kabbala hat etwas Ironisches an sich. Sie beschäftigt sich mit einem Nebelschleier, der als Geschichte der mystischen Tradition das Korpus, den Raum der Sache selbst umhängt, ein Nebel freilich, der aus ihr selber dringt.

Bleibt in ihm, dem Philologen sichtbar, etwas vom Gesetz der Sache selbst oder verschwindet gerade das Wesentliche in dieser Projektion des Historischen? Die Ungewissheit in der Beantwortung dieser Frage gehört zur Natur der philologischen Fragestellung selbst, und so behält die Hoffnung, von der diese Arbeit lebt, etwas Ironisches, das von ihr nicht abgelöst werden kann. Aber liegt solch Element der Ironie nicht vielmehr schon im Gegenstand dieser Kabbala selber, und nicht nur in ihrer Geschichte?

Der Kabbalist behauptet, es gäbe eine Tradition über die Wahrheit, die tradierbar sei. Eine ironische Behauptung, da ja die Wahrheit, um die es hier geht, alles andere is als tradierbar. Sie kann erkannt werden, aber nicht überliefert werden, und gerade das in ihr, was überlieferbar wird, enthält sie nicht mehr. Echte Tradition bleibt verborgen; erst die verfallende Tradition verfällt auf einen Gegenstand und wird im Verfall erst in ihrer Grösse sichtbar.

Commentary

The "philologist" of this aphorism is equivalent to the "historian" of a mystical discipline, although Scholem often liked to call himself a philologist, by which he indicated the importance of establishing the textual and linguistic tradition of the Kabbalah as the key to its history. The problem suggested in the aphorism is, however, common to all the historical disciplines and is the question of what of the essence of the past remains accessible to the historian:

> Does there remain for the philologist something visible in this fog of the law of the subject itself or does the essential disappear in this projection of the historical? The uncertainty in answering this question is inherent in the nature of the philological enterprise itself and thus the hope, from which this work draws its life, retains something ironic which cannot be severed from it.

History is concerned with the sources that have been produced by the past event and the historian can only reach that event through the sources. To what extent, then, can such an indirect procedure yield knowledge of the truth?

But this is the very problem which also confronts the Kabbalist; the "element of irony resides rather in the subject of this Kabbalah itself and not only in its history." The truth of the Kabbalah is, by definition, a secret truth. It can be known, but not in the same sense that one "knows" the perceptual world. The very "hiddenness" of Kabbalistic truth, which is an essential part of its definition, makes it impossible to transmit, for any act of transmission or communication would immediately violate its secret character. Yet, the very word Kabbalah means tradition, or that which has been handed down. The authenticity of Kabbalistic truth is based on the claim that the Kabbalist possesses an authentic tradition which has been handed down to him and which reveals the secrets of the Torah. The Kabbalist is therefore caught in a tension between the secret nature of his truth and his claim that he has received it by a process which would violate that secret: "Authentic tradition remains hidden; only the fallen tradition (*verfallende Tradition*) falls upon (*verfällt auf*) an object and only when it is fallen (*im Verfall*) does its greatness become visible."

Yet, on a deeper level, this problem of the accessibility of the source of a mystical tradition lies in Kabbalistic theology itself. The Kabbalah holds that the source of all creation is the hidden God, *Ein-sof* (the "Infinite"). The hidden God, by definition, cannot be known, yet the Kabbalah, through its theory of *sefirot*, attempts to comprehend something of this God. Thus, Kabbalistic theology is caught in the same tension between the knowability and hiddenness of its subject.

Scholem alludes to this last level in his metaphor of the "veil of fog" which surrounds the subject matter studied by the philologist. The fog is presumably the texts which are available to the scholar, but which do not permit actual access to the truths which they describe. But exactly the same metaphor can be found in that passage in the *Zohar* which describes the first steps of creation with the *Ein-sof*: "'In the beginning'—when the will of the King began to take effect, he engraved signs into the heavenly sphere. Within the most hidden recess a dark flame issued from the mystery of the Infinite, like a fog forming in the unformed (*kutra' begulma*) . . ." In his translation of this passage into German, Scholem rendered the "fog" as *Nebel,* the same term he uses in this aphorism. Thus, the epistemological problem of both historian and Kabbalist is represented by the metaphor which hints at the theological problem of knowing the hidden God.

On the other hand, the problem of the historian differs fundamentally from that of the Kabbalist. Although both confront truths which are inaccessible to ordinary sense perception, the secrecy of Kabbalistic truth is a result of the *transcendence* of God, while the historian deals with events which are part of the world. Historical truth is only "secret" in the sense that what lies beyond the temporal horizon of the historian is unknowable in the perceptual sense of the word, while Kabbalistic knowledge is secret because God is essentially absent. Thus, only by metaphorically conceiving of the past as somehow parallel to the hiddenness of God does the analogy between historian and Kabbalist make sense.

SATZ 2

Die Öffentlichkeit der Hauptwerke der alten kabbalistischen Literatur ist die wichtigste Garantie ihres Geheimnisses. Denn wir sehen nicht mehr, und wann werden wir schon angesprochen? Kein kabbalistisches Werk ist wegen seiner popularisierenden Tendenzen, wegen des angeblich in ihm begangenen Verrats an den Geheimnissen der Tora so angegriffen worden wie das Buch *Emek ha-Melekh* des Jakob Elchanan Bacharach aus Frankfurt am Main, das 1648 herauskam. Aber man öffne diesen Folianten heute, und es zeigt sich, dass unsere Wahrnehmung für diesen Mysterienverrat geschwunden sein muss. Kaum ein unverständlicheres Buch als dieses "Königstal". Haben wir es also wieder mit jener mystisch-anarchischen Politik zu tun, die die Geheimnisse durch Aussprechen besser schützt als durch Verschweigen? Und welche unter allen ausgesprochenen Welten wäre wohl versunkener in ihrer rätselhaften Aussprechlichkeit als die Welt der Lurianischen Kabbala?

Commentary

In this aphorism, Scholem seemingly turns the conclusion of the previous aphorism on its head. Where in Aphorism 1, the greatness of a hidden tradition only becomes visible in a "fallen" or publicized state, the very public character of the Kabbalah in Aphorism 2 guarantees that the mysteries will remain hidden. Yet, the paradoxical fact that publicizing a hidden tradition protects it better than hiding it must stem from the same epistemological principle Scholem develops in Aphorism 1: since the hidden truth cannot, by definition, be expressed, the more one attempts to express it, the more one leads one's audience away from the truth. Here, once again, the issue concerns the meaning of a secret. The German word *Geheimnis* is related to *Heim* (home), suggesting that a secret is that which is not public. The very act of publicizing a secret turns it into something it is not. Once a mystical truth is given public expression, it becomes divorced from the original insight which gave it birth. The reader "no longer sees" and cannot experience what the mystic himself experienced. In this aphorism and in the previous one, Scholem challenges the claim of Martin Buber and others that the reading of mystical texts can cause the reader himself to have a mystical experience.

The issue of the public dissemination of Kabbalistic secrets became an acute one in the century following the Lurianic Kabbalah. While the Spanish Kabbalah of the thirteenth century remained largely an esoteric discipline limited to small circles of *cognoscenti,* the Lurianic Kabbalah was popularized by a number of writers, among them, the author of *Emek ha-Melekh.* Only today, in historical perspective, does it become apparent how mislead-

ing these popularizing texts are and how far from conveying the essential
truth of Luria's teaching: "But open these folios today, and we realize that
our sense that mysteries have been betrayed must have disappeared." But, if
such texts are misleading, then the historian, who is both temporally and
temperamentally outside the small circle of Kabbalistic adepts, has a paradoxical relationship to the original truths: he is able to leapfrog over the
popularizing texts and recover what contemporaries of Bacharach, who were
much closer in time and spirit to Luria, could not understand. The very
incomprehensibility of supposedly popular texts can only be detected by the
historian, while those to whom the texts were directed lived under the "illusion" that they comprehended them. Because of his very distance from the
material, the historian ironically has an insight into the Kabbalah that may
be close to that of the original Kabbalists themselves.

Here, too, one may discern an echo of the Kabbalah itself behind the
aphorism. Luria argued that the initial step in creation was the self-contraction of God and the creation of an empty space (*halal ha-panui*). The late
eighteenth-century Hasidic master, Nachman of Bratslav, suggested that the
empty space could only be comprehended through silence. Public treatment
of these mysteries or, for that matter, any verbal expression would therefore
contradict their essence. If one accepts Nachman's mysticism of silence, then
the Lurianic Kabbalah suffered a paradoxical fate: precisely that Kabbalistic
system whose mysteries could only be approached through silence was the
subject of a public campaign. The popularization of this quintessentially
secret doctrine succeeded to the point where it became virtually the sole
"public" Jewish theology of the seventeenth and eighteenth centuries. It is
perhaps in this spirit that Scholem concludes the aphorism with the paradoxical question: "And which among all of the worlds might indeed be more
submerged in its enigmatic expressibility than the world of Lurianic Kabbalah?" That this fate of the Lurianic Kabbalah was a case of "mystical-
anarchistic politics" may be an allusion to the nihilistic outgrowth of Luria's
system: the Sabbatian movement of the seventeenth century. For, the very
public campaign that spread Luria's teachings made possible, at least in
Scholem's interpretation, the phenomenon of a mass messianic movement
with an antinomian Kabbalistic theology.

SATZ 3

Charakter der Erkenntnis in der Kabbala: die Tora ist das Medium, in
dem alle Wesen erkennen. Die Symbolik des "leuchtenden Spiegels", die von
den Kabbalisten auf die Tora übertragen wurde, ist dafür aufschlussreich.

Die Tora ist das Medium, in dem sich die Erkenntnis spiegelt; verdunkelt, wie es das Wesen der Tradition mit sich bringt, strahlend im reinen Bezirk der "schriftlichen", das heisst aber unanwendbaren Lehre. Denn anwendbar wird sie nur, wo sie "mündlich", das heisst aber tradierbar wird. Die Erkenntnis ist der Strahl, in dem die Kreatur von ihrem Medium aus zu ihrer Quelle vorzudringen sucht—unabwendbar im Medium bleibend, denn noch Gott selbst ist ja Tora, und die Erkenntnis kann nicht herausführen. Es ist etwas unendlich Trostloses um die Aufstellung der Gegenstandslosigkeit der höchsten Erkenntnis, die auf den ersten Seiten des Buches *Sohar* gelehrt wird. Die mediale Natur der Erkenntnis enthüllt sich in der klassischen Form der Frage: Erkenntnis als eine in Gott gegründete Frage, die keiner Antwort entspricht. Das "Wer" ist das letzte Wort aller Theorie, und erstaunlich genug, dass sie so weit führt, von dem "Was" hinwegzukommen, an dem ihr Anfang haftet.

Commentary

The Kabbalistic background to this aphorism is perhaps more important than to any of the other aphorisms in the series. Many of the terms Scholem uses are translations of technical Kabbalistic terms related to the *sefirot* symbolism and can only be understood in that context. Knowledge is represented by the *sefirah hokhmah* which is the highest *sefirah* that can be known. Beyond *hokhmah* lies the realm of the hidden God and His will (*keter*). The *sefirah tiferet* is designated as an "illuminating mirror" (*Die Symbolik des "leuchtenden Spiegels"*) which stands in the middle of the system and which transmits light from the *sefirot* above to the *sefirot* below. In Kabbalistic symbolism, *tefiret* also stands for the written Torah, while the *sefirah malkhut*, which mediates between the world of emanation and the lower worlds, is called the "oral Torah." The light from *hokhmah* darkens as it emanates into the lower *sefirot*, from *tiferet* to *malkhut* and, ultimately, into the lower worlds. This is what Scholem means when he writes: "darkened, as the essence of the tradition requires, [knowledge] emanates into the pure realm of the 'written,' that is, of unusable teaching." This "knowledge" only becomes "usable" where it is "oral," meaning that it can only be transmitted and understood in our world where it has passed through the "refracting mirror," which is the Kabbalistic designation of *malkhut*.

What, then, does Scholem mean when he says that "the Torah is the medium in which knowledge is reflected" and "knowledge is the emanation through which man seeks to penetrate from its medium to its source—remaining inescapably in the medium . . . ?" On the literal level, the Torah is regarded as the medium through which all knowledge from God is conveyed, but since God Himself remains forever hidden and inaccessible, one can never attain the source of this knowledge. Here we have a restatement of the same issue raised in Aphorisms 1 and 2 of the hidden nature of the source of revelation. But on a symbolic, mystical level, the Torah is also the system of the *sefirot* as a whole through which the light from *Ein-sof* emanates. This system can be known, but the source of the emanation—the hidden God—cannot. Yet, the *sefirot* are not emanations *outside* of God; they are part of God's substance. Therefore, one who attains knowledge of the *sefirot* (the mystical Torah), attains direct knowledge of God. The ambiguous or equivocal nature of this knowledge is that it is *both* of God and not of God: it is knowledge up to the *sefirah hokhmah* but not of the hidden aspect of God. He who possesses the "highest knowledge" (viz. *hokhmah*) seemingly possesses everything, but also nothing at all. Hence, Scholem's concluding lines to the aphorism:

> There is something infinitely despairing about the lack of an object of this highest knowledge which is conveyed in the first pages of the book *Zohar*. The fundamental nature of this knowledge is revealed in the classical form of the question: knowledge is a question rooted in God to which no answer corresponds. The "who" is the final word of all theory, which, surprisingly enough, leads so far away from the "what" to which its beginning is bound.

If our earlier analysis of the relationship of historical to Kabbalistic knowledge is correct, then might this aphorism also allude to the ambiguous nature of the historian's quest for the whole truth?

SATZ 4

Die materialistische Sprache der Lurianischen Kabbala, besonders in ihrer Deduktion des *Zimzum* (der Selbstverschränkung Gottes), legt den Gedanken nahe, ob die Symbolik, die sich solcher Bildern und Reden bedient, nicht etwa auch die Sache selbst sein könnte. Solch materialistischer Aspekt der Kabbala war im Grunde in dem Moment mitgegeben, als das Gesetz des lebendigen Organismus als Grundanschauung in ihre Theosophie eingefügt wurde. Es verschlägt dabei wenig, ob man nun sagt, wir seien diesem Gesetz unterworfen, weil es das Gesetz des Lebens der Gottheit selber sei, oder ob man es nur "gleichsam" auch auf die Gottheit "überträgt". Der Wirkungskreis des Gesetzes umfasst eben, wie immer man es drehen mag, alles unterschiedslos. Es lässt sich argumentieren, dass die Ausführungen der

Kabbalisten über den *Zimzum* nur dann widerspruchlos und sinnvoll sind, wenn sie von einem materiellen Substrat handeln, sei dies nun *En-sof* selber, sei es sein "Licht". Die Vorwürfe an die häretischen Theologen der sabbatianischen Kabbala, sie hätten die geistigen Mysterien materialistisch missverstanden, zeigen, wohin die Reise gehen konnte, wenn man einmal versuchte, nach der inneren Logik der Bilder zu denken. Von Anfang an ist ein dialektisches Moment in diesem Materialismus der Lehre vom *Zimzum* und vom Bruch der Gefässe mitgegeben. Die Vorstellung der sabbatianischen Kabbala des Nathan von Gaza, wonach in *En-sof* selber ein "gedankenvolles" und ein "gedankenloses" Licht sich auseinandersetzen, aber ineinander strahlen, ist nur die radikalste Art, diesen Prozess eines dialektischen Materialismus an Gott selber durchzuexerzieren. Die Auffassung der Kabbalisten als mystische Materialisten dialektischer Tendenz wäre zwar durchaus unhistorisch, aber alles andere als sinnlos.

Commentary

The problem of this aphorism is stated at the outset: "The materialistic language of the Lurianic Kabbalah, especially in its theory of *tzimtzum* (the self-contraction of God), raises the question of whether the symbolism which avails itself of such images and expressions might not also be the thing itself." Does a mystical, symbolic language merely "represent" its subject or is the language an essential part of the "thing itself?" We shall see how Scholem returns to this issue of the theory of mystical language in later aphorisms. The specific problem of whether the Lurianic Kabbalah should be understood literally or metaphorically plagued all the disciples of Luria and continued to be a crucial issue in eighteenth-century Hasidic theology. If Luria had meant that God literally contracted Himself, then there would be a place where there is no God—a heretical proposition! But if Luria had meant such statements metaphorically, the whole system loses much of its originality and meaning. Scholem points out that the problem of "materialism" (that is, of whether statements concerning God should be understood as pertaining literally and physically to God), originated not with Luria, but even earlier, in the thirteenth-century Kabbalah, when "it adopted the law of the living organism as a basic conception in its theosophy." This "law" must refer to the notion that the *sefirot* constitute the "body" of God. Once the Kabbalists began to use such language, they opened themselves up to the charge that they meant the body of God not in a spiritual but a material sense.

If one can legitimately call those Kabbalists who understood the Lurianic theory of creation literally as "materialists," then it would be necessary to extend such unhistorical language and call them additionally "dialectical materialists." If God literally absented Himself from the empty space He had created, creation would have a dialectical logic: the Becoming of the world would be the result of a movement of Being through Nothing.

Such thinking could lead to heretical positions as it did in the radical thought of the Sabbatian theologians of the seventeenth century: "The conception of the Sabbatian Kabbalah of Nathan of Gaza according to which a light 'full of thought' and a light 'devoid of thought' confront each other in *Ein-sof* itself, even as they radiate into one another, is only the most radical way of imparting this process of dialectical materialism to God Himself." By understanding the process of divine contraction literally, Nathan of Gaza had to posit two kinds of light within the hidden God Himself: a light full of thought and a light devoid of thought. The *Ein-sof* could not contain only a light full of thought since "thought" is identified with one of the emanated *sefirot*. Such a light would be limited and would place limitations on the infinitude of the hidden God. The concept of a light devoid of thought was therefore necessary to preserve the unlimited character of the *Ein-sof*, but Nathan understood this light as the source of the "roots of evil" (*shorshei ha-dinim*). Thus, in Nathan's theology, the *Ein-sof* itself is caught in a dialectical conflict between two contradictory principles. The unknowable, hidden God loses both His unknowability and His inner harmony.

SATZ 5

In der Auffassung der alten Kabbala über das Verhältnis von *En-sof* und dem Nichts hat sich letzten Endes dasselbe Gefühl für die Dialektik im Schöpfungsbegriff Ausdruck geschaffen wie nachher in der Idee des *Zimzum*. Was besagt denn im Grunde die Scheidung zwischen *En-sof* und der ersten Sefira? Doch eben dies, dass die Wesensfülle des verborgenen Gottes, die jeder Erkenntnis (auch der intuitiven) transzendent bleibt, im Urakt der Emanation, in der reinen Wendung zur Schöpfung überhaupt, zum Nichts wird. Das ist jenes Nichts Gottes, das in der Perspektive ihres Weges den Mystikern notwendig als die letzte Stufe des "Entwerdens" erscheinen musste. Aber hier bleibt den Kabbalisten das Bewusstsein eines letzten Abgrunds, des Abgrunds im Willen, der sich als das Nichts darstellt. Von diesem Akt an, im Abgrund dieses Willens, ist in der Tat nun schon alles gegeben. Denn Gottes Wendung zur Schöpfung ist ja eben die Schöpfung selbst, wenn sie auch uns sich nur in unendlichen Abstufungen und Prozessen darbietet. Aber in Gott ist dies alles ein einheitlicher Akt. In diesem Sinn steht allerdings die prinzipielle Unterscheidung zwischen *En-sof* und der ersten Sefira in Verbindung zur pantheistischen Problematik: in dieser Unterscheidung wird sie weitge-

hend eingeschränkt, und zwar aus dem bei Moses Cordovero besonders deut-
lichen Bewusstsein heraus, dass der Übergang von *En-sof* zur ersten Sefira,
der Urakt, einen unendlich bedeutungsvolleren Schritt darstellt als alle von
da an erfolgenden Schritte zusammen. Unter diesem Gesichtspunkt darf man
auch die entschiedene Ablehnung der Identifikation von *En-sof* mit dem
Nichts (*'ajin*) bei allen Kabbalisten von etwa 1530 an sehen. Hier scheint ein
Gefühl dafür mitzuwirken, was mit dieser These von der Identifikation der
zwei Begriffe gefährdet wird: ihr fehlt das dialektische Moment im Schöpfungsbegriff. Es ist dieser Mangel an Dialektik, der diese These dem Pantheismus gegenüber hilflos macht. Ohne Transzendenz reicht hier das Nichts
ins Etwas herab. Man könnte sagen, dass jene Kabbalisten der Frühzeit, die
zwischen *En-sof* und *'ajin* nur eine Differenz der Namen, nicht aber des
Wesens statuieren wollten, damit in der Tat den ersten Akt aus dem Welten-
drama gestrichen haben, der die dialektische Exposition des Ganzen enthält.
So erhielt dann jene Theorie von der Identität ihre pantheistische Wendung:
die Schöpfung aus Nichts ist nur noch eine Chiffre für die Wesenseinheit
aller Dinge mit Gott. Das "Erlebnis" konnte ja nie weiterdringen als bis zum
Nichts, und aus diesem realen Erlebnisgrund mag sich auch jene pantheistische Identifikation des *En-sof* und des Nichts bei den alten Kabbalisten oft
genug herschreiben. Der Mystiker, der seine Erlebnisse undialektisch verar-
beitet, muss beim Pantheismus anlangen.

Commentary

In this aphorism, Scholem enlarges upon the dialectical logic of the
Kabbalah to which he alluded in Aphorism 4. The dialectics of the Kabbalah
begin with the relationship between the *Ein-sof* and the first *sefirah*, frequently referred to as *'ayin* (Nothingness). Scholem formulates this fundamental relationship as follows:

> the essential plenitude of the hidden God, which remains tran-
> scendent with respect to all knowledge (even intuitive knowledge),
> becomes Nothingness in the primal act of emanation, an act
> which is above all the pure turning toward creation. This is that
> Nothingness of God which necessarily had to seem to the mystics,
> from the basic perspective of their path, to be the ultimate stage
> in the process of "profanation" (*des Entwerdens*).

Some of the early Kabbalists saw no essential difference between the first
sefirah (sometimes also called the divine "will") and *Ein-sof* itself, while for
the others, the emanation of the "abyss of the will" (or Nothingness) was
in fact the first act of creation. According to traditional monotheistic theol-

ogy, the world was created by God *ex nihilo,* meaning that God and the
world are fundamentally different. Such a theology is the very antithesis of
pantheism. But those who conceived of God as identical to Nothingness
radically reinterpreted *creatio ex nihilo* to mean that the world emanated
directly out of God. This doctrine therefore bordered on pantheism since it
held that the world shared in the divine substance. On the other hand, those
who held that Nothingness was an emanation of *Ein-sof* and not identical
with it were able to maintain the absolute transcendence of the hidden God
by erecting a dialectical barrier between Him and all subsequent emanations.
This second theory of the status of the divine Nothingness was therefore
closer to the traditional antipathy to pantheism.

It was this anti-pantheistic understanding of Nothingness that took hold
in the later Kabbalistic tradition and was given new expression in the sixteenth century. Moses Cordovero argued that all of subsequent emanation
and creation was already contained in the movement from *Ein-sof* to the
first *sefirah.* He posited an infinite number of dialectical steps in this first
movement such that the "will" of God approaches, but is never quite identical
to the Infinite. In Isaac Luria's theory later in the century, the hidden God
must first create an empty space—a Nothingness—in order to make a place
for the world. This was the radical theory of *tzimtzum* or the self-contraction
of God. Thus, centuries before Hegel's *Logik,* the Kabbalists understood the
importance of a dialectical logic of creation. It was not so much that they
anticipated Hegel as that the theological necessity of avoiding pantheism and
maintaining God's transcendence led to dialectical thinking: "without transcendence, Nothingness extends down into Somethingness." In this way,
mystical and rational modes of thought converged in a remarkably similar
logic.

The conclusion of the aphorism deals with the reason why the early
Kabbalists might have inadvertently ended up in pantheism:

> "Experience" (*Erlebnis*) was never able to attain more than Noth-
> ingness and one might well ascribe the early Kabbalists' panthe-
> istic identification of *Ein-sof* and Nothingness to their own real
> experience. The mystic who treats his experiences undialectically
> must end up in pantheism.

The mystical experiences of the early Kabbalists (of which we possess little
direct information) could never yield knowledge of the hidden God, but only
of a mystical Nothingness. The mystic who relies on his experience rather
than on theoretical reflection might confuse *Ein-sof* with Nothingness, a
mistake that the theoretical or theosophical Kabbalist presumably would

never make. On what basis Scholem believes that experience might only attain a perception of Nothingness is unclear. But what may explain this passage is the word Scholem uses for experience: *Erlebnis*. We have here an allusion to his youthful polemic against Martin Buber's *Erlebnismystik*, which Buber propounded until approximately 1917 when he began to evolve his dialogic philosophy of *Ich und Du*. Buber's "mysticism of experience" led to a sense of unification with the cosmos, which could be understood as pantheism. Scholem not only rejected Buber's mystical philosophy but also argued that Jewish mysticism was essentially different: it was not a mysticism of experience but rather a theosophy in which the individual identities of God and the mystic are maintained. As opposed to Buber's mysticism, and, indeed, to much other historical mysticism, Scholem insisted that there is little evidence of a pantheistic *unio mystica* in the Jewish sources. The early confusion of *Ein-sof* with *'ayin*, with its pantheistic and experiential overtones, was soon corrected in the mainstream of the Kabbalah.

SATZ 6

Die Kabbalisten haben die volkstümliche Ausbreitung tiefmystischer Lehren erstrebt. Die Rechnung für solch verwegenes Unterfangen hat nicht auf sich warten lassen. Sie wollten eine mystische Verklärung des jüdischen Volkes und des jüdischen Lebens. Die kabbalistische Folklore ist die Antwort aus dem Volk, und—wie man nicht ohne Schaudern feststellen muss—sie ist auch danach. Aber dass es eben zu einer Antwort überhaupt kam, das ist doch bemerkenswert. Wie die Natur, kabbalistisch gesehen, nichts ist als der Schatten des göttlichen Namens, so kann man auch von einem Schatten des Gesetzes, den es immer länger und länger auf die Lebenshaltung des Juden wirft, sprechen. Aber die steinerne Mauer des Gesetzes wird in der Kabbala allmählich transparent, ein Schimmer der von ihm umschlossenen und indizierten Wirklichkeit bricht hindurch. Diese Alchimie des Gesetzes, seine Transmutation ins Durchsichtige, ist eines der tiefsten Paradoxe der Kabbala, denn was im Grunde könnte undurchsichtiger sein als dieser Schimmer, diese Aura des Symbolischen, die nun erscheint. Aber im Masse der immer steigenden, wenn auch immer unbestimmter werdenden Transparenz des Gesetzes lösen sich auch die Schatten auf, die es auf das jüdische Leben wirft. So musste am Ende dieses Prozesses logischerweise die jüdische "Reform" stehen: die schattenlose, unhintergründige, aber auch nicht mehr unvernünftige, rein abstrakte Humanität des Gesetzes als ein Rudiment seiner mystischen Zersetzung.

Commentary

The historical context of this aphorism is the process by which the Kabbalah, following the expulsion from Spain in 1492, gradually became accepted by most Jews to the point where it substantially influenced the course of Jewish history. One of Scholem's most famous, if not most controversial, theses was that the Lurianic Kabbalah, once popularized in the seventeenth century, became the impetus for the Sabbatian movement which, in turn, so revolutionized the Jewish world that it laid the groundwork for the secularization of the eighteenth and nineteenth centuries. Jewish secularization meant the dissolution of the authority of Jewish law, represented here by Reform Judaism, which rejected the *halakhah* as normative and prescriptive for daily life. Scholem "logically speaking" (if not historically) claims that the roots of this abrogation of the law lay in the immanent dialectic of Jewish history, and, specifically, in the Kabbalah:

> Just as nature, Kabbalistically seen, is nothing but a shadow of the divine name, so one can also speak of a shadow of the law, which is cast ever longer over the Jews' way of life. But in the Kabbalah, the stony wall of the law gradually becomes transparent; a shimmer of the reality surrounded and circumscribed by it breaks through. . . . But along with this ever increasing, if also ever more indistinct transparency of the law, the shadows which the law casts over Jewish life dissolve. The end of this process must, logically speaking, be Jewish 'Reform:' the shadowless, backgroundless, but no longer irrational, purely abstract humanity of the law as a remnant of its mystical dissolution.

The Kabbalah treated the law as symbolic, just as it treated nature as a "shadow of the divine name." One must follow the law not for its own sake or because it was commanded, but for the sake of the divine secrets which it symbolizes. Where the rabbis had seen the law as a "hedge" protecting Jewish life (what Scholem calls here the "stony wall of the law"), the Kabbalists transmuted the law into transparency by rendering it symbolic. What made this procedure paradoxical is that the reality symbolized by the law is the divine mysteries. That which is revealed by this "alchemy of the law" is that which is most obscure and secret. Once again, the Kabbalist is involved in a paradox of revealing what is by definition hidden. If in Aphorism 2 Scholem argued that the very act of publicizing Kabbalistic secrets protected them, here he seems to suggest that dissemination of the Kabbalah subverted the very legal tradition that gave mysticism a social framework.

Although Scholem does not mention the Sabbatian movement in this passage, he surely has it in mind when he refers to the "mystical dissolution" of the law. The logical consequence of turning the law into a symbol was the antinomianism of the Sabbatians. From mystical antinomianism, it was but a small dialectical step to the rational antinomianism of the Reformers: rationalism and irrationalism are not polar opposites but are instead intimately interconnected. In this way, the dialectical logic of the Kabbalah led to the dissolution of the very tradition of which it was an intimate part. Making a secret public transforms it into a force for destruction.

One cannot read this aphorism without noticing the ambivalent language which Scholem uses with respect to both the Kabbalah and the law. The popularization of Kabbalistic ideas gave birth to the demon of Sabbatianism. The Kabbalah created its opposite: Jewish Reform for which the symbolic irrationality of the Kabbalah was anathema. Given his fundamental hostility to Reform Judaism, Scholem would surely have to regard the Kabbalah in an ambivalent light: the Kabbalah was ultimately responsible for the sterile rationalism of the nineteenth century. At the same time, the language he applies to the law is even more uneasy. The law is a "stony wall" which casts "ever longer" shadows around the life of the Jews. This language comes close to the Enlightenment critique of medieval Judaism as enmired in obscurantist legalism. Indeed, Scholem elsewhere asserts that the *halakhah* is "a well-ordered house" in need of an "anarchic breeze" to give it vitality. For Scholem, the Kabbalah was this anarchic breeze and it was due to the Kabbalah that the Jewish legal tradition did not become a sterile fossil. As opposed to the adherents of the Enlightenment, Scholem holds that it was the Kabbalah rather than modern rationalism that allowed light into this gloomy world. But it was a light that, in Sabbatianism, ignited into a fire that consumed traditional Judaism and left in its wake the sterile rationality of the nineteenth century.

SATZ 7

Als das eigentliche Unglück der Kabbala darf man vielleicht (wie bei vielen nicht nach Hause gekommenen Formen der Mystik) die Emanationslehre betrachten. Die Einsichten der Kabbalisten betrafen Strukturen des Seienden. Nichts verhängnisvoller, als der Zusammenhang dieser Strukturen mit der Emanationslehre zu konfundieren. Diese Konfusion pervertiert ihre aussichtsreichsten Ansätze zugunsten der bequemsten und denkfaulsten aller Theorien. Cordovero wäre als Phänomenologe eher nach Hause gekommen denn als Schüler Plotins. Der Versuch, das Denken der Kabbalisten ohne

Benutzung der Emanationslehre aufzubauen (und zu Ende zu denken), wäre
die Begleichung der Schuld, die ein echter Schüler Cordoveros auf sich zu
nehmen hätte, wenn es einmal einen geben sollte. In der Form der theoso-
phischen Topographie, die die kabbalistischen Lehren in der Literatur an-
genommen haben, bleibt ihr sachlicher Gehalt unzugänglich. Der Widerstreit
des mystischen Nominalismus und der Lichtsymbolik in den kabbalistischen
Schriften stammt aus dieser unausgetragenen Spannung zwischen ihren be-
deutendsten Intentionen und ihrer Unfähigkeit, ihnen zu reinem Ausdruck
zu verhelfen.

Commentary

This is probably the most obscure of all the aphorisms. Scholem uses
terms like "phenomenology" and "nominalism" whose meanings are less
than clear, even in the best of circumstances. The core idea of the aphorism
is that the neoplatonic theory of emanation, which is typically associated
with the Kabbalah, is actually misleading. The neoplatonists asserted that
the emanations were outside of the One, the source of the emanations, while
in the Kabbalah, the *sefirot* are within God. The Kabbalah therefore attempted to describe activity within God Himself that led to the creation of
the world while neoplatonism did not account for how the process of emanation began in the first place. Because the neoplatonic theory of emanation
failed to confront this most difficult of questions, Scholem considers it "intellectually lazy." The Kabbalah, on the other hand, attempted to reconcile
the tension between the One and the Many *within* the divine sphere itself.
Moreover, the God of neoplatonism was utterly impersonal, while the Kabbalah sought to preserve both the personal God of the Bible and the impersonal God of the philosophers by the relationship between the attributeless
Ein-sof and the *sefirot*.

The Kabbalah was therefore led to a dialectical theology which is notably
absent in neoplatonism. As we have seen in earlier aphorisms, lack of a
dialectic leads to the danger of pantheism: without a dialectical moment—a
moment of non-Being—the One would "swallow up" the Many. Indeed, the
direct connection between the One and the Many in neoplatonism would
seem susceptible to the pantheistic interpretation it received from such medieval Jewish philosophers as Abraham ibn Ezra. The light symbolism of
neoplatonism conveys this sense of a direct emanation from the One to the
Many and it is probably due to the fact that the Kabbalah adopted this
symbolism from neoplatonism that its emanational theory has been mistaken
for that of the neoplatonists.

How this distinction between neoplatonism and the Kabbalah can be connected to twentieth-century phenomenology is unclear. Husserl's phenomenology eschewed a discussion of Being or Essence in favor of individual beings or essences. Scholem claims that the Kabbalah was also concerned with the "structures of beings" (*Strukturen des Seienden*), a term that he borrowed from this school of philosophy. Yet, what does it mean that the Kabbalah was concerned with individual essences rather than a universal Essence? Perhaps what he has in mind is that the dialectical theology of the Kabbalah established the principle of individuation within God Himself, thus giving legitimacy to the essential distinctions between individuals in the lower worlds. This emphasis on singular individuals, based on the distinctions between the *sefirot,* was perhaps the result of the desire to avoid any pantheistic formulations. Where neoplatonism failed to solve the problem of individuation and thus was threatened by pantheism, the Kabbalah postulated the movement from the impersonal One to the many attributes of the biblical God within the divine itself.

Similarly, the reference to "mystical nominalism" may be connected to the tendency in medieval nominalism to cast doubt on universal essences and to emphasize instead the singularity of individual beings. But more importantly, the Kabbalah might be called a school of "mystical nominalism" as a consequence of its notion that only names (or signs) signify essences although, as opposed to the philosophical nominalism of William Ockham, the Kabbalah took the divine names to be essential attributes of God rather than merely subjective significations.

In what sense, then, might Moses Cordovero be considered a "phenomenologist?" Although there are statements that look pantheistic in Cordovero's Kabbalah, as Joseph Ben Shlomo has shown, Cordovero was a fundamentally theistic thinker. In order to preserve God's transcendence, Cordovero postulated an infinity of "divine wills" (the first *sefirah*) which approach the *Ein-sof* dialectically but never actually merge with it. With this theory, Cordovero gave the most rigorous expression to the dialectical relationship between the hidden God and His revealed attributes. Thus, if neoplatonism had failed to hypothesize any movement within the One, Cordovero searched farther within *Ein-sof* than any previous Kabbalist for the dialectical turn from the One to the Many.

Finally, the obscure final phrase of the aphorism concerning the "irreconciled tension" between the "most important intentions" of the Kabbalists and their inability to bring them to "pure expression" is also deliberately evocative of phenomenology which made "intentional acts" an important part of its thought. But what exactly Scholem may have had in mind here is unclear. In any event, the aphorism closes by pointing out a fundamental

tension between the Kabbalah and phenomenology. Phenomenology claims
to be able to make coherent and intelligible statements about the "structures
of beings." But the Kabbalah, as we have repeatedly seen in these aphorisms,
is trapped by the essential inexpressibility of its truths. Perhaps the adoption
of neoplatonic language to describe a theosophy radically different from
neoplatonism guaranteed that the Kabbalah would reach a linguistic dead
end: it attempted to express an inexpressible truth in language that could
only be misleading. If this is the case, then perhaps neoplatonic language
safeguarded its essential secrets.

SATZ 8

Es gibt in der Kabbala etwas wie einen verwandelnden Blick, von dem
zweifelhaft bleibt, ob man ihn besser als einen magischen oder als einen
utopischen Blick bezeichnen sollte. Dieser Blick enthüllt alle Welten, ja das
Geheimnis von *En-sof* selber, an dem Ort, an dem ich stehe. Man braucht
nicht über das zu verhandeln, was "oben" oder "unten" ist, man braucht
nur (nur!) den Punkt zu durchschauen, wo man selber steht. Diesem verwandelnden Blick sind alle Welten, wie einer der grossen Kabbalisten gesagt
hat, nichts als die "Namen, die auf dem Papier von Gottes Wesen aufgezeich-
net werden".

Commentary

Scholem seems to be referring here to the Kabbalah's doctrine of mi-
crocosm-macrocosm. All the worlds, from upper to lower, are parallel: the
sefirot are symbolically the body of God which has the same anatomy as the
human body. Thus, by examining oneself, one can arrive at the mysteries of
the divine. The "transforming view" of the Kabbalah "reveals all worlds,
even the mystery of *Ein-sof* itself, at that place where I stand. One need not
argue what is 'above' and what 'below.' One need only (only!) see through
one's own vantage point." From this point of view, the Kabbalah appears
much closer to modern humanism as a philosophy than it does to traditional
God-centered theology. To be sure, such a "humanistic" formulation of the
Kabbalah would have been alien to the Kabbalists for whom the focus was
God rather than man. But it is surely a legitimate, if unhistorical, development of Kabbalistic thought: by turning Kabbalistic images upside down,
man as the image of God becomes the measure of all things.

The relationship between the lower worlds and God can also be understood as the relationship between names (human language) and the Name
(divine language): "For this transforming view, all worlds are . . . nothing

more than 'names recorded on the scroll of God's essence.'" The Kabbalists regarded the name of God (or the names of God) as equivalent to God Himself. Since all worlds proceed from God, the lower worlds may be thought of as linguistic derivations from the divine name. The relationship between human language and divine language, which is the subject of the next aphorism, makes it possible to comprehend the divine essence: since our language derives from God, we can grasp divine truths by examining our own language. Otherwise, God would remain irretrievably transcendent and unknowable.

Although a "theoretical" Kabbalist would not regard these insights as having "magical" properties, there is a sense in which the interconnectedness of all worlds is "transforming." Because this world is a mirror of the world of emanations, the actions of human beings directly influence the divine realm. The mystical importance of human activity took on a specifically messianic or utopian dimension in the Kabbalah of Isaac Luria in the sixteenth century and ultimately led to the messianic activism of seventeenth-century Sabbatianism. Thus, the Kabbalah developed a mystical form of utopian humanism foreshadowing dialectically the secular utopian movements of a later era.

SATZ 9

Ganzheiten sind nur okkult tradierbar. Der Name Gottes ist ansprechbar, aber nicht aussprechbar. Denn nur das Fragmentarische an ihr macht die Sprache sprechbar. Die "wahre" Sprache kann nicht gesprochen werden, sowenig wie das absolut Konkrete vollzogen werden kann.

Commentary

This aphorism is a commentary on the relationship between divine and human language alluded to in the previous passage. The divine language which is also the name of God "can be pronounced but cannot be expressed, for only that which is fragmentary makes language expressible. The 'true' language cannot be spoken, just as the absolutely concrete cannot be realized." As Scholem puts it elsewhere, the name of God is "absolute, meaning-bestowing, but itself meaningless . . ." The name of God is the source of all human language, but it is not itself meaningful in the sense that human language has meaning (that is, signifies something). The divine language only acquires meaning (becomes "expressible") as it is "translated" into human terms. But this act of translation only communicates part of the divine truth since human language is necessarily fragmentary or limited while God's language is infinite. Yet, because human language has its source in the divine, it is not arbitrary; rather, it is the legitimate, if the only, vehicle we have for expressing ultimate truths. Thus, the Kabbalistic attempt to transmit divine mysteries is caught, once again, in a paradox: it uses human language to speak of that which is, by definition, inexpressible. But its enterprise is not doomed, because its language is guaranteed by the divine origin of language. Because language has this equivocal meaning, it is capable of communicating the divine truths, but not in a direct, unmediated fashion. The dialectical relationship between divine and human language requires that the divine truths (which Scholem here calls *Ganzheiten* or "totalities") be communicated "in an occult fashion." Only that which is cloaked in mystery can truly communicate a mystery; only when the linguistic form fits the theological content can language escape its merely human limitations and signify that which is infinite.

This aphorism is directed against the existentialist theology of Karl Barth and his Jewish interpreter, Hans Joachim Schoeps. In a 1932 review of a work by Schoeps, Scholem wrote: "The word of God in its absolute symbolic fullness would be destructive if it were at the same time meaningful in an unmediated way. Nothing in historical time requires concretization more than the 'absolute concreteness' of the word of revelation." The absolutely concrete word of God cannot be comprehended by human beings directly, as existentialists such as Barth, Schoeps and Martin Buber thought. Instead, this word must undergo a process of mediation, of translation into human terms, which is the historical tradition. Thus, the commentator on the tradition rather than the ecstatic, who claims direct communication from God, is the true *homo religiosus*. In this sense, the historian, who deals with the sources of tradition, is a secular manifestation of the religious personality, for both translate the inexpressible truths of their subjects into the fragmentary language of human beings.

SATZ 10

Hundert Jahre vor Kafka schrieb in Prag Jonas Wehle (durchs Medium seines Schwiegersohns Löw von Hönigsberg) seine nie gedruckten und von seinen frankistischen Schülern dann vorsichtig wieder eingesammelten Briefe und Schriften. Er shrieb für die letzten Adepten einer ins Häretische umgeschlagenen Kabbala, eines nihilistischen Messianismus, der die Sprache der Aufklärung zu sprechen suchte. Er ist der erste, der sich die Frage vorgelegt (und bejaht) hat, ob das Paradies mit der Vertreibung des Menschen nicht mehr verloren hat als der Mensch selber. Diese Seite der Sache ist bisher entschieden zu kurz gekommen. Ist es nun Sympathie der Seelen, die hundert Jahre später Kafka auf damit tief kommunizierende Gedanken gebracht hat? Vielleicht weil wir nicht wissen, was mit dem Paradies geschehen ist, hat er jene Erwägungen darüber angestellt, warum das Gute "in gewissem Sinne trostlos" sei. Erwägungen, die fürwahr einer häretischen Kabbala entsprungen zu sein scheinen. Denn unübertroffen hat er die Grenze zwischen Religion und Nihilismus zum Ausdruck gebracht. Darum haben seine Schriften, die säkularisierte Darstellung des (ihm selber unbekannten) kabbalistischen Weltgefühls für manchen heutigen Leser etwas von dem strengen Glanze des Kanonischen—des Volkommenen, das zerbricht.

Commentary

Scholem's relationship to Franz Kafka as an unwitting product of a "heretical Kabbalah" deserves an essay in its own right for what it tells us about Scholem himself. In a letter written in 1937 to Zalman Schocken in which he discusses his reasons for choosing to study the Kabbalah, Scholem anticipated almost verbatim what he says in this aphorism: ". . . many exciting thoughts had led me (in the years 1916–1918) . . . to intuitive affirmation of mystical theses which walked the fine line between religion and nihilism. I later (found in Kafka) the most perfect and unsurpassed expression of this fine line, an expression which, as a secular statement of the Kabbalistic world-feeling in a modern spirit, seemed to me to wrap Kafka's writings in the halo of the canonical." For Scholem, Kafka expressed the conflict of the secular Jew still bound to his tradition: on the one hand, he believed deeply in the existence of "the Law," but, on the other, he regarded the Law as fundamentally inaccessible. The notion of the hiddenness of the source of revelation was surely Kabbalistic, but where the Kabbalists claimed to be able to penetrate these secrets, the secular Jew remained impotently paralyzed outside the first gate of the Law. Thus, Kafka represented the nihilistic (or antinomian) secular consequence inherent in the Kabbalah, a theme which Scholem developed in his historical studies of eighteenth-century Frankism.

The radical theology of the Frankists led to speculations in which the literal message of the Bible might be inverted altogether such as the notion that paradise had "lost more with the expulsion of man than had man himself." This type of inversion was already one of the characteristics of the way some of the Christian Gnostics of late antiquity read the Bible, and the similarity which Scholem pointed out between the Gnostics and the Frankists in terms of theology can therefore be found also in their similar biblical exegesis. But Kafka, perhaps moved by some deep "kinship of souls," also employed such inversions in his parables on classical stories. These parables may be understood as Kafka's attempts to penetrate those religious texts by reading them, in Walter Benjamin's expression, "against the grain." For the secular Jew, as for the radical Kabbalist, the truth is now alien and hidden; the texts handed down by tradition do not reveal this truth if read literally. Only by reading the texts against their literal intent can the reader reveal what is hidden.

This interpretation of Kafka as a heretical neo-Kabbalist appears first in letters which Scholem wrote to Walter Benjamin in 1934 in response to Benjamin's essay on Kafka, published in the *Jüdische Rundschau*. Scholem took strong exception to Benjamin's denial of the theological element in Kafka, and particularly the theological problem of the inaccessible Law (*halakhah*) which Scholem held was the key to understanding Kafka's *Trial* and the parable "Before the Law." He wrote to Benjamin: "Kafka's world is the world of revelation, yet from that perspective in which revelation is reduced to its Nothingness (*Nichts*)." The Kabbalistic overtones to this remark are evident in the word "Nothingness," the divine abyss that stands between the mystic and comprehension of the hidden God. Unlike the Kabbalist who claims to be able to penetrate, if only partially, the mystery of the *'ayin*, Kafka remained confounded by the utterly incomprehensible nature of revelation. Here the paradox of comprehending the incomprehensible, which characterized the historical Kabbalah, as we have seen in these aphorisms, became fully apparent, as it only could from a secular viewpoint. No wonder, then, that Kafka ended up in an abyss of despair and regarded his writings as failures deserving only to be burnt.

A correct understanding of Kafka therefore required a correct understanding of theology. Here Scholem's polemic against Hans Joachim Schoeps, mentioned in the commentary on the previous aphorism, becomes relevant once again. In his essay on Kafka, Benjamin had mentioned Schoeps as one of those who incorrectly found in Kafka a position similar to his own theology. Scholem agrees with Benjamin, but for the reason that Schoeps's theology was wrong. It is the theological position which Scholem found in the Kabbalah and which he himself adopted that should be identified in Kafka: "The *unrealizability (Unvollziehbarkeit)* of that which is revealed is the point at which, in the most precise way, a *correctly* understood theology (as I, immersed in my Kabbalah, imagine it and as you can find it given rather responsible expression in that open letter against Schoeps which you know) and the key to Kafka's world come together. Not, dear Walter, the *absence* (of this theology) in a preanimistic world, but its *unrealizability* is its problem." Thus, the problem for theology is how to realize and comprehend in the finite world of human beings the infinite revelation of God. The realization of revelation in the medium of the historical tradition is necessarily inadequate and even paradoxical, as these aphorisms repeatedly assert. This was the problem for the Kabbalists and it was also the problem, in its most acute form, for Kafka. Interestingly enough, Benjamin came to this conclusion himself several years later in a formulation which seemingly anticipates Aphorism 1: "Kafka's real genius was that . . . he sacrificed truth for the sake of clinging to its transmissibility, its haggadic element. Kafka's writings . . . do not modestly lie at the feet of the doctrine, as the Haggadah lies at the feet of the Halakhah. Though apparently reduced to submission, they unexpectedly raise a mighty paw against it. This is why, in regard to Kafka, we can no longer speak of wisdom. Only the products of its decay remain."

For Scholem, the historian, the "products of decay," the tradition produced by vanished wisdom, were equally all that remained. The historian works in the deepest darkness, always striving like Kafka for some communication from the Castle, for some revelation from the mountain which was the site of the primordial revelation. As he wrote to Schocken: "For today's man, that mystical totality of systematic 'truth' whose existence disappears especially when it is projected into historical time, can only become visible in the purest way in the legitimate discipline of commentary and in the singular mirror of philological criticism. Today, as at the very beginning, my work lives in this paradox, in the hope of a true communication from the mountain, of that most invisible, smallest fluctuation of history which causes truth to break forth from the illusions of 'development.'" Like the Kabbalist, the historian works with the fragments left by tradition, but he nourishes the hope that through immersion in these fragments, he, too, may have a revelation of the "secret" truth. Yet, by the very nature of his enterprise, his experience of the past (and of God, if that is what he seeks) must be indirect and never immediate.

CYNTHIA OZICK

The Fourth Sparrow: The Magisterial Reach of Gershom Scholem

Gershom Scholem is a historian who has remade the world. He has remade it the way Freud is said to have remade it—by breaking open the shell of the rational to uncover the spiraling demons inside. But Freud, in fencing himself off from tradition, was hobbled by the need to invent everything on his own, through case history, trial and error, drug research, venturesome ingenuity, hunch and speculation above all. The little gods he collected, and the vocabulary he borrowed, took him partially and intuitively to Greek and primitive sources. All the same, in purposefully excluding himself from Hebrew origins—in turning Moses into an Egyptian, for instance—Freud inevitably struck loose from an encompassing history of ideas, ending in sensation and in a thesis of individuality suitable to the ardent physician he was; his new formulations stuck close to biology and family drama.

If Freud is regarded as an engine of thought and a sorcerer of fresh comprehension—as one of the century's originals, in short—there are nevertheless those who, without necessarily reducing Freud's stature, think the oceanic work of Gershom Scholem envelops Freud's discoveries as the sea includes even its most heroic whitecaps. Or, to alter the image: Freud is a peephole into a dark chamber—a camera obscura; but Scholem is a radio-telescope monitoring the universe, with its myriads of dark chambers. This is because Scholem's voyage brought him past those boundaries Freud willfully imposed on himself. Freud dared only a little way past the margins of psychology; whereas Scholem, whose medium was history, touched on the

From *Art and Ardor*. © 1983 by Cynthia Ozick. Knopf, 1983.

very ground of human imagination. Freud claimed Hannibal as his hero, but Scholem delved beyond the Greek and Roman roots of the classical European education common to them both. Scholem went in pursuit of the cosmos—and that took him straight to the perplexities of Genesis and the Hebrew language. Freud shrugged off religion as "illusion," and ended his grasp of it with that word. Where Freud thought it fit to end, Scholem begins.

In his restrained little memoir, *From Berlin to Jerusalem: Memories of My Youth,* Scholem recounts how even in boyhood he was drawn by mysterious magnets to the remote heritage his parents had deliberately denied him. The elder Scholem was a Jew who, like many Jews in the Germany of his generation and afterward, longed for a kind of social invisibility. The proprietor of a print shop, he thought of himself as a properly bourgeois German; he intended his four sons to distinguish themselves by growing up indistinguishable—he required them to be turned out as educated Germans with no recognizable Jewish quirks of intellect or passion. The two older boys obliged him; the two younger, Werner and Gerhard, were infected by a powerful Jewish desire to repair a morally flawed world. Werner became a Communist, and, to his father's outrage and shame, was court-martialed for treason, having taken part in an anti-World War I demonstration while wearing a German military uniform. Gerhard Hebraized his identity fully, called himself Gershom, sought out the Yiddish-speaking East European Jewish intellectuals he was expected to scorn, and became a Zionist. In the father's eyes the activities of both sons were "anti-German." The Marxist was unreachable in jail. The Zionist the father threw out of the house. The Marxist died in Buchenwald. The Zionist chose Jerusalem, and emerged as the monumental scholar of Jewish mysticism whose huge researches and daring insights have infiltrated and significantly enlarged the religious imagination of our age.

Scholar, yes—but also rediscoverer. When Scholem began his investigations, the antirational elements in Judaism had long been deliberately suppressed, both by tradition itself and by the historians. Though there are mystical moods in the vastnesses of Talmud, they are almost by-the-by: what dominates is the rabbis' ethical and juridical genius, in the intellectual and rationalist sense. Scholem set out to rescue from distaste and neglect, indeed from ill-repute and shame, those wellsprings of metaphoric vitality that lay in Kabbalah, a proliferating system of symbolic descriptions of creation and revelation deemed capable of seizing the quality of holiness itself. These ancient ideas, some of them bordering on a kind of Jewish Gnosticism, were hidden away in numbers of texts, some forgotten, some misunderstood, some condemned, some—like the Zohar—ringed round with traditional strictures. Scholem cut through disdain and rejection to begin, single-handedly, his life's task of reconstructing the story of Jewish mysticism.

Kabbalah—grounded in a belief in divine disclosure and the irrepressible hope of redemption—was historically both an inward movement and an outward one. When joined to messianic currents, it exploded the confines of esoteric reflection and burst into real event. The most startling event occurred in the seventeenth century, just after the massive Chmielnitzki persecutions of Polish Jews, when a popularly acclaimed redeemer, Sabbatai Ṣevi, and his prophet and theologian, Nathan of Gaza, set their generation on fire with the promise of an imminent return to Zion and an instantaneous end to exile and its oppressions. Scholem's inexhaustible masterwork on this subject, *Sabbatai Ṣevi: The Mystical Messiah,* divulges with philological, historical, and psychological force the amazing tale of that Sabbatian adventure: how it broke out spectacularly among the Jewish masses, and how it launched reverberations that penetrated into the next two centuries. The would-be deliverer, broken by threats of execution by the Turks—who held the Holy Land—saved his life and abandoned his followers by converting to Islam, bringing a furiously spreading cataclysm of redemptive fever to a tragic and bewildering anticlimax.

Sabbatai Ṣevi is a titanic investigation into the substance and effect of illusion. It explores the rise, in the years 1665 and 1666, of a messianic movement among a profoundly subjugated people, only just recovering from the Inquisition and the Iberian expulsion, thrown into yet another devastation—the catastrophic massacres of the Jews of Poland that began in 1648 and continued until 1655. But the Sabbatian movement was not merely the response of hope to cataclysm. Sabbatai Ṣevi, born in Smyrna, Turkey, did not declare himself the true messiah of the Jews only to abolish their dispersion and restore to them their historic territory; the idea he represented was a cosmic redemption, the cleansing and renewal of all things, the retrieval of the sparks of holiness from the husks of evil which, according to Kabbalistic thought, bind them fast.

In the wake of Sabbatai Ṣevi's annunciation came an incalculable penitential wave. The messiah's work could not be completed until the world was cleared of sin, and everywhere—over the whole face of Europe, in Turkey, Morocco, Palestine, Egypt, wherever Jews lived—sanctification made vivid claims in the form of an astonishing spiritual roiling characterized by penitential exercises and charitable works. While the Gentiles around them gaped, Jews stopped in their daily tracks, gave up their livings, sold their possessions—the city of Leghorn, which had a large Jewish merchant class, nearly came to a halt—and prepared to journey to Jerusalem. Though there were doubters, no community of Jews went untouched by the messianic fervor. Legendary reports of the redeemer spread from land to land—a pandemic of ecstatic expectation.

The personality of the messiah himself is remarkably well-documented. He was plump, young, attractive. He had a beautiful singing voice, which he liked to show off in the synagogue, chanting psalms. An undistinguished writer, he was poetic in act rather than word. He was not intellectually notable, although the study of Kabbalah, which formed his character, demands unusual conceptual gifts: Kabbalah is a kind of Einsteinian mysticism—the brilliance of its inventions is precisely the brilliance of an original physics. It is no easy, amoral occultism, rather the vision of a universal moral restitution willed so acutely that only an alteration in the perception of the cosmos can account for it. Without the Kabbalah, Scholem explains, there could have been no Sabbatai Ṣevi to inaugurate the messianic dream, and no messianic dream to inaugurate the career of Sabbatai Ṣevi.

But he was, above all, a man of afflictions, subject to periods of "darkness," which then gave way to phases of "illumination." In short, a classic manic-depressive; and, worn and perplexed by his suffering during the cycle of bleakness, he traveled from Jerusalem where he was tolerated as peculiar though harmless, to Gaza, to receive a healing penance from a twenty-year-old Kabbalist named Nathan. Nathan was a young man of genius—a natural theologian, given to bending Kabbalah with the craft of a chess master plying new openings. Sabbatai Ṣevi confessed that now and then, in moments of exaltation, he conceived himself to be the messiah—and Nathan, all at once irradiated, confirmed him as exactly that, conferred on him his mission, and theologized his madness.

The madness expressed itself in what was termed "strange acts." When the mania came on him, the messiah's face grew rosy and glowing, and, lifted up by glory, he would compel his followers to engage in unprecedented and bizarre performances. He made changes in the liturgy, pronounced the unutterable Tetragrammaton, called women to the Ark, married himself to the Scrolls of the Law, turned fasts into feasts; once he crammed three holidays into a single week; another time he declared that Monday was the real Sabbath. The glad tidings of the messianic age began to supersede the Law by eroding its strict practice—prayerbooks were amended to include the new messiah—and meanwhile the awakening to redemption burgeoned among all classes of Jews. One widespread group was especially receptive—

those refugees called Marranos, who had survived the Inquisition in the guise of professing Christians, all the while secretly maintaining themselves as Jews. Their Catholic inheritance had inclined them toward worship of a Redeemer, and their public apostasy prepared them for the strangest of Sabbatai's strange acts: his conversion to Islam.

The political meaning of the ingathering of the exiles into Turkish-held Palestine was not lost on the sultan and his viziers, who smelled, in so much penitence and prayer, a nuance of insurrection. Sabbatai Ṣevi was arrested in Smyrna, where he had come home under the triumphant name of King Messiah, Savior and Redeemer. He was offered one or the other: execution or apostasy. He chose to save his life, and with that one signal tossed thousands of his shocked and disillusioned followers back into the ordinary fact of exile, to be swallowed up once again by unmediated, unmiraculous history. But masses of others, the "believers," continued to nurture their faith: for them the messiah's act was a sacred mystery shielding an arcane purpose. An underground literature and liturgy sprang up; Nathan promulgated a new theology of paradox to account for the apostasy, wherein the inward reality of belief was held to be more forceful than the outer reality of happening. The "true" truth is always the concealed truth. The holiness-at-the-core is the real revelation even when it is clothed in seeming evil. The sacred and the profane change places. The Sabbatians came at length to an astounding prayer: "Blessed art Thou, Lord of the Universe, who permittest that which is forbidden."

The crisis of theology brought on by the messiah's apostasy led the believers to abandonment of traditional rabbinic Judaism, and from there with astonishing directness to Reform Judaism, anarchism, Enlightenment, revolutionary utopianism, nihilism, antinomianism, orgiastic excess—all the stupendously complex, often contradictory, strands of ideology that are implicit in the imagination released from the yoke of Commandment. All this was the effect of illusion. We are not finished with Sabbatianism yet, nor with the bafflements it suggests about the mentality of its heirs (Justice Brandeis was descended from a Sabbatian family), or the antiquity of the impulse nowadays called Zionism, or the psychological atmosphere surrounding the development of Christianity in its earliest years, or the whole history of Christianity over the centuries. The career of Sabbatai Ṣevi hints that every messiah contains in himself, hence is responsible for, all the fruits of his being: so that, for instance, one may wonder whether the seeds of the Inquisition somehow lie even in the Sermon on the Mount.

Scholem's interpretations of these extraordinary matters were in themselves shockwaves for those who depended on the conventional histories. Instead of being merely a false messiah and mystagogue who inflamed a desperate people with his maniacal delusions, Sabbatai Şevi was now seen as a forerunner of the impassioned idealist Zionism of the nineteenth century; and Nathan of Gaza's formulations, instead of being mere popular nonsense, were revealed as the heir to a deep poetical tradition, dense with luxuriant imaginings and an inspired fecundity of moral feeling: the Kabbalists' yearning was to release the encapsulated divine sparks that would cleanse the world of evil. And beyond all that, Scholem maintained that the disintegration of orthodoxy through the development of Sabbatian mysticism led indirectly to circumstances that favored eighteenth-century Enlightenment and nineteenth-century Reform Judaism. This last—rational stirrings growing out of the heart of an intensely nonrational movement—is only one of Scholem's innumerable contributions to fresh seeing. Scholem's magisterial historical intuition, his capacity to enter and overwhelm several philosophical traditions at once, above all his reclamation of Kabbalah, empowered intellectual-rationalist Judaism to reharness the steeds of myth and mysticism, and to refresh the religious imagination at many wells and springs along the way.

These immense ideas, spilling over from Scholem's histories into literature and even into literary criticism, have made Scholem into one of the great modern masters: a knower who, through the scrupulous use of knowledge, refashions and dominates the way we look at ourselves and our notions of the world.

But even these perplexities are not all. The major wonder is about mysticism itself, about human imagination itself, and how it runs free in religion. Scholem and Deuteronomy do not agree; for Scholem, mysticism is endemic in the sacral orchestration of the human mind, and should not be set aside. But Deuteronomy's agnostic wisdom (29:28) concerning the effort to penetrate the nature and purposes of God is antithetical: "The secret things belong to the Lord"—which is to say, they are not for us.

About the paradoxical personality of Gershom Scholem himself, I once speculated in a story:

> The draw of the irrational has its own deep question: how much
> is research, how much search? Is the scientist, the intelligent phy-
> sician, the skeptical philosopher who is attracted to the irrational
> himself a rational being? How explain the attraction? I think of
> that majestic scholar of Jerusalem sitting in his university study
> composing, with bookish distance and objectivity, volume after

volume on the history of Jewish mysticism—is there an objective "scientific interest" or is all interest a snare? Is the hidden cauldron not an enticement and a seduction to its investigator?—Or, to say it even more terribly: it may be that the quarry is all the time in the pursuer.

Accordingly, when I set out to see Scholem, I went with his memoir under my arm, impatient to put a single question—that notorious conundrum all readers who are fascinated by his explorations surrender to: Does the scholar of Kabbalah possess a hidden self (as Kabbalah speaks of a hidden "true" God)? Is there some secret sharer within, an unrevealed soul? Is there, in brief, a shadow-Scholem?

Scholem is quick to answer: "The scholar is never the whole man." Then he does a thing that seems ordinary at the moment, but will turn out to be as tantalizingly wily as a reply from the Delphic oracle—he crosses to his wide scholar's table and hands me a piece of paper, a newspaper review. It concerns Scholem's relations with his great friend, Walter Benjamin. Who Benjamin was, and what he was to Scholem, can be surmised from the dedication prefixed to Scholem's seminal volume, *Major Trends in Jewish Mysticism*: "To the memory of the friend of a lifetime whose genius united the insight of the Metaphysician, the interpretive power of the Critic and the erudition of the Scholar." Benjamin, a breathtaking essayist, a literary thinker drawn to Marxism, unable to share Scholem's Zionist convictions all the way, remained in Europe until it was too late. To avoid being murdered as a Jew he took his own life in 1940, at the age of forty-eight. (Scholem, a Zionist since his teens, arrived in then Palestine in the 1920s.) The two brilliant polymaths pursued their mutually enriching exchanges for years; when they were separated, the talk went on copiously, in stunning essaylike letters. The German edition of their correspondence was reviewed in the London *Times Literary Supplement* by George Steiner. "Perhaps you will find the shadow-Scholem *here*," Scholem says; it is Steiner's review he has put in my hands. Among other stringently mournful speculations, I am astonished to read: "Scholem cannot forgive." I am astonished to read it because it has been delivered over to me as a kind of confession. Or perhaps not. The allusion, in any case, is to the Jews of Germany who deceived themselves into believing Germany would accept and absorb them. Presumably Benjamin was among them.

And it is these Jews—this pitiable phenomenon of a passionately loyal citizenry longing only to be good and peaceable Germans—who comprise the furious hidden text of *From Berlin to Jerusalem*. Writing of the bloodthirsty days of Nazi-dominated Munich, Scholem comments: "I had long since made my decision to leave Germany. But it was frightening to encounter the blindness of the Jews who refused to see and acknowledge all that. This greatly encumbered my relations with Munich Jews, for they became extremely jumpy and angry when someone broached that subject." In Frankfurt, Scholem broke off his friendship with Franz Rosenzweig, the remarkable author of *The Star of Redemption,* a vigorously original meditation on Judaism; in spite of his "intense Jewish orientation," Rosenzweig still hoped for "a Jewish community that considered itself German." "Thus I had," Scholem concludes, "one of the stormiest and most irreparable arguments of my youth." And again: "In view of the task of radical renewal of Judaism and Jewish society, Germany was a vacuum in which we would choke."

It is more than an irony, it is an ongoing wound, that *From Berlin to Jerusalem,* incontestably a Zionist book, continues the fraternal drama in its dedication to the Marxist brother who chose Communist "Humanity" over Jewish fate. But if Werner is not yet absolved, neither is Benjamin. "He paid dearly for his flirtation with Marxism," Scholem tells me. Not far from where we sit in the dining room, a long row of books commands an endless shelf: they are all by Walter Benjamin.

We are having this conversation over lunch in Scholem's house in Jerusalem, on green and flowering Abarbanel Street. The books climb and spread over all the walls of every room. Scholem is famous for loving chocolates, so I have brought some, but warily: he is famous also for knowing which chocolates will do and which won't. "Why am I being bribed?" cries Scholem—a very lofty elf with bold elfin ears and an antic elfin glee advertising tricks and enigmas—and I am relieved that my offering has passed muster. The pilgrimages to this house have been many. The critic Leslie Fiedler has been here. The historian Lucy Dawidowicz has been here. The scholar Yosef Yerushalmi has been here. The novelists Mark Mirsky and Norma Rosen have been here. Jorge Luis Borges has been here, in homage, but Scholem disclaims it: "Borges wrote all his work beforehand, before he read me." Patrick White, the Australian Nobel Prize winner, acknowledges Scholem's influence, particularly in the novel *The Riders of the Chariot.* Yale professor Harold Bloom's startling schematic borrowings, in *Kabbalah and Criticism* and elsewhere, prompt Scholem to quip: "It's a free country."

He seems pleased by these varied manifestations of his authority. What he does object to is the questionable uses his prestige is sometimes put to. "I was naïve," he explains. "I believed that if scholarship came, it would drive out charlatanism. Instead, the charlatans go on as before—only now they use me as a footnote." (The charlatans are presumably occult faddists who have appropriated Kabbalah.) He tells how his work is now frequently subject to a kind of veiled plagiarism: "One man wrote a book on Kabbalah and referred to Scholem in a few footnotes. But all the rest of the book was also Scholem!"

Lunch is cold spinach soup, ambrosial in the perpetually patient sunheat of a Jerusalem afternoon; roast veal in a pastry crust; and, for dessert, Mrs. Scholem's homemade pink ices, concocted of fresh strawberries. The meal is elegant, in an atmosphere new to me—is it the way the light laps over these Biblical hills like some heavy celestial ray, is it a redolence of 1912 Berlin? Mrs. Scholem has been thinking about my question—the question about the shadow-Scholem. She shakes her head; she looks grave, but in a riddling way. "I know what the shadow is. And I found out only three years ago. I know it only three years." It has nothing to do with Benjamin; it has nothing to do with any of that. Will she tell? "No, I won't tell." It is a joke and it is not a joke. Later, when I plead with her to tell after all: "Maybe when I am one hundred years old. Until then I won't tell." Scholem, elfin, enjoying this: "What is 'information'? Nothing at all. Use your judgment. Use your imagination." It is as if he does not mind being invented. We begin to speak of the "theater of the self." "I call myself a metaphysical clown," Scholem says; "a clown hides himself in theater." I ask whether Walter Benjamin ever hid himself that way. "Benjamin never played theater." How much of Professor Scholem is theater? Scholem: "Ask Mrs. Scholem." Mrs. Scholem: "One hundred percent."

We turn over the pages of Scholem's memoir and study the photographs. There is one of Scholem and his three brothers, all of them under the age of fourteen. "His mother called them the four sparrows," Mrs. Scholem supplies. In the picture Gerhard, the smallest, is only six. I am suddenly emboldened to speculate—though not out loud—about the flight of the last sparrow; it seems to me I know by now what the shadow-Scholem must be. It is the shadow cast by the sparrow's wings on the way from Gerhard to Gershom. It is the capacity to make one's life a surprise, even to oneself—to create the content of one's own mind, to turn out to be something entirely unexpected. Nothing in the narrow Berlin of Gershom Scholem's youth prepared him for where he stands now. When, I inquire, did he begin to sense what his destiny would be? He reflects; he resists. And then: "About the age of twenty. You get the feeling of going in a straight line." And how would he account for this realization of a special intellectual calling? The rejoinder is so plain, and yet so obscure, that it shocks, like the throwing of three ordinary stones. "I wanted to learn about Judaism. I wanted to learn Hebrew. I wanted to learn as much as I could." Mrs. Scholem: "He went to the bottom of the question. Curiosity." Scholem: "Yes, curiosity."

But that cannot satisfy. And, in fact, the particulars of Gershom Scholem's journey, as he describes them in *From Berlin to Jerusalem,* do not quite satisfy either, although they are meant to yield the story of "going in a straight line"—they leave out the mystery of self-surprise. Everything strange remains strange. The eccentricity of an education against all likelihood, begun in parental contempt, seized in contradiction of everything influential—society, the times, the drift and pulse of contemporary scholarship, Germany itself—is not unraveled. The secret of how that miraculous rupture and awakening came about, leading to Scholem's rise as one of the whirlwind masters, teachers, wideners and imaginers of our age, is not revealed. The closest Scholem comes to it is in a single sentence. Alluding to his attraction to Kabbalah, he remarks, "Perhaps I was endowed with an affinity for this area from the 'root of my soul,' as the kabbalists would have put it, or maybe my desire to understand the enigma of Jewish history was also involved—and the existence of the Jews over the millennia *is* an enigma, no matter what the numerous 'explanations' may say."

Yet Scholem will go no further in self-disclosure, or even self-conjecture, than he has already gone; perhaps he cannot. "There will be no second volume of memoirs," he warns. This book, another on Walter Benjamin that follows it, and the volume of correspondence with Benjamin—a trinity of biography, autobiography, and portraiture—are all we are to have in the way of personal history.

What the memoir delivers—and it is, after all, a shining little book—is a pageant of characterizations, rife and roiling, in spots diaphanous, elsewhere speedy, skeletal, and spare. It is all a slender chain of shimmering beads on a string: quicksilver sketches of a hundred brilliant encounters—Rubashov, who became Shazar, Israel's third President, living next door to Scholem in a boarding house packed with brainy but impoverished young Russian Jews; the philosophers Martin Buber and Hermann Cohen; Agnon, the Nobel-winning genius whose stories Scholem was the first to translate and to teach; Simmel, the prototypical self-estranged Jewish intellectual (to whom Buber "sometimes pointed out . . . that a man like himself ought to be interested in seeing to it that men of his type did not disappear"); Franz Rosenzweig; numbers of intellectual young women, German, Jewish, and half-Jewish; and glimpses of Benjamin himself. There is plenty of comedy, some of it melancholy, such as Hermann Cohen's comment to Franz Rosenzweig, reproaching the Zionists, "Those fellows want to be happy!"—"the most profound statement," Scholem writes, "that an opponent of Zionism ever made."

Still, everything flashes by with the quirky velocity of picture cards—people (Scholem is sensitive to looks), ideas, influential books (Kafka especially), Talmud study ("the dialogue of the generations"), extraordinary observations. Though crowded with radiant susceptibilities—for learning, for ideals, for intellectual friendships—yet these anecdotal portraits all run by too quickly. What we want from a memoir, I suppose, is something like the sensation of watching Hans Castorp's thoughts open into new depths before our eyes; or the actual texture of a mind in struggle that John Stuart Mill's *Autobiography* chillingly renders. One aches for a Thomas Mann to make a fat Bildungsroman of Scholem's early life—to unfold, for instance, the falling-away of mathematical ambition in the young scholar (who began as a powerful mathematician). What a marvel it would be for those paternal and fraternal crises to play themselves out in dramatic scenes; for the late nights of boarding-house cake-nibbling and philosophy to shout themselves across the page; for the playful and gifted mother who took such twinkling pleasure in writing Scholem's school compositions to draw nearer to us—for every unforeseeable and perplexing wave in Scholem's life to break into novelistic plenitude! But no, the enigma with its aura of conjecture still glimmers—it is there for us to pluck at or reinvent. The shadow persists. The plenitude, and the revelations, are in the work.

HYAM MACCOBY

The Greatness of Gershom Scholem

The study of Jewish mysticism would have offered a tremendous challenge
to any ambitious scholar, but it took a Scholem to realize the true possibilities. For he sensed from the start that these materials were not just a heap
of rubble, requiring a job of scholarly tidying-up. He saw that they constituted an intellectual system of great power which had played a highly important role in the history of Judaism and had indeed contributed to its
continuing vitality. The system was not of the rational or philosophical type,
but was the product of the mythological imagination, which Scholem regarded as an essential element in religion and in community life alike. Not
that he succumbed to the temptation of regarding Jewish mysticism as the
only "true" or authentic Judaism. Rather, he adopted a model of balance,
or dialectical tension, in which mysticism formed one of the opposing poles,
with rationalism forming the other. (Here Scholem differed from both Buber
and Bin-Gorion, who were content to be dislocated from the central movement or balance of Judaism and to identify themselves with dissident or
peripheral trends, thus developing a "counterhistory" of Judaism.)

But the first task, to which Scholem addressed himself with Germanic
thoroughness, was simply to collect the scattered materials of Jewish mysticism, many of which had never been published in printed form. Scholem's
early bibliographical works listed the various manuscripts and books and
thus made an ordered study and assessment possible. The next task was to

From *Commentary* 76, no. 3 (September 1983). © 1983 by the American Jewish
Committee.

bring some method to the dating of these materials and thus to gain an idea of the history and development of mystical theories and notions. This required, above all, accurate philology, i.e., mastery of the language of the documents. Scholem's philological expertise, acquired through unbelievably hard work on the part of one not brought up in Hebrew or Aramaic studies, enabled him to provide convincing solutions to the main puzzles of the documents, and to dispose of the amateurish hypotheses about dating that had hitherto reigned in the field. Thus Scholem was able to work out how Jewish mysticism changed over the course of time. This had never been previously understood. Before Scholem's investigations, Jewish mysticism had been regarded as a seamless whole, both by its devotees and by its opponents—its devotees considering it too holy to be divided into historical periods, its opponents considering it undifferentiated nonsense.

The materials of Jewish mysticism, as Scholem demonstrated, belong in the main to two different periods. In the earlier period, mystical thought centered on the *Merkavah* ("Throne" or "Chariot") of God. This Merkavah mysticism was to be found in the so-called *Hekhalot* tracts, deriving from Palestine, which describe how mystics (identified as talmudic figures like Rabbi Akiva and Rabbi Ishmael) journeyed through the seven heavens, surviving dangers from fearsome angels, to reach the Throne of God where they achieved a vision of the Deity. Such astral journeys, it appears, took place in a trance, induced by fasting and prayers.

The later mysticism is that which is called "Kabbalah," and it underwent its classical development in Spain in the thirteenth century. This kind of mysticism is much more elaborate than the earlier Merkavah mysticism. It contains a complicated system of theosophy by which the nature of God and His mode of creation are explained through the concept of the ten *Sefirot,* or emanations, mediating between God and the world. Rather than trance-experience, Kabbalah comprises a kind of mystical philosophy, demanding study and contemplation. The chief literary work of Kabbalah is the *Zohar,* and on it is based the subsequent history of Jewish mysticism. The *Zohar* inspired new developments, notably the Kabbalah of Isaac Luria (sixteenth-century Palestine), the messianic movement of Sabbatianism (seventeenth century), and the hasidic movement beginning in the eighteenth century. Indeed, so enormous was the impact of the *Zohar* that it was in time accepted by Jews as a divinely inspired work, equal (at least) in status to the Mishnah and Midrash, and surpassed only by the Bible, to which it gave the esoteric key.

Scholem's work on the documents of early Jewish mysticism, or Merkavah mysticism, led eventually to his dating their basic content much earlier than had previously been thought. The beginnings of Jewish mysticism were moved back from the early Middle Ages to the first centuries of the Christian era, thereby confirming the sparse indications in the Talmud of mystical activity within rabbinic circles. This did not mean, however, a reinstatement of the traditional Orthodox view that Jewish mysticism derives from primeval, even antediluvian, times. Unlike the kabbalists themselves, Scholem did not regard the biblical prophets, for example, as mystics. In his view, mysticism was a phenomenon that succeeded the dying away of biblical prophecy, and represented an attempt to bridge the resultant gap between man and God.

Scholem's work on the later Jewish mysticism, or Kabbalah, and its main literary expression, the *Zohar*, resulted not in a confirmation of early origins but, on the contrary, in a demonstration of its medieval character.

Written in Aramaic, once a Jewish vernacular but in the Middle Ages far less well-known than Hebrew and therefore more impressive, the *Zohar* claims as its author a famous sage of the mishnaic period, Rabbi Simeon ben Yohai. He in turn is represented as having learned his secret wisdom from previous sages stretching in an unbroken chain back to Adam; hence this mystical knowledge is given the name "Kabbalah," meaning "tradition." Scholem offered a comprehensive and convincing proof that almost in its entirety the *Zohar* was written by a thirteenth-century author, Moses de Leon, and as an original composition rather than a compilation of previously existing materials. The full proof is one of the most brilliant arguments in the history of literary criticism; it is lucidly summarized in the fifth lecture in Scholem's *Major Trends in Jewish Mysticism* (1941).

To be sure, there had always been those, ranging from the ultra-Orthodox Jacob Emden to the Enlightenment historian Heinrich Graetz, who had denounced the *Zohar* as a forgery (and Graetz had argued that the forger was Moses de Leon). Yet against this, there was the sheer heterogeneity of the *Zohar*, which is more like a whole literature than a single book, comprising not only a commentary on the Torah, but a number of separate treatises, written in apparently different styles, with titles such as "The Book of Concealment" and "The Secret of Secrets." Many scholars had come to the conclusion that the *Zohar* was partly medieval, but that it also contained a nucleus of genuinely ancient material. This plausible hypothesis was the one with which Scholem began his investigations, for it seemed inherently unlikely that one person could have produced such a massive literature on his own. Nevertheless, he finally concluded that this was indeed the case, apart from three components which he declared to be even later than the main body of the *Zohar*, being a rather weak imitation of it by another hand.

What then are *we* to think of the *Zohar*, if it is proved to be a medieval work masquerading as an ancient one? Scholem's reaction was quite different from that of the indignant Graetz. He pointed out that what is called "pseud-epigrahic" literature has played a great part in the history of religions; many books of the Bible and Apocrypha belong to this category. The device of putting one's ideas into the mouth of some great figure of the past is not just a deceitful way of attracting attention, but a method of self-annihilation by which the writer opens himself to thoughts beyond his normal capabilities.

Having solved the question of the authorship and date of the *Zohar*, and having detached this question from the issue of moral blame (for forgery) with which it had been entangled, Scholem was able to look at the *Zohar* as the classical expression of Spanish-Jewish mysticism in its period. Yet far from relegating the Kabbalah to one particular historical age, as its denigrators wished to do, he showed that it was a stage in a continually developing movement of thought, one with both a past and a future.

It was, finally, Jewish mysticism in its full historical development that engaged Scholem's synthesizing intellect. He wished to ascertain the factors that unified the isolated Merkavah mystics of the early talmudic period with the *Zohar*, with the complicated theosophic scheme of Lurianic Kabbalah, with the trauma of Sabbatian messianism, and with the charismatic communal leaders of the hasidic movement of the eighteenth century. In doing so he aimed to show how Jewish mysticism changed from an esoteric by-path on the fringes of the Jewish community to an active communal force capable of influencing the course of Jewish history. This very large project necessitated a scholarly stance very different from the usual specialization in one historical period; it required, in fact, an investigation ranging over eighteen centuries.

Scholem saw in all forms of Jewish mysticism a paradox of rebellion and conservatism. On the one hand, mystics are rebels against the staidness of normative Judaism, with its orderly this-world orientation and its concept of a transcendent God; against this, the mystic tries to create bridges between the lower and the upper worlds. On the other hand, Jewish mystics have been concerned not to abandon Judaism but to revitalize it: to put new meaning into traditional prescriptions, prayers, and practices, and thus to defend them against the encroachments of skepticism. Scholem sees this double aim as setting up a tension that has both threatened the disintegration of Judaism and, at the same time, has enabled Judaism to surmount the dangers of petrification. Only by walking this tightrope has Judaism retained sufficient adventurousness to avoid fossilization. Only by risking disaster has it avoided the greater disaster of grinding to a halt.

Scholem was hardly blind to the dangers of mysticism, or unsympathetic to the arguments against it made at various times by Jewish religious authorities. Although the rabbis of the Talmud did not outlaw mysticism—on the contrary, they greatly respected it—they nevertheless limited it as an activity to a carefully circumscribed elite. And they constantly warned against its perils: the mystic, aiming to ascend to regions far above the humdrum, mundane world, could end with a contempt for ordinary everyday living that amounted to heresy. A famous cautionary story in the Talmud tells of four rabbis who entered the "garden" (*pardes*) of mystical experience; only one of them, Rabbi Akiva, emerged unharmed.

Mysticism in the talmudic period was involved, in a way not yet fully understood, with the doctrine known as Gnosticism, and adherence to this doctrine, the rabbis understood, could lead to complete alienation from Judaism. For there was a tendency to explain the split between the mundane and the spiritual by postulating a split in the universe itself; at its most extreme, this led to a doctrine of Two Powers, the lower of which was the creator of this unsatisfactory earth, while the higher power could be approached only by purging oneself of the dross of the corporeal.

This dualism was Gnosticism proper. Jewish mystics, believing in One God who created the earth, did their utmost to avoid it. Yet their very undertaking made Gnosticism an ever-present danger. Scholem, indeed, was inclined to see the origin of Gnosticism itself in an internal revolt against the "anti-mythological stance" of the Jewish religion, an attempt to put back into the concept of God the color, movement, and narrative interest that had been drained from it by the shift from polytheism to monotheism.

It is certainly true that the Bible has nothing to say about the biography of God or the geography of His dwelling place, while Merkavah literature, with its elaborate angelology and its descriptions of the seven heavens leading to the Throne room of God, does something to supply the need for mythological content. In the subsequent development of Jewish mysticism, the mythologizing urge was given ever more imaginative play, and, as an inevitable consequence, the tendency to dualism increased. In the Kabbalah, God's biography and geography receive fantastic elaboration. God is even provided with a wife, and, eventually, with a cosmic love story, spanning the centuries of past and future, with tragic episodes and a happy ending. The early mystics had voyaged through space to reach the Throne of God; the later mystics voyage through God Himself (they call this the "upper Merkavah"). Geography and biography merge: the seven heavens become transformed into seven regions of God Himself, with further regions to explore beyond.

A strong impetus to the Kabbalah, Scholem argued, was given by the coldness of the categories of Jewish medieval philosophy, in which the anthropomorphisms of the Bible and Talmud were allegorized and rationalized into philosophical abstractions taken from the Aristotelian system. Maimonides' doctrine of the attributes of God can still be discerned under the kabbalistic system of the *Sefirot,* but changed and personalized as if in a dream. The attributes awaken to life and form themselves into strange patterns and relations, some of them sexual. They combine into organic forms—sometimes that of a man, sometimes that of a tree. Instead of philosophizing the anthropomorphisms of Bible, Talmud, and Midrash into abstract categories, the Kabbalah makes them even more concrete, but on a cosmic scale. If the Bible speaks of the "hand" of God, this to the kabbalists is not just a metaphor for His influence on events, but a real hand, so real that all human hands are unreal in comparison, since they achieve what reality they have only by partaking of the reality of God's hand. The Kabbalah thus rebels against the gulf between the spiritual and the material—a gulf created by the very effort of philosophy to generalize and conceptualize.

Rationalism separates, while mysticism denies separation and seeks to demonstrate that the universe forms a continuum. Thus the Kabbalah opposes not only the rationalism of philosophy, but also that of the Talmud, which separates man from God by regarding the commandments of the Torah as applying to the human situation only, and not as a means of affecting the inner essence of God. The commandments in their talmudic elaboration tend to assume the aspect of a mere set of rules, many of them arbitrary, for the patterning of individual and communal behavior. The mystic rebels against this limited role, and reasserts the link between the visible and invisible worlds: the commandments become prescriptions for affecting the life of God and for promoting reconciliations among the various parts of the cosmos. The Kabbalah asserts always that what we experience on earth is what God experiences on high. Our suffering is an adumbration of the cosmic suffering of God. The whole cosmos is yearning to achieve healing and wholeness, and the commandments performed on earth by men have a vital role in bringing about this longed-for denouement.

Yet if all this gives a new urgency and importance to the performance of the commandments, it also sets the stage for their abolition, when they have completed their cosmic task. The very idealization by which the Kabbalah elevates the commandments to mystical or magical status sows the seeds of antinomianism, or the abrogation of Law.

It is in just this way that the Kabbalah had an extraordinary and revolutionary impact on Jewish ideas of the messianic age. The early mysticism of talmudic times, the Merkavah mysticism, had no messianic significance at all, because it was confined to a very small circle of initiates who were interested in obtaining a personal vision of God on His Throne. When, however, after many centuries, Jewish mysticism surfaced again, first in Germany and then in Spain from the eleventh century onward, it had acquired characteristics which were eventually bound to produce an overt messianism of fateful import for future Jewish history.

Spanish Kabbalah contained a theory of history: an account of how the world had been created, what had gone wrong with it, and how it might be put right. In effect, it was a huge magical system by which the initiate might expect to produce effects on a cosmic scale, including the overcoming of the evil powers retarding the coming of the messiah. This new system placed enormous potential power in the hands of the mystic. The magical use of the commandments and prayers at the hands of some great soul (confident or deluded enough to believe that he knew exactly how to turn the key) might cause reconciliations and recombinations in the worlds above that would result in a *tikkun,* or "mending," and this beneficent readjustment of the cosmos would have, as its inevitable corollary on earth, the coming of the messianic age. The mystic did not have to wait patiently for the coming of the messiah, as the rabbis had enjoined; he could do something to make it happen.

These practical potentialities would only be realized on the political stage, however, when the Kabbalah had developed sufficient prestige to foster a mass movement. In the Spanish Kabbalah, this was far from being the case, and mystics were still small in numbers and uninfluential. But the expulsion from Spain in 1492 gave a tremendous shock to the whole Jewish people, and it was in the wake of that shattering event that a new great surge in kabbalistic thought and activity took place, this time in Palestine in the sixteenth century in the town of Safed. It centered on the extraordinary personality of Isaac Luria, known as the Ari. Here the kabbalistic belief in the correspondence of the human and the divine led to the daring doctrine that the disaster of exile and expulsion was not just part of Jewish history but part of the biography of God. In order to create the world, God had had to exile part of Himself from Himself; and this creative withdrawal (*tzimtzum*) or exile was what was being reenacted on earth by Israel. This gave a positive function to the exile that both comforted and stimulated hope;

and new attention was given to the stages of *tikkun*. The personality of Luria, together with the charisma of his gifted circle of followers, leading a holy life in Palestine, captured the interest and devotion of almost the whole Jewish world.

Kabbalistic ideas, for the first time, now became the norm in Jewish rabbinical teaching everywhere, and prayer books were altered to conform with Lurianic notions of the mystical efficacy of prayer and the role of the commandments in uniting the split in the upper worlds and reconciling God with His exiled consort, the *Shekhinah*. Mysticism, from being a solitary activity reserved for the very few in talmudic times, regarded as too dangerous for general knowledge, had become part of the education of every learned Jew.

At the same time, dualistic tendencies already apparent in the *Zohar* received new emphasis in the Lurianic Kabbalah (which was put into writing by Luria's disciples, Luria himself being mostly, like Socrates, a fount of oral, not written, wisdom). The evil against which the mystic pitted himself was not psychological, as in talmudic Judaism, but cosmic, forming (though this was unspoken) a part of the constitution of God Himself. The whole of cosmic history became the story of God purging Himself of evil.

A fascination with the demonic, absent from the classical Judaism of the Bible and Talmud, thus became increasingly a feature of kabbalistic thinking and practice. Judaism now developed a doctrine of Original Sin which stemmed from a period even earlier than the sin of Adam—from the time of the cosmic disaster known as "the breaking of the vessels," a concept invented by Luria.

Our knowledge of this historical development of Jewish mysticism is due, in major part, to the work of Scholem. This work, as I have mentioned, offended many people—the Orthodox because of his late dating of the *Zohar*, and the heirs of the Enlightenment because of his demonstration of the importance of the role of mysticism in Judaism. Scholem's next step, however, was even more unpalatable. He resuscitated the unsavory incident of the pseudo-messiah Sabbatai Sevi, which most people thought best forgotten, and showed that it was of central importance in Jewish history, arising logically and inevitably out of the Kabbalah.

Sabbatai Sevi (1626–76) was a strange and tortured personality who came from a milieu saturated with the concepts of the Lurianic Kabbalah. He alternated between moods of deep depression and moods of manic exaltation, when he thought himself the messiah and exuded a self-confidence that carried all before it. In his moods of exaltation he would commit in public "strange acts" involving the breach of important Jewish laws (for example, he would eat forbidden fat). To these acts, shocking to his audience, he attached a mystical significance; but in his ordinary moods he adhered strictly to all rabbinical and biblical laws.

On his own, Sabbatai Sevi would not have gained widespread adherence. He was dismissed by most people as unbalanced, and he himself believed in his messianic mission only by fits and starts—and even when he believed in it, he was more concerned to provide impressive charismatic exhibitions than to build a movement or engage in the necessities of propaganda. It was only when Nathan of Gaza, a man of great gifts and industry who was widely respected as a scholar and kabbalist, became converted to a belief in Sabbatai that a messianic movement of historical importance became possible. It was Nathan who provided the link with the Lurianic Kabbalah and with the whole previous history of Jewish mysticism, and who brought all the energy of this centuries-old aspect of Jewish religious experience to the exploitation of the compelling contradictions of Sabbatai's character. At the same time, Nathan, accepted as the prophet who by tradition would accompany the messiah, was able to mobilize nonkabbalistic messianic expectations as well. By the time the movement acquired mass support, it had become a mixture of talmudic, folkloristic, and kabbalistic elements capable of appealing to a wide spectrum of the Jewish people.

Gershom Scholem's great work, *Sabbatai Sevi: The Mystical Messiah* (Hebrew, 1957; English translation, 1973) is the apex of his achievement, combining as it does detailed, patient scholarship with his characteristic originality, cutting through the confusions of all previous writers on the subject and leading to new formulations of wide significance for the history of religion. The work is, however, disconcerting in many ways. The Sabbatian movement ended in utter bathos. The messiah-figure who had aroused such hopes throughout the Jewish world, when given the choice of death or conversion to Islam, accepted conversion. This ignoble collapse, for the vast majority of Jews, meant the end of the movement, and it then became of great concern to conceal the extent to which Sabbatai had received both official and mass support. Part of Scholem's work consisted in exposing the extent of this cover-up, and here he aroused the anger of other scholars who felt he had gone too far.

Even more controversial was Scholem's assessment of the antinomian aspect of the Sabbatian movement. He showed how the Sabbatian movement had put forward doctrines usually regarded as the antithesis of Judaism, and yet these doctrines were not repudiated by the learned and pious scholars

who flocked to Sabbatai's banner. For example, Sabbatai claimed divine status by signing his letters "Shaddai," one of the biblical names of God. (He
also made great play of the fact that the name Sabbatai Sevi and "Shaddai"
were equivalent in the system of numerology known as *gematria*.) One would
have thought that, as far as pious Jews were concerned, this would have
spelled an end to his claims; and indeed some Jewish leaders were horrified
by this blasphemy and withdrew their support. But what is surprising is how
many Jewish leaders took this claim to divinity in their stride.

One could argue that the development of the Kabbalah, especially in its
Lurianic form, had prepared the way for this by according the messiah a
cosmic status that he did not have in talmudic Judaism, and also by dividing
the Godhead into so many layers or departments that it was possible to
identify the messiah with one of these aspects without deifying him completely. Nevertheless, the fact is that the very thing that had been held to
make Christianity idolatrous was now accepted without protest by a large
portion of the Jewish people and their leaders. On the basis of this, Gershom
Scholem came to the startling conclusion that there is *no fixed* definition of
Judaism; Judaism is simply everything that it has been historically, and must
therefore include a doctrine of the deification of the messiah, at least as one
of its possible manifestations.

The Sabbatian movement proved similar to Christianity in another important respect: its abrogation of the Torah and declaration of the advent
of a new law. This aspect was not fully developed in the lifetime of Sabbatai
Sevi himself; yet he did introduce many innovations of a liturgical character,
incorporated new festivals, and by his own performance of "strange acts"
signalized that there could be mystical power in the breaking of the law as
well as in its observance. This clear tendency to antinomianism was, however,
again accepted by the majority as within their understanding of the character
and function of a messiah.

After the apostasy and death of Sabbatai Sevi, these antinomian tendencies were intensified by those who remained faithful to his memory. The
whole Torah was regarded as abrogated, or at most as in force only until
the expected return of the messiah. Many Sabbatians regarded Sabbatai's
apostasy as itself an act of mystical significance, the last of his "strange
acts," and decided to follow his example. They formed the Dönmeh sect,
continuing to believe in Sabbatai secretly while outwardly behaving as Mus-
lims—a weird regression to the condition of the Marranos under Christianity. Finally, the Sabbatian sect known as the Frankists turned antinomianism
into a regime of sexual license and deliberate ceremonial breaches of Jewish
law. Their "sanctification" of sin, together with their gnostic theology, made

them the spiritual heirs of such gnostic libertine sects of the ancient world as the Carpocratians.

Scholem wrote with a certain sympathy even about the wildest excesses of Sabbatian antinomianism, with its doctrine of salvation through sin. For he saw this development as a logical and understandable outcome of the anarchic forces within the Kabbalah—forces which were invoked for the defense of Judaism against rationalism but which contained their own destructiveness. Moreover, he characteristically considered Sabbatianism a creative as well as a destructive force. By breaking the mold of the Law, it released new energies and new religious and political possibilities. Scholem pointed out the part taken by Sabbatians, or ex-Sabbatians, in the French Revolution; and also what he claimed was a strong Sabbatian influence in the growth of the Reform movement in Judaism—a movement usually regarded as rationalist in the extreme, far removed from mystical fantasies. According to Scholem, the genesis of new ways of thought is more catastrophic and agonized than later beneficiaries suppose; the Enlightenment itself owed more to kabbalistic and neoplatonic occultism than to sober common sense. When one looks at the maelstrom of ideas underlying the discoveries of Kepler and Newton, one is forced to agree.

Indeed, the rise of modern science, as Alexander Altmann and others have pointed out, owes much to the Kabbalah. Normative Judaism, preoccupied with morality and the duties of family and community life, kept its gaze on this world and dismissed cosmological speculation with the talmudic injunction against asking "what is above, what is beneath, what was before, and what will be hereafter." The Kabbalah, turning its gaze from earth to heaven, produced a daring cosmological scheme of soaring range, precursor of the vast schemes of modern astronomy and atomic physics. Even more important, the Kabbalah was concerned with hidden *forces* in the universe, and with the possibility of harnessing and manipulating them; this has been the key concept of modern science and the secret of its power. So it was paradoxically the irrationalism of mysticism, rather than the rationalism of Talmudism, that turned out to have more in common with the ultra-rationalism of science.

Scholem's work on the paradoxically creative power of antinomianism aroused opposition from many quarters. He was accused of glorifying antinomianism, and also of exaggerating its part in the fundamental thought of the Kabbalah. Here there was considerable misunderstanding. Scholem called himself a "religious anarchist," but he did not mean by this that he sided with the antinomians. He meant that he did not believe that there was a norm or orthodoxy in Judaism in comparison with which all other trends were to be condemned as heresies or as inauthentic. Any trend that made use of Jewish concepts and that did not seek to turn people away from Judaism (as, for example, Christianity did) was part of the whirlpool that formed the historical reality of Judaism, showing its vitality by the ceaseless opposition, conflict, and ebb and flow of ideas. The later forms of Sabbatianism, by their utter rejection of Orthodoxy, made the same error of one-sidedness as did the rigid Orthodox who sought to repudiate the vivifying concepts of Jewish mysticism. The health of Judaism lay in the interplay of opposites, and thus in the acceptance of the whole of Jewish tradition, not just part of it.

The later history of the Kabbalah was seen by Scholem as an attempt to recover from the destructiveness unleashed by Sabbatianism. The hasidic movement of the eighteenth century retained the Lurianic and Sabbatian concept of a kabbalism-for-the-masses rather than for a circle of mystical initiates, but the dangerous, antinomian genies released by this concept were put back into the bottle. The Law was reasserted, and new effort was put into the "joy of the commandment." To this end, Scholem argued, it was essential to play down, or "neutralize," the messianic aspect of Kabbalism. In Hasidism, the messianic fervor and sense of renewal that Sabbatianism had created were internalized, and divorced from overt political action. The tzaddik, or communal leader, became a kind of interim messiah, presiding over his Hasidim in a timeless little enclave in which it was "always Sabbath." The feeling of near-worship of Sabbatai Sevi was transferred to the tzaddik in his particular circle, but without the universal reference that could lead to actual deification. Hasidism, therefore, was a kind of watered-down Sabbatianism, owing its tone to the previous, now-discredited movement.

This was a characterization that gave great offense to present-day Hasidism, who hotly denied any historical or theoretical link with Sabbatianism. And Scholem also "offended" against the conception of Hasidism made popular by Martin Buber as a mysticism that glorified everyday life. Scholem sharply criticized this as an idealization which ignored the gnostic influence filtered through the Lurianic and Sabbatian movements. Hasidism, he wrote, did not actually glorify everyday life but considered it to be sunk in the power of evil (the "husks" or kelipot, left over from the "breaking of the vessels"); it was the duty of the Hasid to redeem all everyday things from these demonic influences. In Scholem's view, Buber lacked a historical sense and was unaware of the continuous tradition of Jewish mysticism, which he preferred to regard as a series of unconnected outbreaks of invaluable mystical insight.

Scholem's conflict with Buber was not merely a matter of the scholar correcting the romantic. Scholem too was a romantic, although of a different kind—a kind for whom accurate historical scholarship provided the necessary fuel. This leads to the interesting question of Scholem's own beliefs. Should we think of him merely as the historian of Jewish mysticism, recording its vicissitudes with academic detachment, or was he himself more deeply involved? There is certainly no question of Kabbalism in the traditional sense, which could only rest on a fundamentalist belief in the *Zohar* as an ancient work. Scholem never disguised his judgment that the Kabbalah represents a way of thinking that is now thoroughly outdated. Nevertheless, he held that it should be studied not merely as a dead historical phenomenon but as an ingredient in our own intellectual and spiritual lives.

That ingredient is not so much philosophical as mythical. Whereas normative Judaism struggles to be anti-mythological, setting a space between God and man, the Kabbalah (and its antecedent, Merkavah mysticism) seeks a place for myth. In the consequent conflict between myth and anti-myth lies the vitality of Judaism. Scholem did not regard myth (or mysticism) as a single universal phenomenon, as Aldous Huxley did in speaking of the "Perennial Philosophy." Each manifestation of myth is specific to a particular culture and is saturated with the historical experience of that culture. Jewish myth and mysticism, despite many details borrowed from outside, form a specifically Jewish phenomenon.

Scholem owed a considerable intellectual debt here to the ideas of Jung, which he encountered in the circle of Erich Neumann, the founder of the journal *Eranos*—though, characteristically, Scholem was never a full member of this circle, but participated in its gatherings only as an interested onlooker. Jung believed that the individual psyche contained two poles, rationality and myth, which always sought equilibrium: an excess of rationality would lead inevitably to a compensating swing to mythical thinking. This is the pattern that Scholem applied to the collective Jewish psyche.

Scholem, however, did not invoke particular psychoanalytic concepts, such as Jung's archetypes, or Freud's Oedipus complex, to explain Jewish mysticism; he considered such an approach reductivist. The phenomena of Jewish mysticism are for the most part communal rather than individual; to interpret them as the outcome of psychological conflicts on the individual level would be like trying to explain art in terms of atomic physics. Like the sociologist Emile Durkheim, Scholem regarded the world of communal life as more than just the aggregate of the individual lives of which it is made up.

And here, on the issue of the individual versus the community, we touch on the relationship between Scholem the scholar and Scholem the Zionist. It is in this relationship, I believe, that the real bond between Scholem and Jewish mysticism is to be found. For there was something mystical in Scholem's philosophy of Zionism.

Scholem thought of the Jewish historical entity as forming an organism with its own life and principles of development. His quarrel with the *Wissenschaft des Judentums* was that it treated Judaism as a corpse to be dissected. The selectivity of *Wissenschaft* scholars in choosing for study only those aspects of Judaism which could bear scrutiny by the respectable German bourgeoisie was, in Scholem's eyes, motivated by the desire not so much to "bring Judaism up to date" as to abide by the pious maxim, *de mortuis nil nisi bonum*. Moritz Steinschneider, one of the major luminaries of the *Wissenschaft* school, actually said openly that his task was to give the remains of Judaism a decent burial. Scholem reacted against this notion with all the force of his being.

Not only did his scholarship differ from that of the *Wissenschaft*, but his Zionism too differed from the Zionism of those who repudiated the history of the Diaspora and thought of themselves as making an entirely new start. He regarded Zionism as something both new and very old: as a new expression of the ancient energies of the Jewish national organism, and as further proof of the ability of that organism to perpetuate itself by fresh responses to the challenges of history. Zionism itself, moreover, was an assertion, made by the Jewish national organism, of the same kind that had been made unequivocally by the Kabbalah when it claimed an eternal, even divine, status for the Jewish nation (by identifying it with the *Sefirah* called *Malkhut* and with the *Shekhinah*). Further, Scholem saw the Kabbalah as the historical precursor of Zionism—in a way that could not be predicated of normative, non-mystical Judaism. For the Kabbalah had not waited passively for the exile to end in God's good time, but had grappled agonizingly with the fact of exile, had given it metaphysical status, and had prepared a technique and a timetable for ending it and breaking through to a new mode of national being. This, in the Sabbatian movement, had led to disaster, but the breaking of the orthodox mold thus achieved had prepared the way for political Zionism.

For Scholem, as we have seen, this was the pattern of progress: creativeness was attained only through destruction and disaster, in which, however, the traditional was not repudiated but transformed. It is thus not surprising (at least in retrospect) that the young Scholem, inspired with Zionist feeling, should have reached out for a form of Judaism which he instinctively knew to have in it the seeds of destruction and creation, the

movement of life and new birth, despite its outward appearance of uncouth-
ness and even weirdness. It was by no means the choice of an academic,
looking for a "subject" in which he could make his mark, but rather a
spiritual choice and commitment.

Scholem had a vision of the wholeness of Jewish experience, and it was
this vision, especially as it affected his deep attachment to Zionism, which
acted as the motivation of his stupendous effort of scholarship. But it is
necessary to distinguish sharply between this vision of wholeness and the
relativism which has often been advocated in other branches of modern
Jewish scholarship. Scholem attacked the idea of a "normative" Judaism in
the sense of a dominant strain or direction of thought against which all other
tendencies were deemed insignificant. But he did not seek to negate all unity
or discernible pattern in Jewish history, or to divide off succeeding ages or
generations in such a way as to deny their continuity one with the next.
Least of all did he try to explain succeeding movements solely in terms of
the social, economic, or sociological substrata prevailing at the time. His
main aim was to display the *dialectical* character of Jewish culture: the presence within it of a perennial conflict between the forces of conservation and
the forces of change, or between reason and instinct, or between orthodox
theology and mythology (all ways of putting the same thing). In place of a
single tradition, he postulated *two* traditions, each with its history and continuity—a tradition of orthodoxy and a tradition of dissent, or, in Freudian
terms, a tradition of the ego and a tradition of the id. These were in continual
conflict, but the conflict itself was another tradition.

It is only at this point that one may suggest certain limitations in Scholem's approach. For him, talmudic Judaism is the domain of the ego, while
mysticism is the domain of the id. But is this quite correct? Talmudic Judaism, after all, has its own dialectic, of halakhah (law) and aggadah (lore).
How does this opposition relate to the dialectic of Talmudism and Kabbalism?

The aggadah is the mythology of the Talmud, the embodiment of its
abstract ideas in stories, picturesque, impossible, and wild. Only part of this
aggadah, however—indeed, a very small part—is mystical in character.
Whereas the Kabbalah, as it developed in the Middle Ages, regarded itself
as the heir of the aggadah and made it even more wild by giving it an entirely
mystical meaning, the aggadah of the Talmud is developed in the service of
non-mystical ideas. The Talmud's is a kind of humanistic mythology that
gives a background of dream and instinctual passion to ideas that are essen-

tially rational: an example is the extraordinary story of the journey through time made by Moses to attend a lecture given by Rabbi Akiva, which he is unable to understand. (This little myth validates the concept of change and progress in the Oral Law.) But besides little humanistic myths, there are the big myths too, which are based on the Bible: the myth of the expulsion from Eden and of the Exodus from Egypt.

Such myths give subliminal support to the values that are articulated more explicitly in the halakhic portions of talmudic Judaism, and these, I would argue, are the values of adulthood. Mystical myths, by contrast, are a flight to infancy, or even as far back as the womb, since they are all concerned to break down the separations set up by individuality and personal relations. Such a flight is not ruled out by the Talmud. Indeed, it is conceded as one of the possibilities of the psyche, albeit one that can lead to knowledge of so basic a kind that it threatens the whole psychic structure, and must therefore be kept within strict bounds. But the Talmud's own characteristic "mysticism" is of the type which Buber incorrectly attributed to the Hasidim: the "normal mysticism" (this term is actually a coinage of Max Kadushin) which achieves closeness to God not by prying into His internal constitution or seeking incorporation into His mysteries, but by going about His business in the affairs of everyday life.

The question, then, is whether the Kabbalah should be regarded not as the unconscious mind of Judaism, but rather as its psychosis. To ask this question is not to return to a pre-Scholem attitude of amnesia and repression, by which the whole tradition is dismissed as if it had never existed. The Kabbalah's space-flight through the geography of God is a descent into the abyss of the human mind and a daring exploration of the origins of creativeness. Nevertheless, to elevate the Kabbalah into a constitutive pole of the dialectic of Judaism may be to accord it too high a status. In order to endow it with this status, Scholem had to exaggerate the indigenousness of the Kabbalah and to play down (though he did not entirely ignore) the derivation of many of its elements from outside sources, such as Neoplatonism, Albigensianism, and indeed Christianity in general. The origins of Christianity itself, Scholem hints (though he never fully argues), can be understood in the light of the career of Sabbatai Sevi. The parallel between Sabbatai Sevi and Jesus, however, is very imperfect (the parallel between Nathan of Gaza and Paul is much stronger). The similarities can best be explained not by postulating a parallel evolution out of the dialectic of Judaism but rather by the direct influence of Christianity on Judaism.

Scholem's distaste for the idea of a "normative Judaism" and his reaction against German selectivity can lead to an unwillingness to acknowledge outside influence, and therefore to a reluctance to distinguish the authentic from the inauthentic. Even Scholem had to admit to reservations concerning the superstitiousness and demon-haunted dualism of Polish Hasidism; here he was almost forced to the point of admitting that some forms of Jewish existence could be inauthentic. But to admit this even in one case is to concede a point of principle: that there is an essence of Judaism in the light of which various Jewish manifestations (for example, Sabbatai Sevi's assumption of divine status) can be judged, and if necessary, condemned. Such an essence is not "normative" in the institutional sense; we may be led by it to condemn aspects of orthodox as well as unorthodox Judaism. But acknowledging it does allow us to retain the possibility of characterizing Judaism as a doctrine or attitude toward life in general, and hence to recognize the universalist implications that reside within the organic national entity that is Judaism. For if there is one thing that has always been characteristic of Judaism, it has been the refusal to identify God entirely with the Jewish people, or to sink into any kind of nationalist idolatry.

Scholem's Nietzschean view of creativity-through-destructiveness certainly has biblical support, in the apocalyptic picture of the "day of the Lord" when great catastrophes will be the prelude to a new dimension of life. Scholem pointed out that this apocalyptic view of the messianic age has alternated in Judaism with a more gradualist view, typified by the rationalist Maimonides, that the messianic age will be continuous with life as we know it and will not necessarily involve cosmic catastrophe. The controversy is strangely similar to that between revolutionary Marxists and gradualist socialists. The apocalyptic view is associated with a deep consciousness of crisis, while the rationalist view is associated with optimism about the possibility of human control of the processes of history.

Scholem may not be correct in identifying the gradualist view with strict adherence to the status quo, or in crediting catastrophism with the creative role. It is by no means clear that the talmudic vision of ordered, peaceful progress is less potent for change than the crisis theology of the Kabbalah— even though, in times of *actual* crisis, the Kabbalah does seem more relevant. We may well take a view typical of talmudic exegesis—that the catastrophic picture of the messianic age is what will happen if humanity deserves no better, while the rationalist picture is what could happen in the admittedly unlikely event that humanity achieves control of its destiny.

For after all, the catastrophic view of the Last Days, associated as it is with the idea of a radical change in the human soul, is in effect a cry of despair over human nature as it is, a prediction, or hope, that God will eventually admit the failure of His human experiment and substitute something more viable. This is a view into which Judaism has often lapsed. But its more durable, and characteristic, view, as projected in the basic myth of the Exodus, is not so deeply pessimistic. Scholem himself, in his political standpoints within the Zionist movement, always stood for control, reason, and optimism, and not for the vertigo of fanatical, magical messianism. Though he did not assign to rationalism the chief creative role in Jewish history, his intellectual practice was that of a rationalist Jew.

These reservations, however, cannot affect Scholem's magnificent achievement of historical reconstruction. After his work, we can no longer think of the history of Judaism as one of outer tribulations but inner calm. The Jewish psyche has been swept by storms of conflict and passion that have brought it almost to the breaking point, while at the same time acquainting it with the heights of human experience. The healing processes of sanity have intervened not only to redirect but also to conceal. Scholem has told the truth fearlessly, and has thus helped us toward a kind of sanity that incorporates within itself the insights made possible only through an understanding of madness.

JOSEPH DAN

Gershom Scholem's Reconstruction
of Early Kabbalah

The historians of Jewish thought who preceded Gershom Scholem were perplexed by a major problem: how to reconcile the fact of the appearance of the first schools of the kabbalah in the late twelfth century with the fact that the period was also the one in which Jewish philosophy, and especially Jewish rationalistic philosophy, reached its peak? How can a historian accept that the first Jewish scholars who dealt in kabbalistic, mythological symbolism, were contemporaries of Maimonides and wrote the first kabbalistic treatises at the same time that Moses ben Maimon was writing his *Guide to the Perplexed*? How could two such extremes exist in the same cultural and historical circumstances?

The problem was especially acute for historians like Heinrich Graetz, who viewed the kabbalah as inherently un-Jewish and polytheistic, the opposite of everything he regarded as meaningful and important in Jewish culture. For Graetz and those of his mind-set the kabbalah represented everything that Judaism should not be, while, alternatively, Maimonidean philosophy was seen as the culmination of Jewish rationalistic monotheism in its purest form. It seemed that the appearance of the kabbalah was timed by an invisible hand exactly to the precious moment of the supreme victory of Jewish rationalistic philosophy, when the spirit of Judaism achieved, at last, its utmost refinement. Naturally enough, Graetz and other Jewish nineteenth century rationalists had to explain away the appearance of the kabbalah as

From *Modern Judaism* 5, no. 1 (February 1985). © 1985 by the Johns Hopkins University Press.

the re-emergence of ancient paganism, and as a reactionary response to the
great achievements of Jewish philosophy. In these circumstances, a serious,
impartial investigation of the background and emergence of the early circles
of kabbalists in Europe was impossible.

Another approach to the problem with which Scholem dealt was that
of the historian of Jewish philosophy David Neumark, who was active in the
first decades of our century. Neumark believed that the elements of irrationalism, mysticism and mythology were always present within Judaism, and
that they emerged in the twelfth and thirteenth century in response to the
atmosphere created by Jewish rationalism. Neumark presented his views in
great detail, supported by impressive erudition and insight. But neither he
nor Graetz could view the kabbalah as an entity justified by and in itself,
possessing its own internal religious and cultural values and meaning. They
believed that the appearance of the kabbalah could not be but a response to
the greater, more important and religiously perfect phenomenon of philosophical rationalism.

It is characteristic of Gershom Scholem's approach to historical problems
and to the work of previous scholars that he did not deny their insights and
claims completely, even though he rejected their attitude towards the kabbalah without reservation. There was in the early kabbalah an element of
response and reaction to Jewish philosophy as Graetz argued; there was in
the kabbalah an element which can be correctly described as the re-emergence
of ancient mythological symbolism which used and transformed philosophical terminology into mystical symbols, as Neumark explained. Scholem did
not disregard these arguments; rather he corrected them by incorporating
them into a more complete and well-rounded picture based on all pertinent
data.

The central fact that Scholem found in the various manuscripts that
preserved the ancient traditions of the early kabbalists was that in the great
centers of Jewish scholarship in Southern France, in Languedoc, a mystical
tradition appeared in the twelfth century. A story about the appearance of
the prophet Elijah in these schools and his revealing great secrets to the
heads of the academies was repeated so often that it could not be declared
a legend and nothing else, especially as the kabbalists preserved certain kabbalistic ideas and quotations of these early mystics, quotes that philological
analysis has shown could, indeed, have been uttered by the early rabbis of
the Provence. The important point that Scholem noted about these traditions
was that they did not speak about a messenger from afar (like Aaron of
Baghdad in Italy and Germany), nor about the revelation of an ancient book
(like the *Bahir*), but about the revelation of the Holy Spirit and the prophet

Elijah; that is, no foreign element seems to have been involved, but, rather, the pertinent new ideas were the product of these Provençal academies, of those distinguished local sages who dealt mainly in *halachah* in the most traditional manner, and who served as leaders to the communities in which they lived.

The first clear kabbalistic traditions which have come down to us are from Rabbi Abraham ben David, known by the acronym the Ravad, who was the greatest talmudic authority in Southern France in the second half of the twelfth century. The quotations that later kabbalists preserved from the Ravad deal with problems such as the creation of the world and the intentions in prayers, and reveal a use of kabbalistic symbolism in an elementary form, probably not yet systematized. The Ravad is especially known for his critique of Maimonides' code of law, the *Mishneh Torah,* and his critical remarks are traditionally printed beside the Maimonidean text. Most of these remarks deal with purely halachic matters, but a few of them have ideological differences at their base. The most important among them is the one opposing Maimonides' declaration that belief in a God who has anthropomorphic characteristics is heresy. The Ravad wrote in response to Maimonides: "some great people, greater than you, believed in this fashion," though he was careful not to include himself in this group. This statement, it should be noted however, need not have been motivated necessarily by kabbalistic mythology; it could be merely a reflection of the fact that a literal understanding of biblical and talmudic anthropomorphism was widespread in this period.

The earliest complete work of kabbalah whose author is known to us is the *Commentary on Sefer Yezirah* by Rabbi Isaac Sagi Nahor ("The Blind"), the son of the Ravad and the accepted leader of the early kabbalists. He was called "the pious," and even mentioning his name was superfluous; everybody knew who "the pious" was. His commentary on *Sefer Yezirah* is a mature, complicated and profound work of kabbalah, which includes most of the basic kabbalistic symbolism concerning the process of creation. According to Rabbi Isaac and all other kabbalists, creation is first and foremost the process of the emanation of the ten divine powers or attributes, the ten *sefirot.* The names and symbols which describe the *sefirot* in this work of Rabbi Isaac are those which became most current in later kabbalah—unlike those of the *Book Bahir,* which are, to some extent, unique to that early text.

Rabbi Isaac became the leader and the teacher of the next generation of kabbalists in the Provence and, especially, in the small town of Gerona in Catalonia, not far from Barcelona. It seems that the kabbalists in northern Spain, which was under Christian control, saw themselves as the disciples of Rabbi Isaac, corresponded with him, listened to his advice and followed his directions. Parts of this correspondence were discovered and published by Scholem, who analyzed them in great detail in order to exhaust the precious historical information contained in them, for this is one of the very few sources for the history of the first stage of the development of the kabbalah.

In these two centers, the Provence first and then Gerona, the most important ideas of the kabbalah were formulated, its systems of symbols received shape, and its struggle with the religious needs of the Jewish people in the Middle Ages began. From these two centers emerged the message that the kabbalah had for Jewish intellectuals of that time, and for the whole of the Jewish people in later centuries.

II

The early kabbalists in the Provence and in northern Spain developed their mystical traditions in an environment in which Jewish philosophy reigned supreme. The intellectual language of Aristotelian philosophy and its terminology were in frequent usage, and Platonic and neo-Platonic ideas were current among Jewish thinkers. While the authors of the *Book Bahir* seem to have been almost completely free of such influences, the mystics in the kabbalistic schools of Europe could not avoid, and probably did not wish to avoid, these intellectual influences.

Since the first years of the thirteenth century the works of Maimonides had aroused controversy within the Jewish world, especially in the Provence. Criticism began with the analysis of the attitude of Maimonides towards messianic redemption and, especially, the belief in the resurrection. The controversy spread quickly, especially after the Hebrew translations of the *Guide to the Perplexed* became known, and the whole scope of Maimonidean philosophy and its implications concerning Jewish beliefs were apparent. In the years 1232 to 1235 a great controversy, which engulfed Jewish scholars from Spain, France and Germany, raged and became one of the most important historical events in the history of Jewish thought in the Middle Ages.

In that controversy some of the most prominent kabbalists of the period took part. One of them, Rabbi Jonah Gerondi, who was a vehement critic of Maimonides, had a part in the beginning of the whole controversy. There was some doubt whether he was a kabbalist, but a letter of Rabbi Isaac the Blind to the kabbalists in Gerona seems to demonstrate conclusively that indeed he was, even though his extant works deal exclusively with ethical problems in a manner devoid of kabbalistic terminology and symbolism. The fact that a member of the Gerona circle of kabbalists was one of the instigators of this controversy is suggestive enough; but he was not alone.

Rabbi Moses ben Nachman, known as Nachmanides, the great commentator on the Torah, was the leader of northern Spanish Jewry at this time as well as the leader of the Gerona circle of kabbalists. There is no doubt about his central place in the development of the kabbalah. The cryptic kabbalistic notes which he included in his commentary served many kabbalists in later generations; commentaries were written on them, and his authority was so great that several kabbalistic works written by other mystics were attributed to him. Nachmanides had a most active role in the controversy. In its beginning he attempted to pacify the various factions and to minimize the differences. Soon, however, he came under attack by the rationalists and was forced to join the opponents of Maimonides.

Scholem emphasized, when discussing this period, that the problem of the role of the kabbalah as such, not only of individual kabbalists who had other roles as well, in the controversy against the rationalistic philosophy of Maimonides should be thoroughly investigated. He himself did not complete a specific study on the subject, but left no doubt concerning his view that the early kabbalists saw themselves, to some extent, as being under an obligation to stop Jewish rationalism from reaching an extreme position intellectually and achieving a dominant place in Jewish culture.

While the problem of the historical involvement of the kabbalists in the controversy around Jewish rationalistic philosophy is most important with regard to an understanding of the social and historical attitude of these mystics, there is another problem which has a bearing on the very content of the teachings of these mystics: their attitude towards philosophy as such, and their use of philosophical ideas and terminology in the formulation of their own mystical symbolism.

A kabbalist who wrote towards the end of that century, Rabbi Moses of Burgos, said concerning the relationship between Jewish philosophy and kabbalah: "our feet stand where their heads are," meaning that the mystics begin where the philosophers end their deliberations. This dictum also claims that there is nothing wrong in philosophy itself; the problem is that the philosophers do not go far enough or that they stop too soon. Kabbalists like Rabbi Moses of Burgos saw themselves as building a theology for which philosophy may serve as a starting point or a basis but from which foundation one must then proceed in non-philosophical ways.

It seems that while Rabbi Moses's dictum is a relatively late one the attitude it reveals was familiar to the early kabbalists in the Provence and in Spain. Sections in the works of early kabbalists like Rabbi Azriel of Gerona could be read as philosophical treatises, especially as far as terminology is concerned. The very distinctive language of the Tibbonite translations of the major works of Jewish philosophy had enormous impact on kabbalistic literature, and their symbolism is often formulated in the same manner.

It is not only the external appearance of kabbalistic language and terminology which reveals the influence of Jewish philosophy. The mystical symbols themselves reflect this impact, though it is important to note the differences as well as the similarities. In contrast to the *Book Bahir,* the works of the kabbalists of Gerona may seem like a rejection of, or withdrawal from, mythological and gnostic formulations and the construction of a "philosophical" mysticism. Scholem has shown, in great detail, in his study of the works of Rabbi Isaac the Blind, and particularly in his analysis of the works of the Gerona circle, that the kabbalists indeed philosophized some of the ideas and symbols that they received in their mystical tradition, but at the same time introduced deep mystical layers into the rationalistic terminology being employed.

The most important field in which mysticism and philosophy collided in this era, while using similar terminology, was in their understanding of the *sefirot,* the ten divine attributes of the Divine in the kabbalistic system, and their hidden, sublime source in the Godhead, called by them *en sof,* "no end." *En sof* was regarded by the kabbalists as a divine realm beyond all description, which cannot even be given a symbol based on any scriptural term, for it is not directly mentioned in the bible. The appelation "no end" was regarded as an accidental term, which has no specific significance; it could as well be called "no beginning" or "no color" or any other negative appelation. It is not a symbol nor a description of a characteristic; just a convenient phrase to refer to something which is far beyond any reference in human language.

This *en sof* is the supreme Godhead, the source of all existence, the beginning of the divine realm, the eternal divine power which was not changed by the creation and will never change. Though it is the source of the divine influence over the world it has no connection with the world and is not influenced by it in any way. A mystic may strive to uplift his soul to the divine hierarchy from one stage to another, but he can never form any mystical contact with the *en sof,* which cannot be touched by anything out of itself. It is not counted among the divine powers, and no mythological terminology, as, for example, that found in the *Bahir,* can ever apply to it.

This picture of the Godhead is reminiscent, to a very large extent, of the philosophical description of the Aristotelian primal cause, the "unmoved mover," the "thought which only thinks itself" and all the other terms used to describe the source of everything, the supreme divinity, in medieval Aristotelian thought. There can be little doubt that the kabbalists in Europe used the philosophical concept in order to describe and characterize their supreme divine power.

To a lesser extent, the same could be said about the ten *sefirot* which emanate from the *en sof* according to these mystics. The concept "emanation" itself is an idea received by the mystics from philosophy, especially from neo-Platonic philosophy, which had a most profound impact on Jewish mysticism as it had on Christian mysticism of late antiquity and the Middle Ages. The vision of the Godhead as an enormous source of light, spreading around itself diminishing circles of light each outside the other, is a central one to the mystics as it was to the neo-Platonic philosophers.

The Jewish mystics in the Provence and Gerona accepted this basic neo-Platonic picture but introduced into it elements which are not found in the philosophical formulations, especially the element of dynamism. That is, while the philosophers usually described a permanent, fixed, structure of the descending steps from the hidden Godhead to the earthly realm the mystics saw an element of movement and change in the same process. The various emanated powers in the mystical structure could undergo processes of rising or falling, of diminishing and enlargement, of intense relationships between them of a mythological nature. And this dynamism allowed, even forced, the kabbalists to generate a more profound and variegated symbolism than was present in philosophical systems.

The structure of the ten *sefirot* themselves is also reminiscent of a philosophical issue—the divine attributes. Some of the *sefirot* are called by the kabbalists by names which include ethical connotations, like Justice, Mercy and Compassion, as we also find in the terminology of some philosophers who defined the ethical maxims not as characteristics of the Godhead but as attributes of divine action in the lower realms. There is a close connection between these two systems and there can hardly be any doubt that the formulation of the system of the ten *sefirot* and their relationship to their source, the *en sof,* in the process of emanation all carry the signs of the profound impact of Jewish philosophical formulations on the works of the early kabbalists.

It should be remembered, however, that while the kabbalistic description of the *sefirot* was influenced by philosophical terminology the system of the *sefirot* is not dependent on that terminology. The *sefirot* as a system of symbols preceded this influence, as witnessed by their description in the *Book Bahir.*

This fact reminds us that it would be a mistake, as Scholem often stressed, to imagine that because the early kabbalah assumed a philosophical garb, and even though the content of some of its symbols reveal the impact

of Jewish philosophy, that, as some nineteenth century Jewish scholars contended, the kabbalah is nothing but a reaction to Jewish philosophy. It must
be remembered that the kabbalah almost certainly existed in some way before
it came into contact with the terminology of the philosophers and that while
in thirteenth century Provence and Spain it did assume the characteristics of
the culture of that time and place it was not dependent on them for its self-
definition. In the coming generations the kabbalah would revert to a mythological symbolism which was very far from the systems adopted and
adapted by the Gerona kabbalists.

III

Some space should be dedicated to the elucidation of the term "symbolism," so often used here to describe kabbalistic terminology and so fundamental to the understanding of Gershom Scholem's explanation of the
nature and development of the kabbalah.

According to Scholem, a "symbol" in the context of the kabbalah is a
term or a description about which nothing further can be said in human
language. It is the maximum linguistic approximation to something which
is actually and permanently beyond full expression by language. Symbols are
terms used not to express what we know but to denote the fact that we
know almost nothing about the substance behind the symbol.

The term "emanation" can serve as a very good example of this necessary feature of kabbalistic symbolism. In Hebrew it is called *azilut* which
is a medieval Hebrew term which evolved, most probably, under the impact
of Jewish philosophy; Scholem found its first appearance in Hebrew in a
poem by Rabbi Judah ha-Levi. Later it was extensively used by the Tibbonites
in their translations of the masterpieces of Jewish philosophy into Hebrew,
translations which were made for the sake of Jewish scholars in the Provence
who were not familiar with the Arabic originals and yet wanted to take part
in the new rationalistic movement. Thus the Hebrew term became popular,
while its meaning remained constant in philosophical discourse.

The mystics used the term in the earliest treatises of European Jewish
mysticism—it is found even in the works of Ashkenazi mystics, and a biblical
connotation was coupled with it to justify its use in Hebrew contexts; it is
even probable that some of these mystics were unaware of the fact that it
was a medieval term, introduced into Hebrew to translate a non-Hebrew
concept. By the time the kabbalists of Gerona used it, it was a commonplace
term in both Hebrew mystical and philosophical literature.

But the problem is: does the term mean the same thing when used in a philosophical work and a mystical one? Or, in other words, what is the difference between a kabbalistic symbol and a philosophical term? According to Scholem, the difference lies in the fact that the philosopher uses the term intending that it mean exactly what it says; he strives for accuracy and unambiguity, trying to formulate his system as clearly as possible, because his philosophical training requires that he logically demonstrate all his conclusions, and this cannot be done unless complete accuracy is achieved. For the philosopher, the terms he uses are vehicles for exact communication between himself and his reader.

The mystic, by comparison, cannot, and does not, use language, or even specific terms, e.g., *azilut,* in the same way, because he deals with contents which are beyond logic, beyond language, beyond human experience; he deals with the mystical, a positive term which really means—the unknown and the unknowable. Accuracy and clarity are out of the question; complete communication is absolutely impossible; if it were possible the contents would cease to be "mystical" and could not convey truths which transcend the parameters of human logic, which is the philosopher's vehicle. The mystic cannot communicate the truth which he has come to know, yet, self-evidently, mystics do compose treatises, even quite lengthy ones, and do attempt some form of communication with fellow mystics, if not with all mankind. They do this, according to Scholem, via symbolism.

For the mystic, "emanation" is not a term describing a process of creation in which the thing created is almost completely similar to its creator. Indeed the term, as employed kabbalistically, does not denote any ordinarily intelligible concept. Rather the term "emanation" is used in this context as a symbol which declares: the subject I am describing is beyond language, beyond human understanding and expression; yet the closest human word to the completely mysterious truth describing the relationship between two other such symbols—this *sefirah* and that *sefirah*—is the word "emanation." No bigger mistake can be made than to maintain that the relationship between the two *sefirot* is "really" one of emanation. If it were so nothing would distinguish the mystic from the philosopher. Yet the mystic's feet are where the philosopher's head is; he begins where the philosopher's logic is exhausted. The symbols cannot convey content, that is, ideas, pictures or feelings in a complete form. They can only give the vaguest hint of that truth which transcends them. But these truths—the mystical ones hinted at by symbols—are so great, so profound, they represent such high religious attainment, that even in this vague and remote form they are much more worthwhile, religiously and spiritually, according to the mystic, than the accurate, clear, but mundane and earthbound truths of the philosopher.

When the mystic, Scholem argued, therefore, uses the term *azilut* he does not and cannot obey the philosophical chain of reasoning, of logical examination and proof. He just gives a hint, which cannot be scrutinized nor criticized. He knows that this term is the closest possible approximation found in human language to a divine truth which, in any other way, is completely beyond human reach.

This is the source of the great freedom that mysticism allows its believers, and which so fascinated Scholem. They can never be taken to account, their ideas analyzed and accepted or rejected. The mystic can always claim, with pure heart and clear conscience, when criticized, that he "never meant it this way" because he really never meant the symbol to be taken literally, i.e., as if it really represented divine truth. That truth is completely beyond communication, and no one can expect the mystic to write it and convey it to the logical human mind. Therefore he can say whatever he feels, being certain that terms like "heresy" do not apply to him, for he had experienced divine truth and tried to convey it by using human words as symbols.

This is also the source of the deep gulf that separates mystics from non-mystics in a religious community. The mystic believes that as God cannot express anything which is untrue, and the truth cannot be expressed in human language, the words of divine revelation incorporated in the holy writ, be it the Bible, the Gospels or the Koran, cannot be understood literally because then they will be conveying only partial truths or even completely false messages. Their divine source proves that they are set in symbolic language, and in order to be understood they have to be read as such. The mystics could not reconcile themselves to the non-mystic's reliance on the literal meaning, while the non-mystics could hardly understand how the mystics discover such unimaginable interpretations of seemingly simple biblical verses.

A case in point is the kabbalistic interpretation of the first chapter of the book of Genesis, the story of the creation. As this chapter presents the beginning of everything, the early kabbalists could not read it as the story of the creation of heaven, earth, fauna and flora. The first event in cosmic history is the emanation of the ten *sefirot* from the hidden Godhead, the *en sof*. These verses should be read, therefore, as the description of this process of emanation, despite the fact that the source of the emanated divine attributes cannot be mentioned even in the symbolic language of the Bible. Rabbi Isaac the Blind and his followers, therefore, understood the first verse of the Bible as revealing how the *sefirot* emerged from the *en sof*: "in the beginning God created heaven and earth" was read as saying: "with the divine wisdom (*reshit*, beginning, is a reference to this power, i.e., the second *sefirah*), the

Godhead, (unmentioned in the verse or anywhere in biblical symbolism), created the Divine Intelligence (*binah*, the third *sefirah*, also called *elohim*, God), and the divine magnificence (*tiferet*, the sixth *sefirah*, which is the central power in the structure of the divine world, and often represents the other five around it, also called "heaven"), and the divine kingdom (*malchut*, the *shekhinah*, the tenth *sefirah*, also called "earth"). Thus this first verse tells of the emanation of the ten *sefirot* in a very brief form, not mentioning the hidden emanator, the *en sof*. Of course, this way of reading is completely foreign and unacceptable to anyone who cannot adapt his mind and feelings to the symbolical reading of Scripture. On the other hand, for the mystic, as Scholem reminds us, reading the story of the creation as if a divine power toiled and brought forth the physical world is unacceptable, terribly trivial and mundane if not completely sacrilegious. For the mystics, the Holy Scriptures are a divine dictionary of symbols. It is not the mystic who has to search through the whole human language to find the appropriate symbol which will express, in the maximal way possible, the hidden divine truths; God himself did it when he revealed His secrets in human language to Moses on Mount Sinai, to the prophets and to the writers who wrote under the influence of the Holy Spirit.

It is not the Scriptures alone that serve the mystic as a treasury of symbols. Creation as a whole, which was made by God, reflects inner divine truths in a symbolic way. Morning and evening, light and darkness, are nothing but earthly symbols of hidden divine processes, which can be understood by the mystic who is aware of their meaning. The same is true about Man: his creation in "God's image" really means that his body and soul reflect in their structure hidden divine truths in a symbolic manner. The study of human psychology, therefore, like the study of physics or cosmology, is, in actuality, the study of the divine symbolism which was used by the Creator when he transformed divine structures into the physical world. Human history, the relationships between nations, natural upheavals and catastrophes, in so far as they are directed by God, are also such symbolic reflections of mystical truth, if read correctly by a mystic. The mystic denies the veracity of all that is learned by the senses or the mind, all that is literal and apparent, if taken as completely true; he believes that all apparent phenomena are opaque reflections of an unknown and unknowable divine truth, of which the earthly manifestations are remote symbols, understood only by those who reject the literal and the logical. "Where their heads are, there our feet stand," where the literal and physical understanding of nature, man, history and the scriptures ends, there begins the deeper understanding of the underlying secrets of the divine world.

Scholem always emphasized the vast difference between symbolism and allegory. Allegory, according to him, means two corresponding layers of truth, one revealed and the other hidden, but the revealed one can be accurately translated to the hidden one and thus reveal the hidden layer. For instance, the presentation above of the kabbalistic interpretation of the first verse of Genesis was, in form, allegorical: the verse says "earth" but means to say "the *shekhinah*," and all one has to do is to translate from one set of words to another. But for the mystic "*shekhinah*" is not a word, corresponding to "earth"; it is a symbol which can be understood by the human mind only as a hint pointing towards something which is far beyond itself. When one "translates" "earth" to "*shekhinah*" one does not explain or clarify anything; rather, one obscures and mystifies the verse, for nobody knows, or can ever know in a logical fashion, what the *shekhinah* really is. We can know many, even hundreds, of different symbols which refer to various aspects of this divine power and its characteristics and functions but we can never know the *shekhinah* as it really is. Symbolism is the maximum we can know, and this maximum is extremely minimal.

In an allegory, the connection between one layer of meaning and the other one is artificial. On an allegorical level, the choice of "earth" to represent "*shekhinah*" is completely arbitrary, because there is no underlying, inherent connection between the two. In mystical symbolism, by contrast, the symbol, even though it expresses only a very small part of the content and meaning of the symbolized power, manifests a real and essential connection to that power. "Earth" and "*shekhinah*" equally represent the hidden divine essence in a remote way, and they are part of that mysterious and hidden entity which is beyond man's reach. This has been frequently described as the relationship between the revealed and hidden parts of an iceberg. The revealed part, the symbol, is really a part of the iceberg, but anyone mistaking it for the iceberg itself will be making a very great mistake, indeed, a titanic mistake.

The study of kabbalistic works is therefore the study of the symbols that the Jewish mystics used when they described the divine world in their intricate system of symbolism. Scholem did not see himself as studying the divine world of the kabbalists as it "really" is, and therefore the question "are there really ten *sefirot*" was for him a completely irrelevant one. He dealt with the symbols, their emergence and development, and especially with their historical impact, and not with the underlying content, which, according [to] the kabbalists, cannot be approached by sensual and logical means.

This understanding of the nature of the kabbalistic symbol is also necessary if one is to arrive at a correct understanding of the kabbalist's standing within the framework of Jewish orthodoxy. Throughout history the kabbalists were, with one notorious exception (the Sabbatian movement), a preserving, traditional and orthodox power, helping Judaism survive in the hostile environments of the European Middle Ages and the Eastern European context of modern times. One may rightfully ask how a movement which describes ten divine powers, and hence is apparently polytheistic, can be a strong force supporting orthodoxy within a monotheistic religious group. The answer lies, of course, in the nature of symbolism. In the literal and physical world "ten" means much more than one, and therefore the clash between monotheism and polytheism. But when symbolism is introduced why assume that in the mystical hidden realm "ten" is "more" than "one"? Such a claim can be put forward only by someone who pretends to know what ten truly represents and what one truly represents; but as the mystic cannot, and knows he cannot, express the mystical content of these symbols it is possible to claim that within the divine realm "ten" is the true essence of "one" and that there is no contradiction between them, one being a specific aspect of the other. This is probably the reason why, throughout history, there has been so little theological criticism of the kabbalah among Jewish intellectuals (except for a few bursts in thirteenth century Spain and in Italy during and after the Renaissance).

It is doubtful whether many of the Jewish non-mystics throughout the ages understood the intricacies of kabbalistic symbolism concerning the *sefirot* and the Godhead, or accepted the kabbalistic way of interpreting scriptural verses. But another aspect of this system of symbols, as Scholem regularly observed, had a profound impact on Jewish religious thought and practice, and demonstrated the orthodox and constructive character of the kabbalah, making it almost immune to all criticism. This is the kabbalistic attitude towards the practical commandments of Judaism, the deeds required of every Jew in his ethical behavior and social and religious life—the *mitsvot*.

In the Middle Ages Judaism found itself in a most difficult situation concerning the rationale for the multitude of *mitsvot* that the Jew was expected to perform as commanded by the Torah and its rabbinic interpreters. The culture of the Middle Ages, under the impact of the Christian spiritualization of religious life and the neo-Platonic disjunction of matter and spirit, tended to identify religious life and progress in one's relationship to God as a process of increasing spiritualization. The level of religious attainment was judged by the purity of spiritual life and by one's distance from matter and everything connected with the physical world. Judaism had to confront this cultural environment, which was hostile to it from the start, with a religious practice which seemed to be concentrated almost exclusively on the practical, physical performance of material deeds. Jewish religious law seemed to decide one's level of religious attainment solely by one's physical and bodily behavior, and not by recourse to any inner spiritual element.

All medieval Jewish theologies and ethical systems, therefore, had to give an answer to the question: how can Judaism claim to be a superior religion when its demands are almost exclusively physical? And each Jewish intellectual camp devised its own answer towards the spiritualization of the religious life in Judaism. Some did it by devising a whole system of spiritual commandments which they claimed were superior to the physical ones, though still founded on the demands of the Torah. For example, Rabbi Bahya Ibn Paqudah in eleventh century Spain introduced mystical elements into his required "Duties of the Heart," elements which Scholem emphasized and described as representing one of the earliest manifestations of Jewish mysticism in medieval Europe. Most philosophers chose a way which gave spiritual reasons for physical deeds, like demonstrating the belief in the unity of God and devotion to him, some even ascribing allegorical meanings to the *mitsvot*. Jewish philosophy as a whole tried to interpret the reasons for the commandments (*ta'amey ha-mitsvot*), in a rational manner emphasizing their social and religious functions.

The Ashkenazi Hasidim chose a more radical way, but also a more conservative one. According to them it is not the physical deed that has a religious meaning but the spiritual effort involved in carrying it out. They did not see the *mitsvot* as supplementing human life and happiness but rather as a trial put before Man by God to test his devotion to Him and his rejection of all worldly temptations, even including one's attachment to one's body. "*Kiddush ha-shem,*" the supreme sacrifice of life for the sake of God's glory, was the example for all the *mitsvot*. Each commandment has an element of sacrifice of a portion of Man's human desires for the sake of heaven. God does not judge a man according to the number of commandments he has performed, but according to the hardships, suffering and sacrifices that a person undergoes in order to perform them. A commandment performed easily is worth much less than the same one performed while overcoming many difficulties. On the one hand, this system insists on the spiritual significance of religious practice, giving no intrinsic value to the physical performance. But on the other hand, this system does not allow the creation of a "spiritual religion" which will neglect the actual commandments and concentrate instead on spiritual values, as most of the philosophical systems seemed to allow. If the actual performance of the commandment is the proof of one's successful negation of the physical world, and every failure in carrying it out proves that one has yielded to worldly temptations, then the only criterion of religious achievement remains the performance of the *mitsvot* and no spiritual substitute is possible; physical success is the only way to spiritual achievement.

The kabbalists, as Scholem emphasized, chose a completely different way, which, historically speaking, proved to be the most successful. It was the one adopted by all orthodox Jewish movements in early modern times and which survives to this very day among the orthodox Jewish groups.

The kabbalists interpreted the commandments as symbols. Every human deed has a counterpart in the divine world. Each good deed contributes something to the process through which it is connected to, and efficacious in, the divine world, and each bad deed is detrimental to that divine process. As it is impossible to know the actual mystical content of these processes, all man knows are the symbols. The content of the *mitsvot,* therefore, is purely spiritual; they involve divine powers and their dynamic life within the divine realm. The physical commandments, however, represent the earthly symbolic counterpart to these divine and completely hidden purposes. The building of a *sukkah,* a tabernacle, certainly does not seem to be a spiritual deed, though its traditional meaning is the remembrance of the redemption from Egypt; one may claim that he has better ways to remember that event than spending a week in Autumn in a loose hut in the yard. According to the kabbalists, however, the *sukkah* really symbolized something connected with the union between the sixth *sefirah, tiferet,* which is the male element in the divine realm, and the *shekhinah,* the female element. The form of the tabernacle is modeled, according to them, after the bridal canopy under which these divine powers are united. Mystical symbolism hints at the spiritual divine processes with which the commandments are connected; a full understanding of these processes being impossible, because the mystical truth beyond the symbols is unknown and unknowable. Therefore, in order to participate in the mystical union in the divine realm a mystic can only adhere to the symbol, perform it as strictly as possible with maximum attention to the minutest detail, for not knowing the significance of such details one can never be sure whether this one is a crucial one or a secondary element in that mystical process. Thus, while the physical deeds themselves may seem to lose their intrinsic importance, the religious message is clear and unambiguous: only by the strict adherance to every physical element in the practical commandments of Jewish tradition can a man achieve contact with the spiritual, divine, content hiding behind them; a content which, being mystical, can never be understood or approached in an intellectual manner, but only with the detailed observance of the commandments as such. Symbolism in this way created a unity between the spiritual and the physical, and strengthened the orthodox element in medieval Judaism.

This basic orthodoxy contributed to the fact that the kabbalah was almost never criticized in the Middle Ages whereas Jewish philosophy came under heavy attack. While the kabbalah was undoubtedly more radical in its ways of thought and concepts, as far as deeds were concerned it was above reproach, formulating a new system of *ta'amey ha-mitsvot* ("reasons for the commandments") which gave new spiritual reasons for their observance. Judaism tended to leave alone any thinker who did not interfere with the practical behavior of Jews; it attacked vehemently anyone attempting to change one of its practices. It may be said that while in Christian history heretics occupy a much more central place than sinners, in Judaism it is very difficult to become a heretic, while it is very easy to become a sinner. The kabbalists were neither: the armor of their symbolism protected them from heresy by claiming that their expressions should never be taken literally, and from sin by seeing the commandments as a set of symbols given to them by God in order to enable the mystics to come close to Him and to participate and influence the inner dynamism of the divine realm.

IV

The early kabbalists in Spain and the Provence, in Scholem's reconstruction, are seen to have concentrated their efforts on the development of kabbalistic symbolism concerning the secret of the creation, the divine processes which governed it, and the further stages of the development of the world. They did not dream as yet that their symbols would, one day, transform Judaism and that mass movements would emerge preaching kabbalistic ideas to the nation as a whole. It seems that from the beginning their orientation was towards small, closed circles and groups dealing with esoteric ideas for their own sake, practising communion with God alone, demanding nothing from the community as a whole. Scholem stressed the esoteric character of the early kabbalistic circles, a character rooted in their theology. Their insistent concentration on the "secret of the creation" (*sod ma'aseh bereshit*) was the result of the way they understood the process of mystical communion with God.

Rabbi Isaac the Blind, in his commentary on the *Sefer Yezirah,* and the other early kabbalists who analyzed in great detail the process by which the first divine attributes emanated from the Godhead and assumed their personalistic character, were not only interested in an academic inquiry con-

cerning the roots of all existence and the emergence of the world as we know
it. They saw the process of emanation as the one which leads down from
the complete unity, a spiritual unity, which existed when all began, when
the different divine powers were still united within the Godhead, until it
reached the enormous plurality of the physical world, where nothing is identical with the other and nothing can be united with anything else. The soul
of the mystic wishes to deny this plurality, to turn away from it, and to be
part of the true divine unity. This unity is a situation of the past and,
therefore, the past has to be sought, understood and a way to return to it
found. For these kabbalists the *sod ma'aseh bereshit* was a divine ladder,
leading down from the early unity within the Godhead to the plurality of
the created world.

If this ladder can be understood in depth, its whole symbolism unveiled
before the eyes of the mystics, the mysteries involved in it embedded in his
innermost soul, then there is a chance that the mystic might repeat the
process, but this time from the end to the beginning. He could, under these
circumstances, attempt to use the ladder of descent in which the divine
powers emanated stage by stage as a ladder of ascension to uplift his soul
towards the sublime unity which always lies above, and before him (in the
chronological sense, because the earlier the time the closer one is to the
complete original unity). "The Secret of Creation" was thus the means by
which the mystic discussed the symbolism which represented not only the
origin of the world, but also the target towards which the mystic tries to
advance—an advance which, historically speaking, is a retreat towards the
past.

This mysticism of a retreat towards a unity with the Godhead which
was in the beginning of all, and diminished during history, is not a national
or community endeavor. It means that the mystic turns his back to contemporary history and has no interest in current affairs and in the advancement
towards a better future. This is an individual path, to be taken by the mystic
alone, as an individual, or probably together with a small group of his
friends; there is nothing here for the masses, no message of salvation or
redemption. This explains the surprising neglect of the messianic element in
early kabbalistic works, from the *Bahir* through the kabbalists in the Provence and Gerona. They repeated the traditional formulae of messianic belief,
but did not add anything to it and did not connect it with kabbalistic symbolism. The symbolism of redemption was, for them, the story of the process
of emanation in the beginning of all, the *sod ma'aseh bereshit*.

This, essentially, is the picture Scholem drew of the esoteric nature of
the early kabbalistic circles in medieval Europe. As kabbalists, they were not

interested in the world around them. As individuals, they could be leaders of communities and of academies and do their best to protect and enhance the interests of their fellow Jews. Thus, the Ravad in his generation at the end of the twelfth century and Nachmanides in the next generation, in the first half and middle of the thirteenth century, were central figures in the contemporary Jewish leadership. Yet nothing of this kind, no element of leadership or historical purpose, is apparent in their kabbalistic works or in the writings of their friends in the circles that were centered around them. As mystics they closed themselves in small groups, produced their obscure symbolism which could not be understood by anyone not initiated in one of these circles, and dealt with their individual kind of redemption and mystical unity which was completely separated from contemporary historical events.

Because of this their first works do not reveal much interest in the more popular and practical side of religion. The theological problems centering around the commandments are not central in the *Bahir*; several of them are interpreted in it in a symbolical, mystical manner, but no clear message can be discerned from these comments. Rabbi Isaac the Blind and the kabbalistic works of the Gerona circle followed the same line; not much is found in them concerning everyday life, ethical behavior and reasons for the ritualistic commandments, even though the basic attitude towards them as symbols of divine processes is already clearly present there. Only in the next generation, in the second half of the thirteenth century, do kabbalists begin to write specific works on this subject.

Scholem discovered evidence proving that the concentration of the early kabbalists in closed esoteric circles was not achieved without opposition and internal strife. In a manuscript he discovered and published he reveals a letter by Rabbi Isaac the Blind to the kabbalists in Gerona, a letter written in the manner of a Rabbi chastizing his disciples. Rabbi Isaac complained in this letter that he had received information that in Gerona people were talking about the kabbalah and its secrets "in the streets and in the market-places," and that the symbols of the kabbalah were becoming public property. Rabbi Isaac admonished the recipients of the letter saying that such wide knowledge of the secrets of the kabbalah must lead to misunderstanding and controversy around the kabbalah, for these secrets cannot be correctly understood by the wide public. He opposed even the writing of kabbalistic books and warned his disciples that if they believed that they could write books and keep them secret they were mistaken, for "there is no cupboard which can hide a book already written."

It seems that Rabbi Isaac directed his criticism especially against Rabbi Ezra and Rabbi Azriel, the founders of the kabbalistic center in Gerona, each of whom wrote several kabbalistic treatises, some of them of book length.

Rabbi Isaac's censure seems to have succeeded for the other kabbalists of Gerona that we know of (who were younger than Rabbi Ezra and Rabbi Azriel), did not write any kabbalistic treatises in the manner of their predecessors, let alone books, and their mystical teachings were incorporated in other works. In short, the members of the kabbalistic center in Gerona accepted, so the facts seem to denote, the demand of Rabbi Isaac not to talk openly about the kabbalah and not to write kabbalistic works thus strengthening the esoteric character of the early kabbalistic circles.

A demonstration of the esoteric character of the early Jewish mystics in medieval Europe is found in the works of a circle of mystics whom Scholem called "The Iyyun Circle," after the central work of this school, *Sefer ha-Iyyun,* "the Book of Contemplation." Scholem listed thirty-two treatises which he ascribed to this group, all of them brief works of a few pages each. Some of these, including the *Sefer ha-Iyyun* and the works closest to it in their terminology and symbolism, do not use the usual kabbalistic system of ten *sefirot* and it seems that it was unknown to them; instead, they use a symbolism of thirteen divine *middot,* attributes, and in this, as in most other ways, they differ from the other early kabbalists. They seem to rely very heavily on neo-Platonic ideas and terminology, color symbolism is very prominent in these works, and there is a more central treatment of mathematical and linguistic elements, following the *Sefer Yezirah* but demonstrating a special tradition concerning its symbolical interpretation. All these thirty-two treatises are either anonymous, or attributed to ancient writers, *tannaim* (teachers of the Mishnah) or *geonim* (seventh to tenth centuries), some to the ancient *Hekhalot* mystics with whom they seem to have had close spiritual ties, and some are attributed to completely fictional figures. There is nothing in these works which could identify either the exact period of their composition or the exact geographical location of the group. Scholem suggested that they probably lived in Southern France in the beginning of the thirteenth century, and the vocabulary they used seems to strengthen this suggestion. The almost exclusive subject of these works is, in various ways, the "Secret of the Creation," and their mysticism undoubtedly was connected with the symbolism representing that process. To this day they remain esoteric and hidden from history, an anonymous and featureless group of enthusiastic Jewish mystics who left their ideas to posterity through the medium of the incorporation of their doctrines in the literature of the later kabbalah.

V

Rabbi Isaac the Blind's warning that the publication of kabbalistic secrets could lead to misunderstanding and controversy proved correct, and, characteristically enough, it occurred concerning the one aspect of active, everyday religious life that the early kabbalists concentrated on and discussed in detail: the meaning and character of prayer.

From its earliest beginnings, Jewish mysticism was specifically interested in the nature of Jewish prayer. *Hekhalot* mysticism (i.e., the mystical teachings of the talmudic era) is concentrated to a very large extent on the *kedushah*, the third benediction among the eighteen, in which the verse from Isaiah 6:4 is recited, and an identification is created between the public praying in the synagogue and the angels praising God around his throne of glory. The *Hekhalot* hymns are very close to the *kedushah* and they denote that the mystical process in the eyes of the ancient Jewish mystics in Israel and Babylonia was connected with the process of prayer. The *Book Bahir*, in a similar way, discusses in relative detail the *kedushah* and the benediction of the priests, hinting at the profound symbolism concerning the divine world hidden within these prayers.

Some of the earliest traditions that we have from the first kabbalists deal with the secret of the intention in prayers. The Ravad himself divided the intention of the "eighteen benedictions" between "the creator" (*yotzer bereshit*, the term used in the *Shiur Komah* for God), and the "prime cause" (*ilat ha-ilot*, the Hebrew term which translated the Aristotelian concept). His meaning in making this division is not completely clear, but it seems that he directed the part of this prayer which praises God towards the highest possible place in the Godhead, while the other part, which deals with earthly requests, to a lower divine power, possibly the third *sefirah, binah*. Rabbi Jacob ha-Nazir, a contemporary of Rabbi Isaac the Blind (or possibly predating R. Isaac), gave a detailed set of instructions concerning the exact *sefirot* to be aimed at during the reciting of the *Shema* ("Hear O Israel") and the division of the "eighteen benedictions" between the divine powers. He also insisted that there is a difference in the intentions relative to the time of the prayer: in daytime—towards the sixth power, *tiferet*, and at night, towards the third, *binah*.

Rabbi Azriel of Gerona was the first kabbalist to dedicate a whole book to the subject, in which he described the symbolism behind almost every word in the prayers and the part of the divine realm to which they relate. In his other works the subject is also prominent: in his commentary on the talmudic *aggadot* Rabbi Azriel included a very profound commentary on the word *amen*, proving that the various words in Hebrew which derive from that root include in a symbolical manner all aspects of the divine world, therefore all the *sefirot* are incorporated and united within the *amen*; this is why the talmud said that "one who says the *amen* after the benediction is greater than the one who says the benediction itself." Many other early kabbalists dealt with the problem of the intention of prayers, including Rabbi Asher ben David, the nephew of Rabbi Isaac the Blind, who was sent by Rabbi Isaac to Gerona to instruct the kabbalists there in the teachings of the school of kabbalists in the Provence. Another Gerona writer on the subject was Rabbi Jacob ben Sheshet, a relatively prolific writer, who dedicated an ethical composition, "Faith and Reason" (ha-Emunah veha-Bitahon) to several subjects dealing with the spiritual observance of the Jewish traditional commandments and norms, including the prayers. This text became a popular one and undoubtedly was instrumental in the spreading of kabbalistic ideas among non-mystics. Rabbi Jacob did not write this study as a purely kabbalistic one; most of it is comprised of talmudic and midrashic sayings, homiletically interpreted by the author in a manner intended to instruct his contemporaries in traditional Jewish ethics. His kabbalistic views are expressed in a subdued manner, but they are still quite obvious to the trained reader (as a consequence this work was later, incorrectly, attributed to Nachmanides).

All this activity concerning prayer did not go unnoticed outside the circles of the kabbalists. This subject was one which concerned every Jew upon whom prayer was incumbent three times a day. The subject of the correct ways to pray, including spiritual intentions, was a major subject discussed in halachic works. Many such books of law dedicated their first chapters to prayer and introduced the legal discussion with a preface dealing with the intellectual intentions. When it became known that the kabbalists had something to say about this interest was aroused, and with it the beginnings of criticism of the kabbalistic approach to this basic subject.

In a collection of documents by Rabbi Meir ben Shimeon of Narbonne, which the author called Milhemet Mitzvah, Scholem found and published a letter by the thirteenth century author attacking the kabbalists for their beliefs in general and especially for their teachings concerning prayer. He described them as polytheists, who "direct the day's prayer to one God and the night's to another God," while on various days and religious festivals one's prayers are to be directed to different powers. He mentioned the Book Bahir, though the quotation he brings is absent from the versions of the Bahir which have reached us. There is no doubt that he was aware, at least in a general way, of the teachings of the early kabbalists and viewed them as a harmful new phenomenon which was to be categorically rejected. It is not surprising that the subject on which he chose to attack the kabbalists was the one which was most directly concerned with everyday religious practice rather than one relating to the theoretical or theological innovations of the kabbalists.

Rabbi Meir's description of the Jewish mystics as representing a mythological and polytheistic revival within Judaism was echoed throughout the ages, and nineteenth century scholars especially repeated it very often. Yet, while Scholem used this document to learn some important details concerning the early kabbalah, the most striking point about this letter is its loneliness. During the next two centuries, when the kabbalah became better and better known among Jewish intellectuals, we hardly find a second opposing voice to join to that of Rabbi Meir's. These basic characteristics—the esoteric circles of the kabbalists, their strict orthodoxy and their fortification of practical observance of Jewish traditional commandments, the prominence of great halachists among the teachers of kabbalah—all these were factors which facilitated the acceptance of the kabbalah as one more feature or aspect of Jewish culture without arousing controversy. It is doubtful whether all those familiar with the kabbalah believed it to be the true "secrets of the Torah" revealed to Moses on Mount Sinai, but their doubts did not bring them to active opposition because it was difficult to show what harm was done by its teachings.

VI

Scholem presented the early kabbalah in the Provence and Gerona in two different, but complementary, historical perspectives. On the one hand, these late-twelfth-century and thirteenth-century mystics were both the product of the culture in which they found themselves and those who contributed to its changes. Everything found in the works of these mystics is profoundly connected to the spiritual world of the early thirteenth century and the major developments within and surrounding Judaism at that time. The three main spiritual drives which Scholem discerned were: (a) the Catharic heresy, the renewed gnostic revolution within European Christianity; (b) the impact of neo-Platonism, both Christian and Jewish; (c) the impact of Aristotelian philosophy and the threat that extreme rationalism presented to traditional religious beliefs and practices. The kabbalists probably were influenced by the first movement, completely absorbed the second, and fiercely opposed the third while offering a profound, traditional, Jewish alternative to it.

In every way these kabbalists participated in the historical developments and cultural trends of their day. Many of them wrote Jewish legal treatises, commentaries on the Bible and the Talmud, responsa on halachic questions, traditional ethical works based on talmudic and midrashic sayings, and other such accepted literary genres. There was nothing revolutionary in their writings either in form or in content. They did initiate new trends, but they did not do it first and foremost as kabbalists but, rather, as Jewish intellectuals and social leaders responding to the needs of the times. It seems that most of them did not devote all their energies to mystical speculation even though it was central to their spiritual and religious experience. The figure of the mystic who is nothing but a mystic can be found at this period only as an exception rather than as the rule. Only later did the kabbalah develop until "kabbalist" became a term which can describe the totality of an author's life and work.

At the same time that these circles of mystics were developing their systems of symbols and responding to the cultural demands of their times they can be viewed, historically, in a much larger perspective, and Scholem complemented the first picture with the second. The appearance of the kabbalah in twelfth- and thirteenth-century Europe was nothing short of a major revolution. The mysticism of the *Hekhalot* and *Merkabah* literature, i.e., the mysticism of the talmudic era, seemingly forgotten as a living force outside the schools of the Ashkenazi Hasidism, suddenly acquired a new vigor and became central, in a much changed form, in a new and dynamic system of symbols. Gnostic tendencies, either inherent in this literature or transmitted independently by other means, suddenly erupted within the major academies of Jewish law in Southern Europe.

Scholem's presentation of the history of these chapters in the development of the kabbalah reflects his deep belief in historical continuity. Indeed there is a linear element in his reconstruction from early Jewish mysticism in the East to the Jewish mystics in the Provence, where first the *Book Bahir* appeared and then the scholars, who had visions of Elijah's appearance to them, developed the system of kabbalistic emanations on the basis of the *Bahir*. This was transmitted to the Gerona scholars, from whom the mystical system spread to other centers in Spain. Some enigmas still exist in this picture, such as the problem of the participation of the Ashkenazi Hasidism in the transmitting of Eastern esoteric gnostic material, and the problem of the *Iyyun* circle and its place in the chain of development of Jewish mysticism in Europe. But on the whole, according to Scholem, there is one stream that leads from *Hekhalot Zutartey* to the *Bahir* and from it to Rabbi Isaac the Blind's commentary on the *Sefer Yezirah* and from there to the works of Rabbi Azriel of Gerona and Nachmanides, and onwards to other mystical circles until the *Zohar* incorporated all of them and brought Jewish theosophy and mythological symbolism to a new level of richness, sophistication and historical impact.

The most meaningful result of these studies by Scholem, from a historical point of view, is that he conclusively demonstrated that it is impossible to separate the history of Jewish mysticism from the history of Jewish culture and religion. The mystics of the Provence and Gerona were not isolated individuals but played a central role, even excluding the mystical dimension apparent in their work, in the unfolding of Jewish culture at that time. As he had done concerning the *Hekhalot* mysticism, i.e., forcing us to acknowledge that it is impossible to separate it from the world of the talmudic and midrashic sages, so, once again, he has in the case of the early kabbalists in Europe revealed them to be an integral part of the culture and literature of their time, their mysticism being an added dimension which contributes tremendously to the understanding of the whole.

Scholem, through his brilliant historical and philological analyses of pertinent texts, has incontrovertibly shown that mysticism is a constantly operating force (though not always with the same strength), in Jewish history. He described the appearance of the kabbalah in Europe as a mythological explosion in the heart of medieval Judaism. But the forces which caused this explosion were not new; they emanated from the constant and enduring mystical dimension of the Jewish religion.

LOUIS JACOBS

Aspects of Scholem's Study of Hasidism

A major theme in Scholem's writings on Hasidism is the relationship between Hasidic thought and Kabbalah. All the early Hasidic works use Kabbalistic terms and vocabulary, the Hasidic masters undoubtedly believing in
the Kabbalah as revealed truth. Yet Hasidism is not simply a later development of Kabbalism in the way, for instance, the Lurianic Kabbalah is a
development of the Zoharic. Hasidism has all the indications of being a new
mystical movement, using the Kabbalah as the basis of its thinking but differing from it in important, though hard to detect, ways. Scholem sees the
originality of Hasidic teaching in its application of the Kabbalistic mysteries
to the inner life of man, to his psychological processes in the concrete world
of the here and now. In Hasidism there is far less concern with the operations
of the Sefirotic realms on high than with their effect on the spiritual life of
man on earth. The doctrine of the Lurianic Kabbalah that there are "holy
sparks" everywhere clamoring to be rescued from the *kelipot,* the husks or
shells representing the demonic side of existence, is understood in Hasidism
to imply the need for man to be constantly engaged in the physical world in
a spirit of consecration. The Hasid is expected to occupy himself in worldly
matters as a means to the true end of human activity, the reclaiming of the
"holy sparks" and their elevation to the sphere of holiness. This is the reason
for the strong opposition in Hasidism to asceticism (although Hasidic masters like Elimelech of Lizensk, still under the influence of the Lurianic Kab-

From *Modern Judaism* 5, no. 1 (February 1985). © 1985 by the Johns Hopkins
University Press.

balah, were ascetics). The typical Hasidic idea of 'avodah be-gashmiyut, "the worship of God through engagement in the physical," means precisely this, that when eating and drinking, when performing the conjugal act and engaging in business, the Hasid should perform yiḥudim, "unifications," i.e., the various combinations of the divine names which provide the essential vitality without which there could be no created, finite universe. In Hasidic legend, when the Maggid of Meseritch, who had heard of the fame of the Baal Shem Tov, visits the master, he is disappointed by what appears to be pointless conversation about horses, unaware that in what seems to be mere frivolous conduct the Baal Shem Tov is really carrying out yiḥudim. It is only when the Baal Shem Tov demonstrates this by making the angels referred to in a difficult Kabbalistic text actually appear that the Maggid is mollified to become an ardent follower of the Hasidic way. Scholem does not refer to this, but it might be noted that the Hasidic fondness for tobacco, especially by the Zaddikim, is based on the same idea. There are extremely subtle "sparks," so refined that they can only find residence in an ethereal substance like the smoke which ascends when the Zaddik smokes his pipe.

Let us begin our review of the various elements in Scholem's study of Hasidism with a brief consideration of his polemical exchange with Martin Buber on this subject. Where Scholem takes issue with Buber's reconstruction of Hasidism is over the understanding of the Hasidic idea of meeting God in the concrete circumstances of this world. For Buber, the Hasidim are giving expression to the idea he has so successfully expounded, the I-Thou relationship. When man enjoys worldly things as gifts from God, when he acknowledges his Creator who has brought these things into being, his "I" meets the divine "Thou." It is well-known that Buber moved in his thought from an original mystical approach to his existentialist attitude, diametrically opposed to the mystical loss of selfhood. For the mystic the "I" is dissolved in the "Thou" or, at least, that is the ultimate aim of the mystic, whereas for Buber, in his later thought, the "I" must retain its full identity for the life of dialogue to be possible. Buber uses very skillfully the Hasidic tales and legends, in which the Zaddikim enjoy the world while having God in mind, to further his own philosophy. In the process he is really giving a new interpretation of the stories (as Scholem admits, in a most persuasive style) until it is realised, as Scholem is at pains to point out, that the stories are based on Hasidic doctrine, on the Torah of the Zaddikim; a doctrine essentially different from Buber's I-Thou. The doctrine is mystical not existentialist. It is all very well for Buber to claim the right to be selective in his use of Hasidic material. Nor does Scholem necessarily deny the value of Buber's thought in its own right. What Buber is not entitled to do is to read his ideas into the Hasidic tales since the tales are based on the doctrine and were told to illustrate that doctrine. The kind of selectivity Buber indulges in, as Scholem remarks, is rather like an attempted reconstruction of Sufism from the fine sayings of the Sufis or, better, the drawing out of Catholic theological doctrines from the tales of the Christian saints. Sufism and Catholicism both have a Gnosis of which the tales of the saints are the expression. By the same token, the Kabbalistic Gnosis, in which Buber in his later period had no interest, is at the heart of Hasidic doctrine, albeit extended in line with the fresh Hasidic emphases. Scholem is surely correct in calling attention to the inescapable fact that Hasidism constantly stresses *bittul hayesh,* "self-annihilation" (there could hardly be a more emphatic rejection of Buber's I-Thou) and ultimate loss of the world. Engagement in worldly things in the here and now is basic to Hasidism but only as the unavoidable means for meeting the divine sparks which reside there waiting to be reclaimed by holy living. The end of the meeting is, as it were, its total transcendence.

Take the legend, quoted frequently in Hasidic writings, of Enoch the cobbler who performed unifications when he stitched the upper part to the lower part of the shoes he made or repaired. In Buber's understanding of this legend, Enoch's unifications were not achieved through his dwelling on the upper worlds while repairing his shoes. The very act of shoe-repairing, carried out by Enoch with a sense of vocation and not simply in order to earn a living, was itself the unification because in it Enoch, as Buber would say, had an I-Thou relationship with his shoes and his customers through which he met the divine Thou in dialogue. The Hasidim, on the other hand, while agreeing that Enoch pursued a worthy occupation (not alone because the world needs cobblers but because there are "holy sparks" waiting to be rescued in the shoes and in the leather), had as their ultimate aim the mystical one of penetrating to the divine essence. They sought the state of oblivion so far as the world is concerned. At the stage when this mystical state is attained there is only the divine Thou, no shoes, no leather, no customers and no Enoch!

Or take Zangwill's essay "The Master of the Name" in his *Dreamers of the Ghetto.* Zangwill, before Buber but as a literary man rather than a philosopher or scholar (it is in the area of scholarship that Scholem finds fault with Buber), tells the tale of a youthful disciple for whom the Baal Shem Tov acts as coachman. The Baal Shem Tov, to the consternation of his companion, stops the wagon he is driving in order to admire a pretty girl who is passing. He explains that, after all, it is God who has created beauty so that one who admires the beauty of women, provided there are no lustful thoughts, is really admiring the Source of all beauty. Buber would presumably agree. The I of the coachman meets the Thou of the girl or rather the Thou of the girl's beauty and this, in itself, is to have an encounter with the eternal Thou behind all created things. In actual Hasidic life, and according to the Hasidic doctrine, the saint who is suddenly presented with a vision of feminine pulchritude would immediately avert his gaze. But he would ask himself why God had brought it about that he inadvertently sees the girl and he would conclude that it is a reminder to him to elevate the pure thought of beauty to the Sefirah *Tiferet*. As soon as he possibly can, the saint is obliged to avoid all reflection on the beauty of the girl, directing his mind in wonder to contemplate on the divine vitality and splendour of which all beauty on earth is no more than an extremely pale manifestation.

This is the basis of the early Hasidic idea of elevating "strange thoughts" (later abandoned as spiritually dangerous except for very few Zaddikim like Yitzhak Eisik of Komarno). As Mordecai Wilensky has shown in his anthology of Mitnaggedic polemics [*Hasidim U-Mitneggedim*], the Mitnaggedim were shocked at the practice of the Hasidim when their prayers were invaded by "strange thoughts" of women or pride or idolatry. (This latter probably means that the Hasid suddenly found the notion entering his head that there might be some truth in Christianity). The Hasidim did not seek to push the "strange thoughts" out of their consciousness but, rather, began to reflect on the divine source of each, the thought being seen as sent by God for that express purpose. The elevation of the "strange thoughts" was effected by the removal of the "strangeness" from the thoughts by attaching them in the mind to the pure worlds on high where there is nothing material and no estrangement from God. Buber, if one understands his philosophy correctly, would not see the thoughts as "strange" at all since it is through them that man's I can meet the Thou behind them. Scholem and his pupils, notably J. G. Weiss and Rivkah Schatz, have shown how all this is repeated again and again in the Hasidic Torah, without an understanding of which it is quite impossible to grasp the meaning of Hasidism, as Buber seeks to do.

Related, though independent of his critique of Buber, is Scholem's attention to the theme of *devekut* in Hasidism. In his famous essay on *devekut*, Scholem describes how this ideal of constantly being with God in the mind is developed in Hasidism. Worldly things are no longer seen as hindrances but as essential means for the attainment of this state. For mediaeval thinkers like Nachmanides *devekut*, attachment to God, can be achieved in spite of worldly concerns. The Hasidim taught that it should be achieved through worldly concerns. Moreover, for Nachmanides and Maimonides *devekut* is a rare state of mind, fully possible only for the very few, extraordinary holy men. Hasidism made *devekut* an ideal for all, though there is an ebb and flow in the life of *devekut*. In later Hasidic thought, too, the ordinary Hasid can only approximate the ideal and even then only through attachment to the Zaddik whose mind is on God. This kind of attachment is totally different from Buber's I-Thou relationship. Scholem stops short of describing it as being absorbed in God or of total loss of selfhood in God but it comes very close to the *unio mystica*.

Precisely because of his recognition of *devekut* as the Hasidic aim *par excellence,* one to which all else is subordinate, Scholem is closer to another contention of Buber against that of Tishby and Dinur. This concerns the role of Messianism in Hasidism. Scholem holds that Buber has gone too far in speaking of the liquidation of the Messianic doctrine in Hasidism but, he maintains, Dinur and Tishby go too far in the opposite direction when they detect Messianic fervour in the forefront of the Hasidic emphases. Scholem prefers to speak of the neutralization of the Messianic element in Hasidism. The Hasidim were completely Orthodox in upholding this basic principle of the Jewish faith and like other Jews hoped for the coming of the Messiah. The hope featured with the greatest prominence in their prayers, which were, after all, the standard Jewish prayers. Nevertheless, Scholem argues, their belief in the coming of the Messiah did not provide for the Hasidim their chief motivation in their religious life. Without, perhaps, realising it on the conscious level, the Hasidim so reinterpreted the Lurianic doctrine of the "holy sparks" in the light of their *devekut* ideal that the *tikkun* ("perfection") referred to repeatedly in the Lurianic scheme was no longer that of the world as a whole, at least not primarily, but of the individual soul. For Luria each individual has his own "spark" of Adam's soul and consequently his own soul-root. In addition there are the "sparks" scattered in creation. Thus each individual has his own task to perform but the "sparks" of divinity he reclaims in creation are not directly connected with the "sparks" in the individual soul. The reclaiming of the "holy sparks" in creation is a group process, a task for all to engage in and eschatological in nature. When all the "holy sparks" have been reclaimed, the *tikkun* will have been completed and the Messianic age will dawn. Hasidism introduced the novel idea that the "sparks" of divinity in creation also belong in some way to the other "sparks" in the individual's soul-root, with the consequence that each individual is required to reclaim in particular those "sparks" in creation which call, as it were, for him and no other to rescue. Furthermore, the main aim of the rescue is for the individual soul to become attached to the "holy sparks" in creation he has reclaimed. Thus the ultimate aim of the rescue of the "sparks" is personal *devekut,* with the general *tikkun* of the world taking second place, though not, of course, denied.

The divergence between Scholem's views and those of Dinur and Tishby would not appear to be particularly strong. For one thing, Scholem admits that he is speaking only of the early Hasidim until around the end of the eighteenth century. After that time, in the circle of the Seer of Lublin, mighty efforts were made to bring the Messiah, to hasten his coming by the performance of *yiḥudim*. Again, as we have seen, Scholem does not deny that the Hasidim did hope fervently for the coming of the Messiah. What is really at issue, then, is the matter of emphasis, and here Scholem seems to be correct. Apart from Scholem's analysis of Hasidic reinterpretation of the "holy sparks" doctrine, where *devekut* is the aim of the religious life it is hard to see why this aim has to wait on the Messiah for its realization. *Devekut* is both possible and desirable, the Hasidim taught, in the unredeemed world, even though, the Hasidim would have maintained that it will be more capable of realization in the Messianic age and will then be of a far more permanent nature. Scholem might also have elaborated on the idea that Messianism, as a group phenomenon, is, in a way, opposed to an interpretation of the religious life in terms of self-perfection and individual spiritual advancement. It is revealing to see how Maimonides, for instance, because of the powerful individualistic thrust of his thought, is hard put to explain why the coming of the Messiah should be necessary at all; why, in other words, a state of national restoration in this world should be required since the ultimate aim of the religious life is for the soul to enjoy God for ever in the World to Come, which, for Maimonides, is the blissful state of the soul after the death of the body. If, in Keats's expressive phrase, this world is a "vale of soul-making" what need is there for a relocation of the vale? Messianism is a matter of time and for the future whereas *devekut* belongs to eternity and the attempt to achieve it belongs to the present.

Scholem takes issue with Tishby who maintains that the vision of the Baal Shem Tov, in which he saw (in his ascent of soul) the Messiah, demonstrates the high degree of the Messianic idea in early Hasidic thought. The vision is recorded in the famous letter by the Baal Shem Tov to his brother-in-law, Gershom of Kutov. The Messiah assures the Baal Shem Tov that when his teachings will have spread abroad the Messianic age will dawn. On the contrary, Scholem retorts, the record of the vision shows the opposite to be true, the Baal Shem Tov expressing his alarm at how long it will take before the Messiah will come. In the relevant text of the letter published in 1781, at the end of the book *Ben Porat Yosef* by Jacob Joseph of Polnoye, the Messiah's reply to the Baal Shem Tov's question: "When will the Master come?" reads (in Scholem's translation): "By this you shall know it: when your doctrine will be widely known and revealed throughout the world and what I taught you will be divulged outwards from your own resources. And they too will be able to perform acts of meditative unification and ascents like you. And then all the 'husks' will perish and the time of salvation will have come. And I was bewildered because of this answer and I was greatly aggrieved by the enormous length of time until this would be possible." Scholem suggests this can only mean that Messianism as a driving power and immediate hope can no longer be reckoned with. The coming of the Messiah is relegated to a distant future.

Incidentally, Scholem and Tishby, as well as other scholars, all accept the letter printed by Jacob Joseph as completely authentic. Some years ago I wrote to Scholem expressing my doubts but he would have nothing to do with such a suggestion, roundly declaring that there is not the slightest doubt that the Letter was written by the Baal Shem Tov himself, even if the claim is rejected that there is still in existence the original Letter in the Baal Shem Tov's own handwriting! Bowing to Scholem's great expertise, I translated the Letter as an authentic missive of the Baal Shem Tov in my *Jewish Mystical Testimonies*. Now I am not so sure. Is it not curious that just at a time when the Hasidic movement was under fierce attack, the Letter should suddenly appear with a message from none other than the Messiah to guarantee the success of the movement? The Letter is presented by R. Jacob Joseph's son-in-law, the editor of *Ben Porat Yosef,* at the end of the book, "for the purpose of bringing merit to the public." Why did R. Jacob Joseph have to wait for his son-in-law to publish the Letter in such a casual way? When I took this up with Scholem he replied that R. Jacob Joseph was a very old man at the time, but does this not make it even more suspect? If R. Jacob Joseph really had in his possession a letter of the Baal Shem Tov, how can it be explained that in his *Toledot Yaakov Yosef,* where he quotes every stray saying of the master, there is not even a hint of the existence of this Letter and not a single reference to its contents? Not that this affects Scholem's argument or, for that matter, Tishby's. There is no doubt that the Letter did appear in the *Ben Porat Yosef* in 1781 so that, whoever compiled it, it is an authentic document of Hasidism and was universally accepted as authentic by the later masters, including the grandson of the Baal Shem Tov, Ephraim of Sudlikov.

Scholem's main scholarly interest so far as Hasidism is concerned was with the movement's earlier manifestations. It would seem that he believed the later writings of the Hasidic masters were basically unoriginal repetitions of the themes treated extensively by the early masters, apart from the fact that having paved the way with his customary, painstaking thoroughness he left the study of other varieties of Hasidic thought to his disciples, among whom every serious student must be counted. Of the systematization of

Hasidic thought in the *Ḥabad* movement Scholem has virtually nothing to say, beyond noting the personal testimony of Dov Baer of Lubavitch (and then not in the context of Hasidism but of personal mystical experience) and the acosmism of Aaron of Starosselje, the disciple of R. Shneur Zalman of Liady. He also calls attention to the neglected but highly interesting acosmic novel by Fischel Schneursohn. In this connection he appears to have held that early Hasidism was not, in fact, acosmic; *devekut* involving no loss of selfhood, although it is still far removed from Buber's I-Thou relationship. I have tried to argue that *Ḥabad* acosmism or panentheism is only an elaboration in more systematic form of ideas already found in the earliest stages of the movement. Scholem himself admits that the early masters were panentheists, believing that all is in God. What the *Ḥabad* thinkers tried to do was to explore in a more radical way the implication of the theory that all is *in* God though it is true that it is not until *Ḥabad* thought that a distinction is drawn between our point of view, where there is a finite universe with real creatures in it, and God's point of view, where there is neither a world nor creatures. Whether such a distinction is logically meaningful is a matter for discussion by linguistic analysts.

Scholem's discussion of how Hasidism uses the Lurianic Kabbalah for its own purposes is very profound and convincing. It was left to others to show that in some varieties of early Hasidism the whole of the Kabbalistic scheme is virtually ignored entirely, though none of the Hasidic masters ever doubted that Luria was inspired. In a remarkable passage from the writings of Menachem Mendel of Premislani (b. 1728), the term *nistar*, the traditional name for the Kabbalah, meaning a "secret," is said to refer to personal religious experience. Scholem has argued that Hasidism is not, as Buber would have it, a purely emotional response. Hasidism, like the Kabbalah, has its gnosis. This is undoubtedly true of many early Zaddikim but, in the passage by Menachem Mendel of Premislani and in the work by Meshullam Phoebus of Zbarazh in which it is quoted, the gnosis of the Kabbalah, that which is in the sacred books, belongs to revealed knowledge—*nigleh*. The books are available for all to study. If a man is incapable of reading the books, for such a man, Menachem Mendel ironically remarks, Gemara and Tosafists are a mystery as well as the books of the Kabbalah. *Nistar*, the secret, is not hidden knowledge, not a gnosis, in Scholem's words, but is the intimate, personal experience of the Hasid who meets his God. It is called *nistar* since that is the nature of every personal experience. It is a secret for the one who has it and cannot be communicated to others.

Scholem has noted how the ideal of *devekut* had its effect on Hasidic attitudes to the traditional high value of Torah study. It is not only that prayer, the activity in which *devekut* can especially be attained, now occupies a higher rung in the ladder of Jewish piety than Torah study, a radical reversal of the traditional view, but the study of the Torah has itself undergone a complete transformation. Torah study, at least in early Hasidism, involves attachment to the spiritual light inherent in the letters of the Torah and is a devotional rather than an intellectual exercise. *Torah lishmah,* "Torah for its own sake," means, in Hasidism, "for the sake of God" whereas, as R. Hayyim of Volozhyn is at pains to point out, for the Mitnaggedim it means for the sake of the Torah and this obviously was the traditional understanding of the matter. Scholem is right in saying that there is a real contradiction between the two concepts. It is hardly possible to know and fully grasp, say, the complicated Talmudic debates if the student has his mind not on the subject matter itself but uses this only as an opportunity for a more intense communication with the divine. It was for this reason that the early Hasidim came down so heavily on the study of the Torah *she-lo lishmah,* with ulterior motives. Where the aim, as for the Mitnaggedim, is to study the Torah in the traditional sense, it is quite possible to engage in such study even though the motive may leave much to be desired. The study of the Torah *she-lo lishmah* is still study of the Torah only it is with the wrong motivation. When, for example, a scholar studies the Torah in order to win for himself a reputation as a learned man, his motive is far from the ideal but he has, after all, studied the Torah and has carried out this religious obligation. It is the motive that is faulty not the deed itself. But if, as the Hasidim understand the matter, the very meaning of Torah study is an exercise in *devekut,* of attachment to God, then where there is an ulterior motive there is no *devekut* and the study is not study at all from the Hasidic point of view. Paradoxically, the Mitnaggedic argument was that the Hasidim did not study the Torah precisely because of their understanding of the obligation in terms of *devekut.* The scholar who studied *she-lo lishmah* at least mastered his subject and had actually studied. The Hasidim who studied *lishmah,* in their sense of *devekut,* could never master the subject and all they were left with was the *lishmah* without the study.

Scholem steadfastly refused to recognise any influence on Hasidism from without. He briskly dismisses Torsten Ysander's attempt to find parallels to Hasidism in the Russian Church and is even more scathing of Yaffa Eliach's suggestion that Hasidic customs as well as the substance of Hasidic teaching came originally from the Russian sect of the Khlysti, a contention which, as Scholem says, is a deplorable example of scholarly irresponsibility, leaving the reader wondering about the state of Jewish studies. He could see no evidence at all for such hypotheses. His strict canons of historical investigation made him eschew what he considered to be mere guesswork. I once asked him how he understood the remarkable parallels which clearly exist between Hasidism and other eighteenth-century revivalist movements and he replied: who can explain the mysterious workings of the *Zeitgeist?* In other words, the parallels are certainly there but there is not the slightest case for any direct influence. Scholem preferred to study Hasidism as a development within Judaism, though, from within, he did acknowledge, and was one of the first scholars to do so, the strong influence of Shabbatianism on Hasidic thought and practices.

Scholem had little to say on some aspects of Hasidic life. He was heard to remark that a study of Hasidic liturgical innovations is likely to prove fruitful but he himself never explored this field. He is similarly unforthcoming on such matters as Hasidic discipleship; dynasties of Hasidic masters; the *kvittel* and the *pidyon nefesh; shirayyim;* the way the Hasidic Torah was composed and transmitted; the Hasidic garb; the Hasidic dance and the role of melody in Hasidic life. Scholem barely touched on the topics treated by Wertheim in his *Halakhot ve-Halikhot be-Hasidut.* Scholem did so much so well but no man can do everything, not even a Scholem.

ARTHUR HERTZBERG

Gershom Scholem as Zionist and Believer

*Then came the fundamental shift in perspective. It came with the rise
of the national movement. We found a firm place on which to stand, a
new center from which there appeared utterly different, new horizons.
. . . The new slogan was: to view our history from within . . . to re-
build the entire edifice of Jewish learning by the light of a Jew who
lives within his people and has no other purpose but to view problems,
events and ideas, in their true light, within the framework of their significance for the Jewish nation.*
—"Mi-Toch Hirhurim al Hochmat Yisrael," *Devarim be-Go*

Gershom Scholem was barely thirteen when he began his revolt against
the assimilation of Jews in Germany. He soon found his way to rabbis who
taught him classic texts. These men not only knew the Jewish law; they
believed it and obeyed it, and under their influence the young Scholem
thought seriously that in order to enter Judaism he ought to follow after
them. "Nonetheless, after I got to know the orthodox life up close, and after
years of ambivalence, I decided not to adopt it," so Scholem told in his
autobiography, *From Berlin to Jerusalem*. However, the tension remained
unresolved for some years more. In the Hebrew edition of the autobiography
there is even a picture of Scholem in Jerusalem in 1925 sitting on Sukkoth
inside a Sukkah with his head covered, studying the Zohar. Scholem had
been attracted to the Kabbalah very early, but here too he never agreed to
study it from within, that is, even briefly to suspend scholarly distance and
become a Kabbalist. In Jerusalem the young Scholem encountered a scholar
of the Kabbalah, of the older kind, who offered to teach him if Scholem

From *Modern Judaism* 5, no. 1 (February 1985). © 1985 by the Johns Hopkins
University Press.

would agree to listen and to ask no questions, to enter the world of the Kabbalah on its own terms. Scholem refused, even though he continued to hold frequent long conversations with this Kabbalist. His earliest path towards Jewish scholarship led him to the work of the nineteenth century founders of modern Jewish studies, the *Wissenschaft des Judentums*. In fact, he had begun to return to Judaism as a thirteen year old under the influence of his reading of a short popular version of Heinrich Graetz's *History of the Jews* which persuaded him that this was indeed his people and that he ought to identify with it. Nonetheless, despite his continuing admiration for Graetz, Scholem's work on the Kabbalah began as a counterattack on his first teacher. In 1945 Scholem completed his avowed break with most of the leading figures of the *Wissenschaft* school, for he accused them, in a stinging essay, of lacking any passion for continuing Judaism. Their historical studies, so Scholem insisted, had been done to classify and entomb the Jewish past, to write its epitaph.

At one point or another in Scholem's career he thus rejected, in whole or in part, German culture as not his own; the Halachah, the law of the rabbis, as a set of prescriptions under which he would not live; the Kabbalah, a world which fascinated him and to which he devoted his life, but which he would affirm as living value only in the most oblique ways; and modern Jewish historical scholarship, the scientific study of the Jewish past, to which he clearly belonged in his method even as he rejected his predecessors. In Scholem's own lexicon the word dialectic is to be found with great frequency. Sometimes this word in Scholem's uses really means ambivalence, that he himself was the field of battle within which opposing forces were at war.

All of these various elements within Scholem were to find their resolution in Zion. Zionism, and not his scholarly studies of the Kabbalah, or even the redefinition of the whole of Jewish history in the light of those studies, is the center of Scholem's intellectual and moral endeavor. The nascent Jewish community in Palestine was the place within which this latterday Archimedes chose to stand in order to forge his lever with which to move the world. He was thus able to live out the paradoxes of both breaking with Germany and with Western liberalism, but while never severing contact with the very culture that he had resoundingly rejected; to be a supreme incarnation of *Wissenschaft des Judentums* while entombing his predecessors for some of whom he had more than a passing admiration; and to believe in God, with enormous respect for both the Halachah and the Kabbalah, while identifying and affirming the secular life of Israel.

Scholem's ship arrived in Palestine in the port of Jaffa a day late, and so he landed on Yom Kippur morning. He hinted on occasion in conversation that perhaps there was some significance to this accident. He never hid his certainty that his journey was a paradigm for other people like himself in the Jewish world. In his autobiography [*From Berlin to Jerusalem*] Scholem quoted a letter which he wrote to a friend at the end of 1924, not much more than a year after he arrived in Palestine, in which he said that "here something more important is happening than anywhere else in the world."

This conviction did not lead him to distancing himself from his many friends in the Jewish intelligentsia whom he had left behind in Europe. On the contrary, he maintained and increased these connections in the six decades of his life in Zion. On his side these relationships were colored and even dominated by the desire to draw his friends after him to Zionism, that is, not merely to an ideology but to *Aliyah,* to casting one's lot with the renewed national community in Palestine. In his close friendship with Walter Benjamin, Scholem worked hard, and unsuccessfully, to convince Benjamin to come. He even arranged a Hebrew University grant to pay for his preliminary Hebrew studies in Germany, but Benjamin soon went off into Marxism. Scholem, ever the Zionist, warned Benjamin that he would find no home there or anywhere else except in the Judaism he was rejecting. Of one of the friends of his youth in Germany he wrote a kind of epitaph, in his autobiography: she would have been a particularly valuable addition to the new Jewish life being born in Palestine and that it was especially regrettable that she did not come. In his later years when most of his visitors among the Jewish intelligentsia were from English-speaking lands, he himself never overtly raised the question of *Aliyah,* but his wife Fania almost invariably did. I can bear personal witness to his increasingly sad, but demanding silence, and of her underscoring in words the meaning of what he was not saying.

In his youth in the 1920s Palestine was indeed the home for a striking number of creative Jewish intellectuals, far more than could be expected in a population of perhaps 80,000 Jews. The young Scholem had no doubt, then, that it was the home of the bravest and the best of Jewry. As the years went by, and especially after the creation of the State of Israel, comparable intellectual forces did not come from the United States, the last available reservoir of Jewish population. The intelligentsia in the expanding America after World War II were less troubled by immediate threats of anti-Semitism, or by feelings of otherness, than any previous generation of Jewish intellectuals in the Diaspora. Nonetheless Scholem believed that his journey would eventually be taken by many. There were more than hints in his conversations, and in occasional comments in his essays on current themes, of the notion that contemporary America might be Weimar Germany. Scholem never seemed to be sufficiently certain of that analysis to insist that anti-Semitism was inevitable even in America, that even there Jews would ultimately be excluded from the majority culture. In a roundtable discussion of the *Galut* in *Maariv* in 1963, he was willing to imagine the possibility of a people that does not regard the Jews living among it as alien. If the Jews cooperate by forgetting that they are in any sense in exile, then assimilation follows. He had American Jewry particularly in mind, among which, in the floodtide of its post-war success in American society as a whole, the word *Galut* had become unfashionable even among the Zionists.

Even though he was willing to imagine successful large-scale assimilation of Jews in the United States, Scholem insisted that America was not really different. The central question was not the possibility of anti-Semitism, which would inhibit assimilation, but rather personal authenticity. The post-World War II intelligentsia in American Jewry reminded him of the kind of people that he had known in Germany. At their most Jewishly and visibly involved, American Jewish writers made their careers out of describing the discomforts in the counterpulls of Jewish and American identity; but this had already been done in Germany in the 1920s by such figures as Jakob Wasserman who had written a very pained and famous book, *My Way as German and Jew*. The description of this tension in Philip Roth's *Portnoy's Complaint*, made Scholem very angry. He denounced the book in 1969 in two letters to *Haaretz*: Roth's portrayal of Jewish marginality was simply pornography; it furnished material for anti-Semites and "the Jews would yet pay dearly for this book." Scholem was a bit uncomfortable about the last remark, for it was out of character with his unapologetic stance, as a Zionist, before the gentiles; but he nonetheless "had to describe a fact." What seems to have prevailed here is the dominant and lasting motif in Scholem's Zionism: the quest for wholeness and authenticity, which was the healthy antithesis to Jewish marginality in the Diaspora, however well or badly that marginality might express itself.

The contributions of American Jews to movements of social protest and the prominence of many individuals in all fields of the larger culture was simply a repeat of earlier experiences in Europe. Scholem had rejected Jewish assimilation in Germany because, even if it worked, it represented the erosion of the true Jewish self. Of course he knew that many of his friends and contemporaries had once identified their Jewishness as the source of the energy which motivated their battle for universal ideals. Such a notion, which asserts that being Jewish does not necessarily lead to Jewish nationalism, Scholem denied on the basis of the first principle: an individual is authentically himself only if he maintains a basic, living connection to his natural community. Such connection to their Jewish identity was weakening among Jewish intellectuals and so Scholem concluded his comments in 1963 on the Diaspora in great pain. "I think that anyone who comes to New York and takes a serious look at what is happening there must inevitably conclude that it is a *Galut*—but it is a *Galut* the existence of which is denied by those who live there . . . Many years ago Ahad Ha-Am wrote his famous essay, 'Slavery in the Midst of Freedom,' which was directed against the assimilationists in Germany, France and Italy. What would he write today against the second and third generation of immigrants from Russia, and elsewhere, who came to the United States and have explained their historic experience in all its importance, as they have, for their own purposes: finding innumerable reasons with which to assert that they are totally at home in this land of many peoples and to deny any consciousness of being in *Galut*? And we are as yet only at the beginning of this road!"

In the light of this compound of sorrow and disdain, why did Scholem spend so much of his later years writing in English and in German and attending innumerable scholarly and intellectual conferences all over the Western world and especially in North America? It was not because he had a passionate desire to teach his chosen subject, the Kabbalah and Jewish mysticism, but because he wanted to suggest something to the intelligentsia as a whole and especially to its Jewish component. A Jew in the *Galut* might need to spend his time painfully balancing out the relationship between his Jewish and his Western identities. Scholem, the Zionist, had left that situation behind in order to express his Jewishness primarily through a lifelong preoccupation with Jewish mysticism. This tradition, as understood from within Judaism, shed its own light on such universal themes as that of order versus creativity in human life. Precisely because he had early chosen to be only a Jew, without hyphen or adjective, not a Western Jew or a German Jew or an American Jew, Scholem felt himself free to speak to Western culture unapologetically and very directly. He was particularly firm in that role because he was supported by, so he believed, a creative new Jewish culture which had been freed to change and to experiment because Jews were now in their own land. There the clash of various contrasting and even inimical ideologies and factions was welcome, because out of these battles a new formulation of modern Jewish existence would arise. To speak for such a world being born, to represent as scholar a neglected area of past Jewish experience of universal interest, Jewish mysticism, the study of which he single-handedly revived in the Land of Israel, was to be at once intensely Jewish and movingly contemporary.

This achievement reflects a basic element in Zionism, for in many of its forms the anti-Semitic Western world was rejected not in order to go native in the Levant, but rather to achieve full equality in European society by recreating the national identity of Jews in their own land. Theodor Herzl clearly thought of himself as a Western, even Austro-Hungarian, kind of political leader who could exercise that role only in a Jewish State. Scholem insisted that his fullest personal stature as scholar was possible only in Zion. In this he identified with a number of East Europeans who were his contemporaries in Germany and later in Israel, such as S. J. Agnon, the writer, and S. Z. Rubashov (later renaming himself Shazar), the scholar-journalist and Zionist politician. In their own view these figures entered the wider culture of the century with their dignity unimpaired and their authenticity asserted, precisely because they were part of the Jewish national renaissance. Agnon would eventually win the Nobel Prize in Literature; Shazar became the president of Israel. The young Scholem, who had refused to believe his father, that an academic career in Germany which would bring him respect in the larger world was really possible, achieved that very purpose by becoming a world famous professor of the Kabbalah and Jewish Mysticism at the Hebrew University. It is thus intelligible why, even after he became a master of Hebrew style, Scholem continued to write in German, and, though he stopped in 1937, he resumed publishing in that language twelve years later. Some of his fairly recent writings on the Kabbalah are still available only in German. In the years that Scholem was not writing German he went over in part to English; his book, *Major Trends in Jewish Mysticism,* was written in that language. It exists to this day only in Western languages and not, surprisingly, in Hebrew.

The break with German and with Western culture that propelled Scholem away from assimilation was thus not total. It was not merely that his Zionism looked outward to Europe, but that it had been defined in the early days of the twentieth century in the way in which only a young intellectual of those days, and of that place, could have defined it. Scholem never believed, from the days during World War I when he, essentially, refused to serve in the army, that liberal or left-wing internationalism would ever ultimately triumph in Germany, or in the world. He was at odds with one of his brothers, Werner, who was a Communist deputy in the *Reichstag* of the Weimar Republic. Nonetheless, as Gershom Schocken has recently demonstrated in an essay in *Haaretz,* Scholem's Jewish nationalism owed much to the example of German Romanticism. True *Gemeinschaft* and unsuppressed feelings were the slogans of some of these advanced young intellectuals at the turn of the century who disliked rationalism in both its bourgeois and Marxist forms. In part his emphasis on the identity of the Jew as primary and *sui generis* came from the enormous influence on Scholem, in his young-est years, of Martin Buber, who used such words as "blood" and "race" to describe Jewishness, before World War I, when these words had not yet been totally contaminated by the Nazis.

Scholem's interest in the Kabbalah began in the years 1915 to 1918. He "filled a number of copy books with quotations, translations and first reflections on the Kabbalah which were still far from any scholarly effort or understanding, but the bacillus of the Kabbalah had taken up permanent residence in my heart." Here too Scholem's relationship to his origins in German culture is more complex than that of a simple break. Late German Romanticism of the early years of the twentieth century brought with it a profound interest in mysticism and in "wisdom from the East." What could be at once more Jewish and more contemporary than to revive a whole gallery of Jewish figures in all their depth and angularity?

Even as he broke with Germany, as alien to him, Scholem remained in connection with those elements in German culture which represented what was in his view a minority tradition, of decency. He took up that conviction again after the Nazi era and, in the last year of his life, he was even willing to accept a German decoration, because the group which granted this pro-posed honor had been among the few, so he told me in personal conversation, which had remained clear of any Nazi taint.

Scholem's relationship to the Jewish culture and models that were avail-able to him in the first decades of the twentieth century is equally complex and dialectical. He seems to have learned a good bit from Moses Hess, even though he makes only one passing reference in his autobiography to having read *Rome and Jerusalem,* the first Zionist classic, published in 1862. Hess had confronted German Jewish assimilation near its very beginnings as an ideology. His reactions were essentially the same as those of Scholem a half a century later. On Scholem's most basic theme, the impossibility of German-Jewish symbiosis and of the necessity for Jews to stop deluding themselves that they can assimilate anywhere, Hess wrote as follows:

> The Germans hate the religion of the Jews less than they hate their race; they hate the peculiar faith of the Jews less than their pe-culiar noses. Reform, conversion, education and emancipation—none of these open the gates of society to the German Jews . . .
>
> As long as the Jew denies his nationality . . . his false position must become more intolerable . . . We shall always remain strang-ers among the nations.

Exactly one hundred years later Scholem wrote in December 1962 to an editor in Germany about Jews and Germans: "In reality there was never a partnership; it was a fiction for which a very high price was paid . . . The German-Jewish dialogue was that of shadows, and it took place in imaginary, non-existent, empty space."

These words are sharper, inevitably, because they were written after the Hitler era. Scholem wrote about German-Jewish symbiosis a bit more calmly in his autobiography [*From Berlin to Jerusalem*], when he looked back on the Kaiser's Germany:

> The lack of judgment of most Jews on all that involved they themselves, while in relation to all other matters they had the power of understanding and far-reaching criticism—a capacity which many justly admired, and also criticized—this power of self-delusion is an important and especially saddening element of the relationship betwen Jews and Germans.

Scholem turned early, along with a number of other young German Jews of his time and place, towards the East European Jews who had recently come to Germany, the very people whom his parents disliked. This was a very conscious rebellion against their parents because these young German Jews saw "in every Jew from Russia, Poland and Galicia who came their way a kind of incarnation of the Baal Shem, or, at very least, of the essence of Jewishness in all its attraction. In my life there was an important purpose to such encounters and to the ties of friendship which came from them." This was exactly the estimate made earlier [in *The Zionist Idea*] by Hess: "These Jews [of Eastern Europe] have preserved the living kernel of Judaism, the sense of Jewish nationality, more faithfully than our Occidental brethren." Scholem was of course much more radical than Hess, for Hess, after writing his book, had remained in Paris and did not choose to go to Palestine to make a beginning for the new life which he defined so well. The young Scholem insisted with heroic force that it was his personal duty to act on these conclusions and not leave them as elegantly stated theory.

This estimate of Scholem's relationship to his earliest readings of Hess is made all the more likely by the nature of his temperament. At various periods in his life he added up his debts to those who had influenced him at the beginning of his career, both by assessing what he had learnt from them and by sharply distancing himself from what he found unacceptable. This is clear and overt in his relationship to Heinrich Graetz. This most important of nineteenth-century Jewish historians was his favorite among the scholars of the *Wissenshaft* School, for, as was said above, it was the reading of an abridged version of his *History of the Jews* which set Scholem as a thirteen-year-old on the path towards Judaism. This debt Scholem acknowledged repeatedly, with a special emphasis on the importance of Graetz's Romantic nationalism in terms of which he conceived Jewish history as the record of a continuing living people. Scholem's lifelong interest in the Kabbalah was, to use a favorite term of his, in dialectic relationship to what he had learnt from Graetz. Something comparable to Scholem's outcry that the Kabbalah had been neglected by Jewish scholarship is to be found in an excursus (Note 3) in the back of the seventh volume of the complete edition of Graetz's history. Graetz began a highly technical essay of some seventeen closely printed pages as follows: "The Kabbalah has long been a field of study which no one has wanted to touch. The pious were afraid to approach it and the modern scholars avoided this abstruse and very difficult subject." Graetz's essay was a first attempt, but he at least knew that Jewish mysticism had ancient roots and that it had been represented in every period of Jewish history. The tone of Graetz's writing about the Kabbalah is objective, as his pages on the false Messiah, Shabtai Zvi, were not. He disliked this outbreak of false Messianism which shook the Jewish world and led to apostasy and to the loss of all restraint among many. Nonetheless, here too there is a long scholarly essay in the appendix to volume 10 amounting to almost one hundred pages in which Graetz wrote the history of Shabtai Zvi and his disciples through the eighteenth century. The theme of the latter part of this study is that the false Messianic underground of the eighteenth century existed, even though its literary remains are now hard to find, and was a powerful force for destroying the unity of the Jewish community.

It is here that Scholem's break with Graetz is apparent and pointed. In the introduction to his *magnum opus,* the two volumes on Shabtai Zvi, Scholem defined Graetz's view of the Kabbalistic flowering after the expulsion of the Jews from Spain in 1492 as an expression of Jewish weakness; that age could not maintain its commitment to reason, because it had been weakened by persecution and therefore the Jewish community could not withstand an outbreak of "obscurantism." Scholem vehemently denied this reading of Jewish history and insisted that the Kabbalah dominated in the sixteenth and seventeenth centuries because "it gave a clear response to the meaning of exile and redemption, a response which linked the historic experience of the Jewish people with that of existence as a whole." Scholem thus changed the understanding of the history of post-Biblical Jewish religion. It was not dominated by reason and law, with an occasional outbreak from a mystical religious underground when the immune mechanisms of Jewish order and reason were weakened by events. Kabbalah and Halachah were both positive forces in Jewish history, in dialectic relation with each other.

The study of Kabbalah thus became Scholem's life work and, as Buber
once said about him, other scholars have made major contributions to learning but Scholem alone created a new field, both in his historiographic interpretations and in his untiring research, which he conducted with the energy
and the brilliance of genius. In his reading of the Kabbalah and Jewish mysticism, Scholem's relationship to the founders of the *Wissenschaft des Judentums* was more complicated than he ever admitted to himself. In 1945
he published an essay under the title of "Reflections on *Wissenschaft des
Judentums*" in which he denounced Abraham Geiger with particular passion.
Geiger was not only a great scholar but also one of the founders of Reform
Judaism. Scholem denounced him for "clerical hypocrisy," and yet he admired Geiger for "the sovereign power which animates a great historian, to
force the facts into his own construction and to explain relationships on the
basis of historical intuition, a dangerous and creative power that Graetz also
possessed." What precisely did Abraham Geiger do with this "sovereign
power?" He assessed Talmudic Judaism as having once been a live and creative period in Jewish history, a reform of the Bible, an adaptation of it to
new circumstances and a break with those elements within it which were no
longer of living value. In Geiger's view rabbinic Judaism fitted that stage of
Jewish history in which the Jews were involved in their own specific national
identity. In the era of the emancipation, when Judaism was now becoming
a universal religion, Reform was setting out to do in its day something
comparable to what the Talmud had done before, that is to revise Judaism
for its newest stage. Therefore the Ritual Law was now superseded and there
remained only the mission of Israel to represent universal moral categories.
     Scholem has said comparable things about the Kabbalah. He made it
very clear in several of his essays that the Kabbalah was no longer alive. The
last representatives of any authentic kind of Kabbalism were older contemporaries of his in Jerusalem in the 1920s, such as Rabbi Abraham Isaac Kook
and the Hassidic Rebbe Arele Roth. No contemporary Jewish life can be
made out of the Kabbalah. On the contrary, the Kabbalah itself can lead
directly and logically to total religious anarchy. Once it is accepted that the
text of the Torah has deeper meanings than its literal ones, and that its
meanings are many, anything that a Kabbalist would like to imagine, including point by point destruction of the literal Torah, in order to free the "spiritual Torah," becomes possible. Scholem rang the changes on all of this in
perhaps his single most famous essay, published in 1937 under the title "The
Holiness of Sin," in which he summarized the ideas which underlie his work
on Shabtai Zvi and his followers, including the explanation of the apostasy
of the Messiah and the breaking of every commandment by some of his most

extreme followers as, in their view, religious necessity. In Scholem's own religious outlook he was frightened of anarchic values, religious or secular, for he kept insisting that he believed in God and that only in the belief in God was there any grounding for morality. Without some moral social order everything was possible, precisely because "God was dead." The writing of the history of the Kabbalah is then an act of telling the past correctly and even a way of suggesting that the present Jewish era, which was inevitably different from both the immediate and even more, from the distant past, had to take account of mystical experience and learn from it as a model, but it did not directly continue it. The grandeur of Scholem's writing, the passion with which he invested his scholarship, and the empathy with which he brings to life a whole host of strange figures has tended to obscure the fact that his writing is an act of magic. Scholem was quite clearly re-evoking these fascinating shades but ultimately, to use the language of his charge against the scholars of the *Wissenschaft* school, in order to bury them with due respect. It was part of the Jewish past; the present was Zionism.

To the degree to which the Kabbalah was alive for him, Scholem used it as a model for a new secular mysticism which had some subterranean links, perhaps, to the believing past. In 1964 he wrote an essay under the title "Reflections on the Possibility of Jewish Mysticism in Our Day." Its concluding passage needs to be quoted extensively. At the end of those reflections Scholem once again raised the issue with which he had dealt as a historian in 1937, that mysticism leads inevitably to anarchic individualism. Jewish continuity has depended, so Scholem asserted very flatly, upon the belief in revealed religion; since that belief is no longer held by many Jews, what can ensure both continuity and community? Ongoing secularization has posed a new question: Can secular life in any sense be regarded as sacred? He finally concluded that "there are those who see in the secularism of our lives and in the building of the Zionist state the expression of the mystical meaning of the secret of the Universe."

Geiger, committed to Jewish Universalism in the era of Reform, had asserted that his Judaism was a call to act in the manner of the Talmud, as he identified it, in a new day. So Scholem—committed more deeply to Zionism than to anything else—asserted that the passion for recreating Israel, the very secular Israel of modern twentieth century men and women, is the ladder on which Jews in his time can ascend to the *Ein Sof*.

Scholem had a comparable relationship to Leopold Zunz, the founder of the scientific studies of Judaism, whom he had attacked with great vehemence, along with Geiger. If Geiger's scholarship was "theological," an apologia for reforming Judaism, Zunz's was "political": he wanted to describe

Judaism in such fashion as to further the cause of the emancipation of Jews. The charge was true. The political purpose of modern Jewish studies was to establish that Jews had made major contributions to the founding of Western culture, and that they had not spent their time throughout all the centuries simply studying the Talmud and pilpulistic commentaries to it. Behold, Zunz proved, there had been Jewish philosophers in the Middle Ages, physicians such as Maimonides, and a whole host of mathematicians and grammarians—in short, Jews who were prominent in every aspect of general culture. Such a people had a right to demand, now, in the modern era, all of the benefits of legal equality that the state extends to its citizens, for the Jews could not be considered alien to Western culture.

Zunz's aim was radically denied by Scholem, who knew that, after legal equality had already been achieved, the Jews were not living happily ever after in Germany. Nonetheless, Scholem admired Zunz for his demonic power as historian, for his capacity to rescue from oblivion, neglected parts of the Jewish past and make them available for those who would make use of this past in the present. Scholem's work on the Kabbalah had, of course, been described by himself in the same way: it was a way of making available for use in the present a neglected part of the Jewish past. The parallelism with Zunz is, however, even deeper. Scholem's "political" purpose was to serve the Jewish national revival. That is why, he asserted, the new Jewish scholarship is different from the kind Zunz founded. In the service of that ideal, Scholem presented his studies of the Kabbalah not only to Jews but to the learned world as a whole, to suggest that the wide interest in mysticism could profit from encountering its Jewish expressionism, and that Jewish culture and spirituality included not only the essentially rational rabbinic law but also, like the other great traditions, it included profound constructions of the human spirit based on the mysterious and non-rational.

In the essay in 1964 which was his final assessment of the relevance of mysticism to contemporary Jewish life he ended a discussion that was obviously very difficult for him to write, as follows:

> For our new life (unless the teaching of A. D. Gordon is to be mentioned here) those of us who are laboring as Jews in the Land of Israel have an interest in the poetry of Walt Whitman. In his *Leaves of Grass*, in which he sang the song of America 100 years ago, he projected a feeling of the absolute holiness of absolute secularity . . . In the coming generations such mysticism is destined to take the form of naturalist, secular ways of thinking, which will have on their surface no trace of traditional religious

concepts, even though the substance of the mystical experience
will be perceived and continue to grow beneath the surface.

Scholem concluded by suggesting that the future of secular mysticism
is in the expansion of the human mind. In context, the clear implication of
his last comment is that Jewish man will experience such a possibility in its
highest within the Zionist community.

In this self-definition the debt to Martin Buber is clear, and so is the
distance from him. Buber taught Scholem this form of Zionism, that within
the authentic, small, renascent Jewish community a new spiritual authenticity
could be experienced by the individual. What Buber failed to do was to go
to Palestine before he was forced to by the Nazis. After his arrival, Buber
continued to look outward from Zion, in the certainty that I-thou encounters
of the highest order were possible even for Jews in the land of the gentiles.
This, Scholem, the Zionist, could not accept.

Nevertheless there is a fundamental truth to Scholem's critique of Geiger
and Zunz. Both of them were ultimately universalists who believed in the
vision of the eighteenth century Enlightenment, that one day human society
and culture would be one and that the process of realizing this vision was
underway in the modern era. Geiger and, even more, Zunz doubted that the
day had quite arrived and they therefore wanted to keep some form of Jewish
separateness alive in the very service of a universalizing ideal. To be sure,
Geiger turned more radical as he got older while Zunz became more conservative and more "Jewish," but they were both fair game for Scholem, the
Zionist. His deepest commitment was to Jewish particularism, to the continuity of a specific people and a specific tradition, and to refreshing it. Even
as he studied the Kabbalah, as historian, in the past tense, he pressed it, at
least obliquely, into service to nourish the new Zionist life.

Perhaps the most astonishing of Scholem's final hints in the last decade
or two of his life about his own views is to be found in the lecture that he
gave in Santa Barbara in 1973 on "Jewish theology today." There at the very
end Scholem, the lifelong exponent of the significance of the Kabbalah, said
the following: "I am convinced that . . . Zionism contains within it religious
content and a religious potential that is far more fundamental than anything
that is expressed by the existing 'religious parties of the State of Israel.' In
the dialectic of Jewish life, the religious tradition continues to be the challenge, *and the fundamental element in that tradition is the Halachah.*" The
circle which began in his youth was thus closed in his later years. Halachah
is no longer, as he sometimes said in his earlier years, a fossil; it is now the
central element of religious continuity. Mysticism is the refresher and cor-

rective, but one can detect a progression in Scholem's later years of growing worry about its anarchic tendencies. The combat of law and mysticism will take place in the new secular Zionist community within which a new Jewish culture is arising. Despite Scholem's past emphasis on the secularity of the Zionist culture, he remained convinced that the religious elements in Judaism were so powerful that "so long as the belief in God is a fundamental phenomenon among all beings created in His image, a faith which cannot be destroyed by any ideology, it appears to me that the absolute secularization of Israel is inconceivable. The continued wrestling with this process of secularization, with both its positives and its limitations, seems to me to be creative and determining."

The issue of religion, of Scholem's abiding faith in God, was the reason for his eventual break with Ahad Ha-Am, the central figure of cultural Zionism. Ahad Ha-Am had proposed at the turn of the century the creation in Palestine of a "spiritual center," a Jewish community of high quality which, though not necessarily of large size, would create a modern Jewish culture which in the very process of encountering modernity in a deeply Jewish way, would invigorate the whole of the Jewish world and act as a model for it. Ahad Ha-Am had a profoundly Jewish education of the kind imparted to rabbis in Eastern Europe in the mid-nineteenth century, but he was an agnostic, and his vision of the new Jewish culture was secular. All his life this Russian Jewish positivist tried to find a way of defining the Jewish national genius as particularly suited to producing a unique morality, but he never found the way to do much more than simply assert this proposition as an undoubted truth. The young Scholem had been attracted to Zionism by East Europeans who were largely followers of Ahad Ha-Am; they saw themselves as on the way, as many of them indeed were, to the Land of Israel, to help create there an elite community which would be Jewish in its sense of historical continuity and morality, and contemporary in its intellectual freedom.

Scholem's journey to Jerusalem was spiritually and even physically in the company of these men, almost all of whom remained his lifelong friends. A good number of his East European contemporaries were in the Labor Movement and Scholem, even though he did not belong to that party, maintained connection all his life with its intelligentsia. Nonetheless what ultimately divided Scholem from Ahad Ha-Am and even from some of his friends in Labor was that he was a believer and that he could not imagine the new Zionist creation in Israel as breaking with faith in God.

In the midst of all of Scholem's scattered essays on contemporary themes, one can thus discern a system. Despite the disguise of tentativeness in much of his writing, that system is based on morality. Here, despite all his strictures against rationalism, Scholem is himself a man of the eighteenth century, the one that he so often condemned. Morality was not, for him, an expression of national genius. It does not represent among Jews any particular propensity for higher values. This kind of thinking leads to chauvinism, and Scholem would have none of that. He therefore insisted, over and over again, that morality is a universal category, that it is no respecter of nations and that it confers no particular roles or benefits. Eighteenth century universalism had been attacked by Scholem to the degree to which it offered modern Jews, and especially Jewish intellectuals, rationalizations by which they could define themselves as a transnational element, beyond the bounds of a specific community or culture; he asserted this very Enlightenment rationalism as a curb against the danger of national autarchy, and especially against Jewish integral nationalism.

Scholem was thus both a mystic and Humanist. He had chosen, early, his own authentic people and their land and he wanted that place not to be "a light unto nations," because the term itself had been vulgarized by its use in modern Jewish apologetics, but certainly a model community. He demanded of it seriousness and absence of militarism and an austere national morality, bordering on pacifism. He thus did indeed belong to such Russian Jewish intellectuals as A. D. Gordon, the *rebbe* of the Labor Movement, who brought with him from Russia a narodnik kind of desire to return to the land, and to the scholars who founded the Hebrew University who, at their best, were trying to continue Jewish religious piety with a secular high-mindedness rooted in history and national consciousness, and, often, an untraditional religious piety.

It was a noble effort. Why was it not joined by large elements of the Jewish intelligentsia in the last two generations? Why did Scholem leave this world in tragedy, with a sense of fulfillment as a scholar but with the feeling that his work as a Zionist was unfinished, and perhaps even impossible? The simplest answer is that throughout the ages, including the last century of modern Zionism, only a minority of Jewish intelligentsia has gone to the Land of Israel, even when they could. Only in their minority, and a very small one at that, did West European Jewish intellectuals come to Palestine before 1933. The bulk of secularized Jewish intelligentsia has for the last two centuries, in situation after situation, preferred to believe that a significant role existed for it in the larger culture, either as critics in unfriendly places or as culture-bearers in good times. The probability that after several generations such an intelligentsia will cease being Jewish, except perhaps in some remaining indefinable aroma, is of concern only to those who, like the young Scholem, have made a deep prior commitment to Jewish particularism. That is an act of some kind of faith. It cannot be compelled by argument; it can only be given life by the example of individuals such as Scholem. In Israel he was a scholar and a spiritual teacher within a society which both gave him room to be his idiosyncratic self and which cared about him. It is this sense of both protecting context and utter freedom which Scholem insisted does not exist for the Jewish intellectual outside Israel; even at his freest, he is within a culture that others not of his kind largely created.

The bulk of Jewish intelligentsia, especially in America today, rejects the notion of Jewish alienation in any sense. Jewish experience, so we have been assured, is now one of the regions of America like Faulkner's South or Duke Ellington's Harlem. Perhaps it is. Scholem did not believe it, and he kept insisting that the increasing number of Jewish intellectuals from abroad, who had become his friends, or his semi-disciples, in recent decades needed to think again. In this dialogue Scholem and those whom he addressed came from quite different situations. His family in Berlin had already traversed the journey from a village, and near poverty, to bourgeois comfort, and from isolation in the ghetto to assimilation. His auditors among the Jewish intelligentsia in America were at least a generation behind him, for they were mostly the grandchildren of immigrants from Eastern Europe and they were still engaged in completing the journey from their grandparents' memories of pogroms and their parents' experience of depression and substantial exclusion even in America to the center of a culture which was increasingly plural, chaotic and large. To be sure, in the last fifteen years American culture has developed major interests in Eastern religion and in mysticism, in general. This development parallels what was happening in Europe in Scholem's youth, and it is largely because of these interests that Scholem's work has become popular in recent years. Few of the Jewish intelligentsia have, as yet, read him the way he wanted to be read. It is useful to quote here the remarks of Harold Bloom in his recent book *Agon* in the essay entitled "Free and Broken Tablets: The Cultural Prospects of American Jewry." Bloom is not very hopeful about the cultural prospects for American Jewry, because he finds this community is not at all oriented to classic texts. The baggage of Jewish learning of those intelligentsia is very skimpy. Bloom therefore invokes Scholem, as the contemporary moral prophet in Jewry, in his insistence on Jewish primary sources and on his regarding nothing Jewish as alien. Even so careful a reader as Bloom has, however, misread Scholem. Bloom declares that "Scholem has never made the mistake of analogizing German and American Jewry." This is simply not true, for, as I proved at the beginning of this essay, Scholem did exactly that. Any Jewry which had fallen away from text was for Scholem on the way out of its Jewishness; a serious return to text led inevitably to exit from the wider culture into the Jewish life being created by Zionism. In his own mind, Scholem had not spent his life trying to purvey knowledge of the Kabbalah even to those lovers of the occult who wanted exact information. His work was his contribution to the sum total of the Jewish national revival; it was part of his Zionist demand on the lives of his Jewish readers.

Scholem's relationship to contemporary Israel had in it, at the end of his days, an element of great sorrow. He often charged the contemporary rabbis with narrowness, for they restricted themselves to ritual matters and were uninterested in the life of the community. In his last years he was witness to a new breed of rabbi, the leaders of Gush Emunim who fulfilled his expectation, at least in its verbal formulation: they and their followers have become vitally involved in public questions in the name of a religious ideal, as they define it. It is no secret that Scholem did not look upon this particular combination of religion and public policy with great joy. He had once declared that the new Jewish settlement in the Land of Israel was the place where all of the clashing elements and schools of thought within Jewry would encounter each other and even quarrel and that what would result from this process and be accepted by a majority would be the new Judaism. Clearly he imagined that such a result would occur within the bounds set by a liberal, humanitarian tradition.

And yet, for all of his unhappiness in much of Israel's current life, Scholem remained unshakeably a Zionist. The issues which the modern age had raised in relationship to the Jewish heritage, the question of what was to be retained or rebuilt and what was to be destroyed, remained in Zion "as yet entirely unsolved, and everything is still open." Scholem continued to believe that Zionism was "a great experiment in human alchemy; through its agency hatred and enmity would be changed at some future time into understanding, respect and fraternity."

HAROLD BLOOM

Scholem: Unhistorical or Jewish Gnosticism

Gershom Scholem, masking truly as a historical scholar, was the hidden theologian of Jewish Gnosis for our time, even as Freud unknowingly was its speculative psychologist and Kafka its poet. Rarely unmasking, Scholem sometimes hinted his truest desires. One of these hints is his sequence of "Ten Unhistorical Aphorisms on Kabbalah," first printed in 1958, which I summarize roughly:

1. "Authentic tradition remains hidden."
2. Secrets are better protected by speech and writing than by silence.
3. "God Himself is the Torah"; so Torah also cannot be known.
4. The Lurianic dialectic is both trope and literal truth, so that the Divine itself is degraded, as in Valentinian Gnosis, or in Nathan of Gaza.
5. Without a negative moment, God and the Creation become One. There must be an Abyss in the Divine Will.
6. Kabbalah transmutes the Law into "transparency," and so, at last, into the antinomian.
7. The "real misfortune" of Kabbalah is its Neoplatonic theory of emanation; the truth of Kabbalah is Cordovero's Gnosis, in which God and the "divine wills" touch but do not coincide.
8. Kabbalah is utopian *or* magical, since even God must be seen

"at that place where I stand." *Tikkun* or "restitution" therefore
can be expressed even as the social messianism of Benjamin
and Bloch.

9. "The name of God can be pronounced but not expressed"; it
must be mediated by tradition, before we can hear it, and even
then must be handed down in fragments, occultly.

10. Kafka, unknowingly, secularized Kabbalah. His writings therefore have for Scholem as for Benjamin and others "something
of the strong light of the canonical, of that perfection which
destroys."

Scholem's historical exegete, David Biale, reads these aphorisms as a
defense of Scholem's own "counter-history" of Judaism. This is surely right.
They are also the sketch of a theory of reading, and also of a new theosophy
founded upon an ancient Gnosis. How much of normative Judaism do they
permit us to retain?

If authentic tradition must remain hidden, then not only institutional
Judaism becomes inauthentic. Scholem's own speech and writing would have
been inauthentic, except that they protected secrets better than an unchar-
acteristic Scholemian silence could have done. As for Torah, it cannot be
known; like Yahweh, indeed since it is Yahweh, Torah cannot be read. On
this account, the Yahwist is not less esoteric than Isaac Luria, or else a radical
trope like the *zimzum* or Divine Contraction is already implicit in the Yahwist. Nathan of Gaza, nihilistically conceiving an Infinite Godhead in Whom
"thought-less" and "thought-full" lights clash continually, enforces the same
paradox as the Yahwist. The *zimzum* is both materially true, a supermimetic
overliteralism, and an extreme metaphor or catachresis. But so also is the
image of Yahweh arguing with Abraham on the road to Sodom. Where the
zimzum is a negative moment in Creation, so Yahweh disputing with Abraham is a negative moment in the Patriarchal history. Without these negative
moments, Yahweh and the Creation threaten to become one. *Zimzum* inaugurates the Abyss in the Divine Will, and the interventions by Abraham
engender another Abyss in that Will, but for which God and the Patriarchal
history might become one also.

But Torah with an Abyss in it is Torah transparent, rather than opaque,
and so Sabbatai Zevi and Jacob Frank are the legitimate heirs rather than
the betrayers of Kabbalah, and of Torah also. The negative moment opens
up, and what appears, by the light of the sparks generated through that
opening, might be called Scholem's final and unstated paradox: Sabbatai
Zevi, Nathan of Gaza, and Jacob Frank are no more and no less represen-

tative of Jewish spirituality than are, say, Maimonides, Judah Halevi, and Franz Rosenzweig. The nihilists and the philosophers alike inhabit the Scholemian Negative, in which the distinction between redemption through virtue and redemption through sin becomes virtually meaningless.

II

Scholem never wearied of finding his true precursor in Kafka, who had shown Scholem (and so the rest of us) how to walk the fine line between religion and nihilism. Kafka himself would have observed what he always intimated in his diaries, aphorisms, parables, stories; that there is no fine line or true way we can walk. Both sides of the line are hedged by nihilism:

> The true way goes over a rope which is not stretched at any great height but just above the ground. It seems more designed to make people stumble than to be walked upon.

Scholem's peculiar genius is that he did not stumble, but walked nimbly upon that rope, which he called neither religion nor nihilism. He called it scholarly history, but no one who reads him deeply could agree with him. The Kabbalah of Gershom Scholem is as much his as were those belonging to the visionaries, Moses Cordovero or Nathan of Gaza. At the close of his thousand page masterpiece, *Sabbatai Zevi, The Mystical Messiah,* Scholem may seem detached from the fate of Sabbatai, and of Nathan his prophet, but to read Scholem's marvelous commentary upon Nathan's *Treatise on the Dragons* earlier in the volume is to participate in a joyous festival of exuberant interpretation. This festival is prepared by some of Scholem's most pungent remarks against those who insist upon an essence of Judaism that would exclude Scholem's sense of the tradition:

> Perhaps it is even unnecessary to look for specific Christian influences where the respective situations are so similar. Early Sabbatianism and the early church went similar ways in accordance with the same psychological laws. But however that may be, the fact remains that at the very beginning of the movement, pure faith, independent of the observance of the Law, was proclaimed as the supreme religious value which secured salvation and eternal life for the believers. We should note in passing that this proclamation did not provoke the reaction one would have expected if some of today's cliches regarding the "essence" of Judaism and of Christianity were correct. As a matter of fact they are not, and

most modern generalizations on the subject of Jewish *versus* Christian religiosity are more than doubtful. There is no way of telling *a priori* what beliefs are possible or impossible within the framework of Judaism. Certainly no serious historian would accept the specious argument that the criteria of "Jewish" belief were clear and evident until the Kabbalah beclouded and confused minds. The "Jewishness" in the religiosity of any particular period is not measured by dogmatic criteria that are unrelated to actual historical circumstances, but solely by what sincere Jews do, in fact, believe, or—at least—consider to be legitimate possibilities.

Scholem's criteria here delight me, because they are so sublimely outrageous. "Sincere Jews" can just as well be read as "sincere nihilists" or "sincere what-you-will" and the "legitimate possibilities" projected by sincerity are charmingly infinite. The "sincere" Nathan of Gaza, as expounded by the indubitably "sincere" Scholem, substituted contemplation of the mystery of Sabbatai for the observance of the Ten Commandments, and aspired towards the final substitution of the study of a Torah of messianic freedom for the mere Torah itself. On Scholem's authority, the antinomian potential of "the religiosity of any particular period" is pragmatically unbounded.

The supposed puzzle of Kabbalah always has been its ability to accommodate itself to the normative Judaism of any era. I say "supposed," because Scholem himself is in the perpetual paradox of bringing to exposure a tradition that can remain authentic only so long as it is hidden. What Scholem has given us, by this principle, which is his own, must be inauthentic, except for the splendid paradox that what he has given us is his own, and therefore is authentic in another sense. Scholem is necessarily what he necessarily could not admit he was: a great revisionist of Kabbalah. His major essays, such as "Tradition and New Creation in the Ritual of the Kabbalists" or "Reflections on Jewish Theology," are transumptions of works like "The Garden of Pomegranates" by Cordovero and *Treatise on the Dragons* of the Sabbatarian Nathan. Scholem transumes Cordovero and Nathan precisely as Milton renders himself early and Virgil and Spenser late; the historian and scholar is also an epic poet of Kabbalah, even as the epic poet is also the historian and scholar of Western poetic tradition.

Scholem's major revision of Kabbalah is informed by a curious paradox. Kabbalah is seen by Scholem as being at once wholly Jewish, and so not truly counter-normative, yet also in its essence as being wholly Gnostic, and so utterly irreconcilable with rabbinical Judaism. Only an enlarged concept of the Negative, more diffuse either than Kafka's or than Freud's, could hold together a Kabbalah of God the father, rigorously keeping His Covenant with Israel, and of the alien God, distantly transcendent, who has no part in our ruined demiurgical cosmos, which fell even as it was created.

III

I want to trace something of the complex development of Scholem's idea of the Negative by examining three of his most powerful essays: "Redemption through Sin" (1937), now most available in *The Messianic Idea in Judaism;* "Tradition and New Creation in the Ritual of the Kabbalists," in *On the Kabbalah and Its Symbolism,* originally published in 1960; "Reflections on Jewish Theology" (1974), now available in *On Jews and Judaism in Crisis.* We can call these instances of early, middle, and later Scholem, with the decisive change intervening between early and middle, a change presumably dominated by consciousness of the Holocaust.

"Redemption through Sin" could impress an American reader as a commentary upon Nathanael West's *Miss Lonelyhearts,* and in particular upon the demoniac figure of Shrike in that extraordinary short novel. I once mentioned the book to Scholem, who shrugged the reference off and lost interest when told that West had changed his name from Nathan Weinstein, was something of a Jewish anti-Semite, and had no overt knowledge of Kabbalah. Yet *Miss Lonelyhearts,* far more precisely and more vividly than anything by Isaac Bashevis Singer, illustrates the spiritual world of Scholem's "Redemption through Sin." I cannot read certain passages in the essay without remembering Shrike:

> The annihilation of every religion and positive system of belief—
> this was the "true way" the "believers" were expected to fol-
> low . . . The descent into the abyss requires not only the rejection
> of all religions and conventions, but also the commission of
> "strange acts," and this in turn demands the voluntary abasement
> of one's own sense of self, so that libertinism and the achievement
> of that state of utter shamelessness which leads to a *tikkun* of the
> soul are one and the same thing.

Scholem is summarizing the aggressive nihilism of Jacob Frank, but one hears in the messianic intensity of the Frankists the desperate, hysterical, savage tonality of West's butcher-bird, Shrike. *Miss Lonelyhearts* proves to be Jewish, ironically enough, in its negations and in its indeliberately Freudian assumptions of total sense. Freud's Negation, with its cognitive return of the repressed, is represented by West's projection as Shrike, while the Freudian affective continuation of repression finds its representative in Miss Lonelyhearts himself, who is the introjection of West's inability either to believe in Christ or to trust in the Covenant of his Jewish father and mother.

Jacob Frank (1726–91) was probably the darkest figure in the history of the Sabbatian movement, yet even in the relatively early "Redemption through Sin," we can observe Scholem entertaining a certain fascination for Frank, particularly when the historian of Jewish esotericism allows himself to observe of Frank that "for all the negativism of his teachings, they nonetheless contained a genuine creed of life." Scholem did not go on to elucidate this "genuine creed," since he presumably did not wish overtly to exalt Frank's nihilistic vitalism. But in the much later encyclopaedic work, *Kabbalah*, Scholem distinguished sharply between Frank as an "adventurer" with a "lust for power" and Frank's "believers" as being "on the whole men of deep faith and moral integrity." It is as though Scholem's authentic sympathy for the Sabbatian movement was so intense that even the deluded Frankists were welcomed into the true traditions of esoteric or Gnostic Judaism.

Scholem's peculiar and complex originality as a supposed historical scholar has imposed some remarkable contingencies upon us. One of these ensued from his fierce desire to find a continuity in Jewish esotericism, so as to establish a counter-tradition to the normative. It is a labyrinthine path that winds from Merkabah mysticism and Jewish Gnosticism through medieval German Hasidism on through the *Zohar* and then through Cordovero and Luria to Nathan of Gaza and the Sabbatians, to culminate at last in the Baal Shem Tov, with Scholem himself as philological yet also theological epilogue. The most tenuous link in the Scholemian chain of esoteric tradition binds the Sabbatians to Lurianic Kabbalah, as though Nathan of Gaza were the true inheritor of the later or modernist Kabbalah. We may seek therefore with some prospect of reward for Scholem's true account of the Negative in his superb essay upon Lurianic ritual, "Tradition and New Creation in the Ritual of the Kabbalists."

Scholem begins here with his central paradox: Kabbalah is a conservative ideology within the frame of Rabbinical Judaism, and yet: "the old God whom Kabbalistic gnosis opposed to the God of the philosophers proves, when experienced in all His living richness, to be an even older and archaic one." This is a rather bold figure, Scholem admits, for the re-entry of myth into monotheistic Judaism, into a religion that, in the Diaspora, engendered a ritual "in which the natural year is replaced by history." Of this normative ritual Scholem remarks, in what I take to be his most memorable and most subtly dialectical sentence: "The ritual of Rabbinical Judaism makes nothing happen and *transforms* nothing." At one pole of the dialectic, this is a critique of normative ritual, as Scholem eloquently makes clear:

> Though not devoid of feeling, remembrance lacks the passion of conjuration, and indeed there is something strangely sober and dry about the rites of remembrance with which the Jew calls to mind his unique historical identity. Thus this ritualism par excellence of Rabbinical Judaism is lacking precisely in the ecstatic, orgiastic element that is always somewhere present in mythical rituals.

That is the Scholem we expect, but the other half of the dialectic follows, shrewder and more powerful in its recognitions:

> The astonishing part of it is that a ritual which so consciously and emphatically rejected all cosmic implications should have asserted itself for many generations with undiminished force, and even continued to develop. A penetrating phenomenology of Rabbinical Judaism would be needed to determine the nature of the powers of remembrance that made this possible and to decide whether other secret factors may not after all have contributed to this vitality.

Scholem had not much use for Freud, who might have helped the revisionist of Kabbalah to see, at just this point, the work of that negation by which thought can free itself, in part, from its sexual past. If the normative ritual frees religious thought from its sexual past, and it does, then there is a partial return of the repressed, by way of a wholly cognitive introjection, while an affective projection or spitting-out of the natural is maintained. Scholem's dialectical balance, unfortunately, is lost when he turns to the description of the Lurianic ritual, which he implicitly praises for what it tries to make happen, for what it hopes to transform. As Scholem rather calmly notes, a dilemma faces "the Kabbalists in their striving to transform Judaism into a mystery religion." That transformation relies upon ritual's assumption of a "role of representation and excitation," a re-sexualization of thought in which the sacred marriage of the masculine and feminine is acted out yet again. A grand Scholemian gusto is manifested in the description of mystical marriages and related moonshines, including marvelous conjurations against the darkly lustrous figure of Lilith, whom a true Kabbalist doubtless has to regard as the patroness of all feminism, since the Kabbalah is nothing if not sexist. This is all good, unclean fun, though it adds little to Scholem's pow-

erful and persuasive point about the fundamental differences between normative and Lurianic ritual.

What needed to be added is accomplished in the powerful late essay,
"Reflections on Jewish Theology," where an ancient and rugged negativity
is introduced by Scholem with a charming shyness, insinuated as it is into a
discussion of the Second Commandment almost as though a Gnostic negation is the only possible interpretation of the Jewish preference for an almost
imageless god. We listen to Scholem here at his most evasive:

> The veneration of an imageless God simultaneously casts doubt
> on the visualizable character that seemed to pertain to everything
> created. Nothing created was worthy of representing what was
> beyond visualization. Therein was also virtually incorporated a
> possible conclusion which by far transcended the comprehension
> of the Biblical and medieval world. Is not the visualizable aspect
> of the world mere pretense; is what is visualizable not merely an
> approximation incapable of expressing the Creation? Is not Cre-
> ation itself in its own way just as much beyond visualization as
> the Creator?

What transcends the comprehension here of the Torah and of the Talmud, and also of the earlier or Neoplatonic Kabbalah, is necessarily comprehended by the later or Gnostic Kabbalah of Cordovero and Luria, in
which true Creation is beyond visualization, because the actual Creation was
a catastrophe, and ensued from the breaking of the vessels. Marvelously,
Scholem sums up Jewish theology in the full accents of Lurianic myth:

> Creation out of nothing, from the void, could be nothing other
> than creation of the void, that is, of the possibility of thinking of
> anything that was not God. Without such an act of self-limita-
> tion, after all, there would be only God—and obviously nothing
> else. A being that is not God could only become possible and
> originate by virtue of such a contraction, such a paradoxical re-
> treat of God into Himself. By positing a negative factor in Him-
> self, God liberates Creation.

Scholem writes as if a negative theology is the only possible theology,
and yet Judaism is scarcely founded upon a vision of the Negative. Characteristically evasive here, Scholem suggests nevertheless that only the Lurianic vision of God is possible for us. Perhaps this is so, though we may
wonder why Scholem worked so much of his life under the evasive mask of
the dispassionate and scholarly historian.

IV

There are many modes of evasion available to us beyond those taught by Scholem, and evasion of and in the spiritual life is a never-ending process. Scholem liked to use the age-old trope of a living body when he spoke of the present and future of Judaism. He refused to speculate upon that future, but clearly he knew that he had supplied us with a Jewish Gnosis, *in his own writings,* and he knew also that only a fraction of us could find our way to such a gnosis independently of him. The enigma of Scholem is that he was himself anything but a mystical messiah. Freud, who refused rationally to assume such a role, nevertheless has become just that for the literalists of the speculation that he inaugurated. Scholem shrewdly aspired to become rather a philological equivalent of Kafka, hinting at a gnosis that we could read between the lines.

I take the notion of "reading between the lines" from Leo Strauss, who chose the normative tradition of Judaism, and who must have known, better than I can, how much Plato had been assimilated into that tradition by the great rabbis of the second century of the Common Era. This assimilation, studied by Elias Bickerman, whose findings then were modified by Saul Lieberman, is quite unmistakeable yet is nowhere mentioned by Scholem, probably both because he took it for granted that normative legalism had profound affinities with Plato's *Laws,* and because he hardly could have cared less. What he did care about was the esoteric or mystical tradition, which in some sense he had reinvented, and there he certainly did resent what he judged to be the Platonic intrusion. His Kabbalah was Gnostic and not Neoplatonic, which accounts for the remarkable aphorism 7 of his "Ten Unhistorical Aphorisms on Kabbalah," where he calls the Neoplatonic theory of emanation, "the real misfortune of the Kabbalah," and remarks that Moses Cordovero ought to be thought of as a phenomenologist rather than a follower of Plotinus.

Scholem's distaste for the theory of emanation is his own most surprising swerve away from Kabbalah, and I think it is the technical center of his theosophical legacy to us. Kabbalah has many built-in self-contradictions, of which the deepest is the irreconcilability between its Plotinean theories of emanation and its Gnostic theories of catastrophe creation. Scholem desired Kabbalah to be wholly Gnostic and yet wholly Jewish, which resulted in his shrewdly desperate insistence that Gnosticism was essentially Jewish in its origins. I am necessarily a hopeless amateur in all scholarly questions relating to Kabbalah, to Gnosticism, and to Neoplatonism, so that what follows is merely an eccentric literary critic's anecdote. Visiting Scholem at his home

in Jerusalem, I had the privilege of listening to his forceful and informed
discourse upon just these matters. When, in my puzzlement, I attempted to
remind him that Gnosticism itself seemed as much a strong misreading of
Plato as of the Hebrew Bible, so that in some strange sense Gnosticism and
Neoplatonism both derived from Plato, Scholem replied triumphantly: "Exactly so. And where did Plato get everything from? Egypt, who had it from
us!"

Nietzsche, not one of Scholem's authorities, taught us that all ancestral
figures are numinous shadows, and also that origins and aims were separate
entities that for the sake of life had to be kept apart. But Gnostics refuse to
separate origins and aims, and Scholem was a Jewish Gnostic, though doubtless he would have preferred to be called a Gnostic Jew. Creation was Scholem's crucial subject, and his rejection of Neoplatonic accounts of creation,
without which Kabbalah is unimaginable, is his most vital act as a revisionist
of Jewish esotericism, since it substitutes a Gnostic dialectics of negation for
the Neoplatonic Negative that ensued both in Christian theology, and ultimately in the negative philosophy of Hegel and all his followers down to
contemporary Gallic deconstructors.

What would an altogether Gnostic Kabbalah resemble? Could we distinguish it from the Alexandrian Gnosticism of Valentinus, or even of Basi-
lides? The figure of Jesus would be gone, of course, but what else in the
Valentinian *Gospel of Truth* would not suit a Scholemian Kabbalah?
Aphorism 7 calls for "an authentic disciple of Cordovero . . . if ever there
should be such a disciple," who would discard the trope of emanation, and
give us an ontological Kabbalah concerned with "the structures of beings."
That authentic disciple could only be Scholem himself. How can he be said
to have so revised Cordovero and Luria as to have given us a Kabbalah finally
purified from the metaphors of Plotinus?

Scholem always emphasized that Kabbalah, like Gnosticism, located disaster within God himself, though no actual Kabbalistic writer before Nathan
of Gaza was nihilistic enough to posit a degradation within the Godhead.
But a multitude of earlier Kabbalists internalized the Neoplatonic trope of
emanation, making of it a process going on within God rather than between
God and this world. Scholem, if we dare to call him a Kabbalist, is certainly
not among the most nihilistic; even he seems a touch startled by the speculative shock tactics of Nathan of Gaza's *Treatise on the Dragons*. But if he
is not the most negative and Gnostic of Kabbalists, Scholem may be the most
internalizing, by which I do not intend "psychologizing," even in the Jungian
mode. I mean that Scholem was not much interested in the *Sefirot,* which
always are the staple of popular Kabbalism. Instead, Scholem joined Cor-

dovero and Luria, and also Nathan, in an obsession with the imagery of catastrophe, with the tropes of the stories that tell how God himself placed himself in exile, how he dispersed himself among the shattered vessels of creation even as he dispersed the Jews among the nations. What the Iberian Expulsion was to Cordovero and Luria; what the Polish massacres of 1648 were to Sabbatai and to Nathan; all that and more the Holocaust was to Scholem. As early as 1937, when he was forty years old, Scholem thought back to his first interests in Kabbalah, of 1915, and of his decision to devote his life to the subject, in 1919, and wrote:

> In no way did I become a "Kabbalist" inadvertently. I knew what I was doing—only it seems to me now that I imagined my undertaking to be much too easy. . . .
> So I arrived at the intention of writing not the history but the metaphysics of the Kabbalah.

In 1937, Scholem also first published his great essay, "Redemption through Sin." A contrast between this pre-Holocaust meditation, and such powerful later essays as "Tradition and New Creation in the Ritual of the Kabbalists" and "Reflections on Jewish Theology" is grimly instructive. "Redemption through Sin" begins with an optimistic aura that the growth of the *Yishuv* in Palestine ought to encourage a sympathy for the Sabbatian movement:

> In these times of Jewish national rebirth it is only natural that the deep though ultimately tragic yearning for national redemption to which the initial stages of Sabbatianism gave expression should meet with greater comprehension than in the past.

There is a curious tone to the ending of "Redemption through Sin," where Scholem expounds his theory that the Sabbatians and Frankists were led by their heresies to the various paths of assimilation, of the *Haskalah* or Jewish Enlightenment, or to European revolutionary movements. In these secular solutions, Scholem finds the irony from which all paradox disappears:

> What they, the members of "the accursed sect," had earnestly striven for in a stormy contention with truth, carried on in the half-light of a faith pregnant with paradoxes.

I do not think that Scholem's understanding of "the metaphysics of the Kabbalah" changed radically after 1945, but his acute consciousness of the Holocaust augmented his already deep sympathy for the Sabbatians, and made him even more of a believer in a Jewish Gnostic version of creation by

catastrophe. *Sabbatai Zevi: The Mystical Messiah* was first published in
Hebrew in 1957, and though I cannot recall one overt reference to the Holocaust in that vast book, I think I would judge Scholem's greatest work to
be the most significant literary response the Jews have yet made to the mar-
tyrdom of two-fifths of their people. There is a subtle difference in the
attitude Scholem takes towards the Sabbatians in "Redemption through Sin"
and his later stance towards them in the study of their mystical messiah. In
the essay, Scholem speaks of Sabbatian nihilism as centered in the "doctrine
so profoundly shocking to the Jewish conception of things that the violation
of the Torah could become its true fulfillment." Twenty years later, Scholem
ended his book on Sabbatai and Nathan with an enigmatic summary of their
nihilistic "faith," by way of repeating a legend told by an Amsterdam Jewish
notary, a few decades after Sabbatai's death:

> In the telling, the supposedly historical facts crystallized into leg-
> end—and a lively, popular legend to boot. And even as the legend
> is told by a nonbelieving chronicler, some rays of "faith" are
> shimmering on it. No doubt this faith had been humiliated and
> discredited. Its hope had been vain and its claims refuted, and
> yet the question compounded of pride and sadness persisted: Was
> it not a great opportunity missed, rather than a big lie? A victory
> of the hostile powers rather than the collapse of a vain thing?
> The two versions of the legend, that of the two ardent believers
> and that of the unbelieving Leyb ben Ozer, have much in com-
> mon, their divergent evaluations of the events notwithstanding.
> The legend of the great actor and impostor, and the legend of the
> elect whose mission ended in failure, together form the legend of
> Sabbatai Şevi as it lives in the memory of the Jewish people.

So even-handed and rhetorically careful is this in its tone, that its vivacity
and outrageousness at first may evade us, which doubtless was Scholem's
cunning intention. What Scholem's Israeli critics angrily asserted seems to
me true enough, and the great book could be retitled *The Legend of the
Mystical Messiah*. Not that Scholem was a Sabbatian; he was rather a Scholemian who awaited what he called "a good Scholemianum," as he charmingly inscribed in my copy of *On Jews and Judaism in Crisis*. We can only
agree with him if we care about what he liked to call "Jewish spirituality";
in relation to that, Jews and Judaism certainly are in crisis. Perhaps they
always have been and always will be in crisis. But, again as Scholem liked to
say, the God of Kabbalah, in all his mystery, needs to be seen "at that place
where I stand," to cite aphorism 8, which adds that from that place, if it is

truly Kabbalistic, a transforming view will reveal all worlds. I certainly am not qualified to stand at a truly Kabbalistic place, but my own vantage point may be fairly representative of at least some of the present and future perplexities implicit in any Jewish spirituality available to American intellectuals. I am aware that I have been characterized by that superb writer of fictions, Cynthia Ozick, as lacking what she calls "Jewish information," to which I can offer little defense or response, beyond wondering who among us can define information as being Jewish or not.

V

I have said that Scholem was a Miltonic figure and ought to be honored as such. Whatever that meant, I would add now that Scholem in relation to Kabbalah and indeed to the pluralism we rightly call Judaism precisely resembles John Milton's own relation to Christian and classical tradition and culture. Milton was a sect of one, who persuasively redefined Christianity and poetry, and made them both Miltonic. Disputing Scholem's scholarship or his historiography is about as pragmatic as disputing Milton's transumption or metaleptic reversal of the poetic and religious tradition. Milton triumphantly made himself early and his rivals belated, and Scholem will do just that to anyone who "corrects" his interpretations of Kabbalah, or his reflections upon Jewish theology. After Freud, we are all Freudians, who write commentary upon Freud, even if we desire otherwise. After Kafka, all Jewish writers are Kafkan, against his desires, and even against their own. After Scholem, a Jew seeking to find Jewish spirituality apart from the normative groupings may be compelled to go through Scholem to find it, because no one else in our time has been able to speak the language of esoteric Judaism with such authority.

Every counter-normative current in Judaism, for at least two thousand years now, has come to sorrow upon the shattered vessels of the Messianic impulse, and Scholem learned caution, I think, by his unrivaled awareness of that sorrow, which nevertheless he declined to interpret as being primarily a sorrow. What I myself am aware of understanding least about normative Judaism is the place it insisted upon making for the expectation of the Messiah. Whether one speaks of Christians or Moslems as heretics from Judaism, or whether one contemplates Jewish apocalyptics, or Gnostics (ancient or modern, Jewish or Christian or pagan), one comes to realize that normative Judaism becomes defensive in regard to its religious adversaries, precisely because the normative tradition is uneasy about its own Messianic burden. Whatever the Messianic impulse has meant before now, it is extraordinarily difficult to see the relevance of Messianic aspirations at this time.

All that Scholem accomplished, in the supposed name of his historical science, would matter little if his legacy were only a new academic discipline. This is far from the reality. Indeed, for a host of contemporary Jewish intellectuals, the Kabbalah of Gershom Scholem is now more normative than normative Judaism itself. For them, Scholem is far more than a historian, far more even than a theologian. He is not less than a prophet, though his prophecy is severely limited by his evasiveness. Freud offered us psychoanalysis as a replacement for Judaism; many of us have accepted the substitution, though in part only. I would suggest that it can be rejected in part only. Kafka offered us nothing except his uncanny artistry at rendering interpretation impossible. The indubitable effect upon all subsequent Jewish writing is to remind us that there is only interpretation, even though a more severe, more harassing master than Kafka never will arise among us. Scholem—less than Freud in speculation, less than Kafka in representation—speaks more to our condition of rupture from the normative than either the analyst or the storyteller speaks, though paradoxically Scholem himself did not incarnate the rupture as they most certainly did.

I would leave the matter there for now, if I could, since obviously I have no authority to speak prescriptively in regard to Judaism, or to speak prophetically in regard to Jewish culture. But I desire to add only one tentative observation. Scholem specifically, Freud more remotely, and Kafka in his ambiguous and ghostly fashion all show us that any normative tradition, rather like any normative personality, is largely a shifting series of masks. What is masked is change, and the necessity for change. Normative Judaism has its massive continuities, but they are neither as massive nor as continuous as they assert themselves to be. I contemplate my many students, and I reflect on how many of them are Jewish in one way or another: confusedly, ambivalently, ambiguously and partly. That is the way things are, the way they are going to be. What offers itself as normative Judaism does not speak to them, as it does not speak to me. Kafka, Freud and Scholem, unlikely but inevitable triad, do speak to my students, and do speak to me. Jewish high culture, intellectually speaking, is now an amalgam of imaginative literature, psychoanalysis, and a kind of Kabbalah. How a Jewish high culture can continue without a Judaism is a most curious question, but if a Judaism yet develops to meet this question, it seems unlikely that such spirituality will have much continuity with the normative tradition. More likely, any such spirituality will receive its Jewish information from the writings of Kafka, Freud and Gershom Scholem.

Chronology

1897 Gershom Scholem is born in Berlin on December 5 to Arthur Scholem, a printer, and Betty Hirsch Scholem. He is the youngest of four sons. Arthur Scholem forbids the use of Yiddish in the home.

1911–14 Scholem starts learning Hebrew, in spite of his father's disapproval. Begins to attend a synagogue regularly and to study the Talmud with an orthodox Jewish Rabbi. Joins the Jung Juda, a Jewish student group, and is active in several young Zionist organizations.

1915 Scholem is expelled from secondary school for writing a letter expressing intense opposition to fighting in the war (World War I). Graduates by preparing on his own for his cumulative exams.

1915–17 Scholem attends the University of Berlin where he studies Mathematics, Philosophy, and Hebrew. He meets Walter Benjamin and is introduced to Martin Buber. Begins reading books on Kabbalah.

1917 Father kicks Scholem out of the house. Scholem moves into the Pension Struck, a kosher boarding house primarily for Russian and Eastern European Jews, where he becomes friends with S. Y. Agnon, H. N. Biakik, Ahad ha-Am, and Zalman Rubashoft, later the third president of Israel as Zalman Shazar.

1917–18 Scholem serves two months in Jena before contriving a discharge as a "psychopath." He continues his education at the University of Jena.

1918–19   Goes with Walter Benjamin to Switzerland and enrolls in the University of Berne. Begins his in-depth study of Kabbalah and first formulates his linguistic theory. Meets Escha Burchardt, whom he later marries and ultimately divorces.

1919–22   Returns to Germany to attend the University of Munich. He changes his course of study from Mathematics and Philosophy and receives a doctorate in Semitics. Presents his doctoral thesis, a translation of and commentary on the Sefer ha-Bahir, which is published a year later under the title *Das Buch Bahir*.

1922–23   Emigrates to Israel. Becomes head of the department of Hebrew and Judaica at the National Library.

1925   Father dies one month before Scholem is appointed lecturer at the Hebrew University of Jerusalem.

1927   Publishes *Bibliographia Kabbalistica* and *Alchemie und Kabbala*.

1930   Publishes *Franz Rosenzweig* and *Kitve ha-yad ha-ha-'ivriyim*.

1933   Becomes Professor of Jewish Mysticism at the Hebrew University.

1932   Publishes *Einige kabbalistische Handschriften*.

1936   Scholem marries Fania Freud.

1937   Publishes *Kontres 'alu le-Shalom*.

1938   Publishes *The Dreams of R. Mordecai Ashkenazi*. Visiting professor at the Jewish Institute of Religion in New York.

1941   *Major Trends in Jewish Mysticism*.

1946–50   Scholem serves as Vice President of the Jewish Cultural Reconstruction, Inc.

1949   Scholem is a visiting professor at the Jewish Institute of Religion for the second time. *The Beginnings of Kabbalah*.

1957   Publishes *Sabbatai Zevi: The Mystical Messiah*; visiting professor at Brown University.

1958   Awarded the State Prize of Israel for Jewish Studies.

1960   Publishes *Jewish Gnosticism, Merkabah Mysticism, and the Talmudic Tradition* and *On the Kabbalah and Its Symbolism*.

1962   Receives the Rothschild Prize for Jewish Studies, and is made Vice President of the Israel National Academy of Science and Humanities. *Ursprung und Anfänge der Kabbalah* and *Von der mystischen Gestalt der Gottheit* are published.

1963   *Judaica I.*

1964   *Jewish Mysticism in the Middle Ages.*

1965   Scholem becomes Professor Emeritus at Hebrew University; publishes *Walter Benjamin*.

1968   Made President of the Israel National Academy of Science and Humanities.

1970   Publishes *The Messianic Idea in Judaism and Other Essays on Jewish Spirituality* and *Judaica II*.

1980   *From Berlin to Jerusalem: Memoirs of My Youth.*

1982   Dies in Jerusalem, February 20.

Contributors

HAROLD BLOOM, Sterling Professor of the Humanities at Yale University, is the author of *The Anxiety of Influence, Poetry and Repression,* and many other volumes of literary criticism. A MacArthur Prize Fellow, he is general editor of five series of literary criticism published by Chelsea House.

ROBERT ALTER, Professor of Hebrew and Comparative Literature at the University of California at Berkeley, is the author of *Rogue's Progress: Studies in Picaresque Novel, Fielding and the Nature of the Novel, After Tradition, Partial Magic: The Novel as Self-Conscious Genre, Defenses of the Imagination, A Lion for Love,* and *The Art of Biblical Narrative.*

DAVID BIALE is Professor of Jewish History at the State University of New York, Binghamton. One of our leading scholars of Judaism, he is the author of *Gershom Scholem: Kabbalah and Counter History.*

W. D. DAVIES is the author of *Christian Origins and Judaism, The Gospel and the Land, Jewish and Pauline Studies,* and *The Territorial Dimensions of Judaism.*

CYNTHIA OZICK was a 1982 Guggenheim Fellow and a recipient of the Mildred and Harry Strauss Living Award from the American Academy of Arts and Letters. She is author of *Trust, The Pagan Rabbi and Other Stories, Levitation: Five Fictions, The Cannibal Galaxy, Bloodshed and Three Novellas,* and *Art and Ardour: Essays.*

HYAM MACCOBY is librarian and lecturer at the Leo Baeck College in London. He is the author of *Revolution in Judea: Jesus and the Jewish Resistance, Judaism on Trial,* and, most recently, *The Sacred Executioner.*

JOSEPH DAN is Gershom Scholem Professor of Jewish Mysticism at the Hebrew University of Jerusalem. His influential publications include *Jewish*

Mysticism and Jewish Ethics and *Gershom Scholem: The Mystical Dimensions of Jewish Thought*.

LOUIS JACOBS, Professor of Rabbinics at the Leo Baeck College, London, is the author of *Principles of the Jewish Faith, Studies in Talmudic Logic and Methodology,* and *A Jewish Theology*.

ARTHUR HERTZBERG is Professor of Religion at Dartmouth College. He is the author of *The Zionist Idea, The French Enlightenment and the Jews,* and *Judaism*.

Bibliography

Agus, Jacob B. Review of *Kabbalah,* by Gershom Scholem. *Jewish Quarterly Review* 66 (1976): 242–44.

———. Review of *The Messianic Idea in Judaism and Other Essays on Jewish Spirituality,* by Gershom Scholem. *Judaism* 21 (1972): 376–83.

Ben-Shlomo, Yosef. "The Spiritual Universe of Gershom Scholem." *Modern Judaism* 5, no. 1 (1985): 21–38.

Bentley, Philip J., comp. "Selected Bibliography of the Writings of Gershom Scholem." *Immanuel* 14 (1982): 142.

———. "Uncertainty and Unity: Paradox and Truth." *Judaism* 33 (1984): 191–201.

Biale, David. "Gershom Scholem and Anarchism as Jewish Philosophy." *Judaism* 32 (1983): 70–76.

Bloom, Harold. *Kabbalah and Criticism.* New York: Continuum, 1975.

Borowitz, E. B. Review of *The Messianic Idea in Judaism and Other Essays on Jewish Spirituality,* by Gershom Scholem. *Theological Studies* 32 (1971): 726.

Cain, S. "Gershom Scholem on Jewish Mysticism." *Midstream* 17 (1970): 35–51.

Chernus, Ira. "Visions of God in Merkabah Mysticism." *Journal for the Study of Judaism* 13 (1982): 123–46.

Cohen, Arthur. *The Natural and the Supernatural Jew.* New York: Pantheon Books, 1963.

Cohen, Gershon D. "German Jewry as a Mirror of Modernity." *LBIY* 20 (1975): ix–xxxi.

Cohes, R. Review of *On Jews and Judaism in Crisis,* by Gershom Scholem. *The New Review of Books and Religion* 1 (1977): 8.

Dan, Joseph. "Gershom Scholem: Historian or Philosopher? An Answer to E. Schweid's Criticism." *Jerusalem Studies in Jewish Thought,* 3, no. 3 (1984): 427–75.

———. *Gershom Scholem: The Mystical Dimension of Jewish History.* New York: New York University Press, 1985.

———. *Jewish Mysticism and Jewish Ethics.* Seattle: University of Washington Press, 1986.

———, ed. *The Teachings of Hasidism.* New York: Behrman House, 1983.

Dekar, P. R. Review of *Sabbatai Sevi: The Mystical Messiah, 1627–1679,* by Gershom Scholem. *Church History* 47 (1978): 245–46.

Dresner, Samuel H. "Hasidism through the Eyes of Three Masters: Buber, Scholem, and Heschel." *Judaism* 32 (1983): 160–69.

Falk, Avner. "The Messiah and the Qelippoth: On the Mental Illness of Sabbatai Sevi." *Journal of Psychology and Judaism* 7, no. 1 (1982): 5–29.

Fine, Lawrence, ed. *Safed Spirituality.* Classics of Western Spirituality Series. Ramsey, N.J.: Paulist Press, 1985.

Frerichs, W. W. Review of *The Messianic Idea in Judaism and Other Essays on Jewish Spirituality,* by Gershom Scholem. *Dialog* 11 (1972): 314–16.

Garber, Z. Review of *The Messianic Idea in Judaism and Other Essays on Jewish Spirituality,* by Gershom Scholem. *Journal of Ecumenical Studies* 10 (1973): 421–23.

Horbury, W. Review of *The Messianic Idea in Judaism and Other Essays on Jewish Spirituality,* by Gershom Scholem. *Theology* 75 (1972): 380–81.

Hourani, Albert. Review of *Sabbatai Sevi: The Mystical Messiah, 1627–1679,* by Gershom Scholem. *Journal of Jewish Studies* 27, no. 1 (1976): 96–102.

Kabbalah: A Newsletter of Current Research in Jewish Mysticism.

Katz, Steven T., ed. "Gershom Scholem Memorial Issue." *Modern Judaism* 5, no. 1 (1985): 1–104.

Kellner, M. M. Review of *The Messianic Idea in Judaism and Other Essays on Jewish Spirituality,* by Gershom Scholem. *Journal for the Scientific Study of Religion* 12 (1973): 129–30.

Lazarus-Yafeh, H. "More about Mysticism and Judaism." *Jerusalem Studies in Jewish Thought* 3, no. 3 (1984): 481–92.

Neusner, Jacob. Review of *Kabbalah,* by Gershom Scholem. *Review of Books and Religion* 4, no. 2 (1974): 10.

Oppenheim, Michael D. "The Meaning of Hasidut: Martin Buber and Gershom Scholem." *Journal of the American Academy of Religion* 49 (1981): 409–23.

Parkes, James. Review of *Sabbatai Sevi: The Mystical Messiah, 1627–1679,* by Gershom Scholem. *Religious Studies* 12 (1976): 262–64.

Piper, O. A. Review of *Jewish Gnosticism, Merkabah Mysticism and Talmudic Tradition,* by Gershom Scholem. *Princeton Seminary Bulletin* 55 (1962): 65–66.

Rapoport-Albert, A. "Gershom Scholem." *American Scholar* 54 (1985): 541–81.

Ross, T. "Scholem, Mysticism and Living Judaism." *Immanuel* 18 (1984): 106–24.

Rubenstein, R. L. Review of *Jewish Gnosticism, Merkabah Mysticism and Talmudic Tradition,* by Gershom Scholem. *Judaism* 10 (1961): 189–92.

Schatz-Uttenheimer, Rivkan. "Man's Relation to God and the World in Buber's Reading of the Hasidic Teaching." In *The Philosophy of Martin Buber,* edited by Paul Arthur Schilpp and Maurice Friedman, 403–34. La Salle, Ill.: Open Court, 1967.

Schwarzschild, S. S. "Gershom Scholem's Recent Writings." *Judaism* 10 (1961): 72–77.

Schweid, E. "In Memoriam: The Jewish World View of Gershom Scholem." *Immanuel* 14 (1982): 129–41.

Signer, M. A. Review of *The Messianic Idea in Judaism and Other Essays on Jewish Spirituality,* by Gershom Scholem. *Studies in Religion* 2, no. 1 (1972): 76–77.

Simon, U. Review of *The Messianic Idea in Judaism and Other Essays on Jewish Spirituality,* by Gershom Scholem. *Religious Studies* 9 (1973): 369–70.

Smith, M. Review of *Jewish Gnosticism, Merkabah Mysticism and Talmudic Tradition,* by Gershom Scholem. *Journal of Biblical Literature* 80 (1961): 190–91.

Snaith, J. G. Review of *The Messianic Idea in Judaism and Other Essays on Jewish Spirituality,* by Gershom Scholem. *Expository Times* 83 (1972): 251.

Stern, D. Review of *On Jews and Judaism in Crisis,* by Gershom Scholem. *Worldview* 21 (1978): 52–53.

Taubes, Jacob. "The Price of Messianism." *Journal of Jewish Studies* 33 (1982): 595–600.

Urbach, E. E., C. Wirszubski, and R. J. Zwi Werblowsky, eds. *Studies in Mysticism and Religion: Presented to G. G. Scholem.* Jerusalem: Magnes, 1967.

Weinberg, J. Review of *The Messianic Idea in Judaism and Other Essays on Jewish Spirituality,* by Gershom Scholem. *Scottish Journal of Theology* 55 (1972): 239–40.

Werblowsky, R. J. Zwi. "Gershom G. Scholem (1897–1982)." *History of Religions* 22 (1983): 199–201.

Acknowledgments

"Introduction" (originally entitled "Kabbalah") by Harold Bloom from *Commentary* 59, no. 3 (March 1975), © 1975 by the American Jewish Committee, © 1976 by Harold Bloom. Reprinted by permission.

"Scholem and Sabbatianism" (originally entitled "Sabbatai Zevi and the Jewish Imagination") by Robert Alter from *After the Tradition: Essays on Modern Jewish Writing* by Robert Alter, © 1969 by Robert Alter. Reprinted by permission of the author and E. P. Dutton & Co.

"The Achievement of Gershom Scholem" by Robert Alter from *Commentary* 55, no. 4 (April 1973), © 1973 by the American Jewish Committee, © 1977 by Robert Alter. Reprinted by permission of the author and *Commentary*.

"Theology, Language and History" by David Biale from *Gershom Scholem: Kabbalah and Counter History* by David Biale, © 1979, 1982 by David Biale. Reprinted by permission.

"From Schweitzer to Scholem: Some Reflections on Sabbatai Svi" by W. D. Davies from *The Journal of Biblical Literature* 95, no. 4 (December 1976), © 1976 by W. D. Davies. Reprinted by permission of the author and the editors of *The Journal of Biblical Literature*.

"Gershom Scholem's Ten Unhistorical Aphorisms on Kabbalah: Text and Commentary" by David Biale from *Modern Judaism* 5, no. 1 (February 1985), © 1985 by the Johns Hopkins University Press. Reprinted by permission of the Johns Hopkins University Press, Baltimore/London.

"The Fourth Sparrow: The Magisterial Reach of Gershom Scholem" by Cynthia Ozick from *Art and Ardor* by Cynthia Ozick, © 1983 by Cynthia Ozick. Reprinted by permission of Alfred A. Knopf, Inc. and Raines & Raines.

"The Greatness of Gershom Scholem" by Hyam Maccoby from *Commentary* 76, no. 3 (September 1983), © 1983 by the American Jewish Committee. Reprinted by permission of the author and *Commentary*. All rights reserved.

"Gershom Scholem's Reconstruction of Early Kabbalah" by Joseph Dan from *Modern Judaism* 5, no. 1 (February 1985), © 1985 by the Johns Hopkins University

Press. Reprinted by permission of the Johns Hopkins University Press, Baltimore/London.

"Aspects of Scholem's Study of Hasidism" by Louis Jacobs from *Modern Judaism* 5, no. 1 (February 1985), © 1985 by the Johns Hopkins University Press. Reprinted by permission of the Johns Hopkins University Press, Baltimore/London.

"Gershom Scholem as Zionist and Believer" by Arthur Hertzberg from *Modern Judaism* 5, no. 1 (February 1985), © 1985 by the Johns Hopkins University Press. Reprinted by permission of the Johns Hopkins University Press, Baltimore/London.

"Scholem: Unhistorical or Jewish Gnosticism" by Harold Bloom, © 1987 by Harold Bloom. Published for the first time in this volume. Printed by permission.

Index